GEOFFREY LEHMANN

POEMS 1957–2013

ABOUT THE AUTHOR

Geoffrey Lehmann's poetry was first published in *The London Magazine* when he was eighteen. His first book of poetry *The Ilex Tree*, shared with Les Murray, won the Grace Leven Prize for Poetry in 1965. In 1981, his *Nero's Poems* again won this prize and in 1994 his *Spring Forest*, published by Faber & Faber, was shortlisted for the T. S. Eliot Prize. He has co-edited three anthologies of Australian poetry with Robert Gray, and their book *Australian Poetry Since 1788* was included in the *Economist*'s best books of 2011. A lawyer by training, he has been partner of an international accounting firm, co-author of five editions of a major taxation text and chairman of the Australian Tax Research Foundation.

GEOFFREY LEHMANN

POEMS 1957–2013

UWA PUBLISHING

First published in 2014 by
UWA Publishing
Crawley, Western Australia 6009
www.uwap.uwa.edu.au

UWAP is an imprint of UWA Publishing
a division of The University of Western Australia

THE UNIVERSITY OF
WESTERN AUSTRALIA

This book is copyright. Apart from any fair dealing for the purpose of private study, research, criticism or review, as permitted under the *Copyright Act 1968*, no part may be reproduced by any process without written permission. Enquiries should be made to the publisher.

Copyright © Geoffrey Lehmann 2014
The moral right of the author has been asserted.

National Library of Australia
Cataloguing-in-Publication data:

Lehmann, Geoffrey, 1940– author.
Poems 1957–2013 / Geoffrey Lehmann.
9781742585604 (paperback)
Australian poetry.
A821.3

Typeset in Bembo by Lasertype
Printed by Lightning Source
Cover image of the author by Charles Blackman.

This project has been assisted by the Australian Government
through the Australia Council, its arts funding and advisory body.

For Gail

Author's note

This contains all of the poetry written by me that I think is worthwhile including in a book. Some poems are substantially revised from earlier versions – sometimes to restore passages deleted from yet earlier printed versions. I have also included some early poems not in my *Collected Poems* (1997) that I have recently revised.

I have benefited greatly from the encouragement, criticism and advice of my wife Gail Pearson in choosing and editing this collection. My friends Robert Gray and Donald Kirby read the text of this book and have given me invaluable encouragement and criticism. I also wish to acknowledge the consistent support for my poetry given by Christopher Koch over several decades.

Contents

SIMPLE SONNETS

I The Stranger	3
II Conversation with a Rider	3
III The Crown	4
IV The Two Travellers	5
V The Search	5
VI The Lake	6
VII The Apricot Tree	6
VIII The Face	7
IX On the Riverbank	8
X Refugee Camp	8
XI In a Foreign Land	9
XII The Last Dragon	10
XIII Across the Border	10
XIV The World	11

EARLIER POEMS

An Image	15
The Traveller Hasteth Through the Evening	15
Emperor Mao and the Sparrows	16
The Last Campaign	17
Lines for a Chinese Tear-jar	18
Christmas Beetle	19
An Aristocrat at the Time of the Emperor Julian	19
Cellini	21
Pope Alexander VI	22
Pope Alexander Farewells His Daughter	23
Meditations for Marcus Furius Camillus, Governor of Africa	
1. *The Dolphins*	24
2. *The Lions*	27
3. *Winter Piece from Africa*	29
4. *A Voyage of Lions*	31
5. *In Old Age*	32

The Emperor Claudius	33
The Pigs	34
My Father	35
Pieces for My Father	38
For William Rainer My Grandfather	40
New Guinea Episode	43
Two Photographs	57
The Song of the House	58
My Father and his Landlady at Young	58
The Poisoned Hand	59
Somewhere Near	60
The Human Element	61
Night Pavan	61
The House	62
Winter Piece	62
Out After Dark	63
Alone in the Afternoon	64
Last Meal	64
For My Aunt Agnes of Walker Street, North Sydney	64
Summer Night	65
For J. A. R. McKellar	65
After the Examinations Chinese-style	66
Kiev Waiting for the Mongol Hordes	67
The Trip to Bunyah: A Letter to Les Murray	67
Rural Life in the Great Depression	69
Student Love	70
Night Flower	73
Elegy for Jan	73
Philosopher and Poet	76
A Poem for Maurice O'Shea	77
The Last Winter – Maurice O'Shea	79
Night Soliloquy – Maurice O'Shea	80
Fall of a Greek City	81
The Kerosene Lamp	82
Colosseum	82
The Painter in Italy: For Lloyd Rees	84
Five Days Late	86
At Bulga	87

Colosseum at a Distance	87
Pear Days in Queensland	89
Garden Piece	91
Snow	91
Plot with Camera on Back of Dog	92
Elegy for Sonnets	93
Roses	93
A Girl Reading a Book in a Country Village	100

NERO'S POEMS

Proem	103
Aqueducts	103
Public Baths	106
Lady Wrestlers	107
For Verritus, a Jockey	107
Acte, an Ex-slave	110
Civilization	110
Rufus	111
Claudia	111
The Gracchiad	112
The Death of Virgil	113
Acte Again	114
Roads and Markets	114
For My Goddess Given by an Unknown Admirer	116
Instructions for a Murder	116
Mother	116
Sweet Suite	119
On the Beat	120
The Night of the Wedding	120
The Morning After the Wedding	121
Ode to the Beauty of the World	121
The New Academy	122
Aqueducts II	124
Epithalamium	125
Notes for a New Civilization	127
Gardens	128
Eating with Friends	131
Our "Sun-god" at Home with Poppaea	132

By the Sea	132
Nero, Hades, Poppaea	134
Lament on the Death of Seneca	137
Potters' Field	137
Bitch Talk	140
My Singing Career	141
The Grand Tour of Greece	141
In Praise of Tourism	143
Advice to Young Poets	145
It's Business as Usual	145
Your Troubadour Emperor	146
Dreams	146
Advice to Emperors	146
At My Tomb	150
Imagined Scenes from the Second Half of My Life	150
A Vision Addressed to Emperors of the Future	151

SPRING FOREST

Getting Started	155
Photographs	155
Hunger and Fear	157
Ex AIF (Australian Imperial Force)	157
The Old Rifle	159
Tools	160
Poverty Ridge	161
Noxious Weeds	162
Down at Hickey's	163
Sparrows	164
Jack	165
Chrysanthemums	167
The Future of the Past	168
Uncle Pat	168
Tommie	170
Mother Church	172
"Menindee"	173
At the Gate	175
Bird-watching with Mr Long	176
Hens in the Saltbush	177

The Light on the Ridge	178
Lines	180
Weather Report	182
The Spot	183
Shifting Gate Posts	184
Against Incendiaries	185
The Pressure Lamp	186
Life Chains	187
Driving at Night	189
Questions for My Horse	190
Outdoors at Night	190
While Fetching Wood	191
Postcard for the National Rifle Association	192
My Daughter	193
Music	194
Calves	194
The Amateur Astronomer	195
The Things	197
The Thrift of Tulips	197
Questions for a Winter Night	198
The Old Bath	199
Impromptu	199
The Evening Star	200
Witnesses	201
Matt Manion	202
Heat	203
A Letter from the Place of Pines	204
Water from My Face	206
Iron and Calcium	206
Alpine Herbfields	207
The Meat Safe	209
Baking at Night	210
With the Stars as My Bed Lamp	212
The Palace Hotel	212
In Praise of Fruit	213
Their Day in Town	214
The Spring Forest	215
Planting Trees in Old Age	216

JMJ	216
The Happy Hour	217
Jack Thompson	218
Night Thoughts Without a Nightingale	222
The New House	224
Electricity	225
Man and Animal	226
The O'Brien Brothers	227
Harry Adams	228
Bush Kitchens	229
George Grogan	230
Drying Out	230
Jim Long and John Manion	231
The Lachlan	231
Ancient Theft	236
Old Testament Country	236
Gladstone Watts and the Crystal Set	237
The Two Wethers	238
Poverty Bush	239
Law	239
The Golden Wall	241
Gilbert and Hall	243
Jack Again	246
Not Yet Found	247
Invicta	247
The Two Tents	248
Botany Lessons from Mr Long	248
The End of the Pacific War	249
A Party of Star Gazers	250
The Daisy Picker	252
Prickly Moses	253
The Old Buck Rabbit	253
Aunt Margaret's Tea Party	254
The Rifle Bird's Song	255
The Old German Sailor	255
At Iambi	256
Jack Once Again	257
Driving at Dusk	258

The Animals	259
Breakfast with a Black Snake	260
Mouse Cricket	261
Betty and the Cockatoo	261
Mr Long's Pet Fox	262
Unlicensed	263

LATER POEMS

The Wandering Tattler	267
Herbal Teas	269
The Antarctic Botanist	272
Tourists and Visitors	275
Not a Winter's Tale	277
Noah's Woods	277
Neighbours	278
Children's Games	283
Death of a Seagull	289
Child in the Dark	290
The Flight of the Children	291
Senryu for Age 40	292
With Father Before Christmas	
The First Year	294
The Second Year	295
The Third Year	297
Ping-pong at Night on the Terrace	298
Lenin's Question	299
Parenthood	300
Harold's Walk	301
Second Chance	304
The Messenger	308
A Short History of Europe	308
Father and Sons	309
The Ring	312
Conversations in a Family Van	313
Thirteen Long Playing Haiku	318
Thirteen Ways of Looking at Twelve Cinnamon Buns	323
Self Portrait at 62	327
Ada – Dies Natalis	332

Self Portrait at 65	335
Travels in Peru	339
Marriage and Seduction	352
Sunglasses	353
Thirteen Reviews of the New Babylon Inn	355
Elizabethan Evening	358
The Rush Cutters	359
Exotic Postcards	359
Why I Write Poetry	365

SIMPLE SONNETS

(1958–2011)

I The Stranger

And I was young and asked, "Where are we going?"
And then we walked by a dark river flowing

Through sunlit plains, but he did not reply.
We walked for days. Once going past a sty

I saw a deaf man feeding with the pigs,
And further on among some poison figs

A child lay dead. One evening from a ridge
I saw a madman on a burning bridge,

Then two red eyes that ran among the graves,
And women shouting at me out of caves.

We stopped to hear a tramp with greying hair
Who sang of summer in the twilit air ...

"So you are curious as to where you'll go?"
He finally replied. Then I said, "No."

II Conversation with a Rider

"With three gold guineas jingling in my purse,"
He said to me, "for better or for worse

"I set out on that dark and windy road
  Past smoking cottages. The roosters crowed,

"The sun came up, the dew steamed and my shield
 Corroded; once a girl called from a field

"But when I reached her she became a stoat.
 I ran through vineyards in a blazing coat.

"One night I cantered straight into a lake
 And saw the dead dance round a burning stake.

"And now this North Sea and a crumbling wall
 Are my last halt with night about to fall.

"A fading signpost points – points as before."
 His horse stamped and a wave broke on the shore.

III The Crown

A young king looked down from a sunlit hill.
The fields were empty and the woods were still.

His crown was hot and heavy on his head,
He tossed it on a gorse bush, but it fled

Downhill, from rock to rock it bounced and leapt.
Skidding down scree, the young man called and wept,

Plunging through ferns and brambles now his hold
Had slipped. He noted where the crown had rolled

And clattering dropped into a stream and sank.
He edged through rushes on the shadowy bank.

It glimmered at the bottom in the sand,
A crayfish clawing at its golden band.

A bird was watching in the hot, still day.
He reached and stumbled, and was swept away.

IV The Two Travellers

A girl was picking parsley near a church,
An old man fished the summer stream for perch,

There was a pear tree; but we had to ride
Through heath and furze and up a mountainside ...

We crossed the snowline, lit a fire and sang
At night and the deserted valley rang,

We slew a dragon, travelled up the pass,
Skirted a town of broken boards and glass.

Dead spirits swarmed across a sandy plain.
Dry lightning, and a blind man gasped for rain.

Years later in a stream we washed our hair
And swam at dusk and slept beneath a pear.

A parsley field and church shone in the sun,
The girl was there. We diced and my friend won.

V The Search

The valley folk were sure that he was dead,
But at an outpost in the hills they said,

"He spoke beneath this fig tree yesterday,
He shared some loaves and fish and went away."

They pointed and we spurred our horses on.
Lost in the hills, at night a strange light shone.

Finding the place where some say he was born
We saw no house, just snow and withered corn.

And hearing of a vine he loved we found
Weeds and a sandy crater in the ground.

There were a million hovels on the plain,
And young and old hunched under yellow rain,

And in the sky from end to end a light
(But not the sun) made trees and streams ignite.

VI The Lake

We reached a lake as night began to fall,
And hitched our horses to a low stone wall.

The lake shivered all night with fugitive gleams.
We slept but had no memory of our dreams,

The sun rose, but with no sound of a bird
And waves broke on the long flat beach unheard.

There was a bleached doll on the wall, and sand.
Only the clouds moved in that arid land.

We picked small succulents growing by the shore.
Our horses fretted, wind blew off the moor,

But there was something dead which held us there.
A shadow laughing at us from the air,

The sun shone, but we could not ride away.
The lake was silent and day followed day.

VII The Apricot Tree

I beat with white fists on the apricot tree.
"Why do you only have six fruit for me?"

"You dare to ask," it said, "when cats have killed
Your bantams and the garlic beds are filled

"With briars and blackberries tearing your silk dress.
You are the author of this wilderness.

"I flowered for you, but how could I set seed
When you forgot the water which I need?"

The sun went down, the wind began to blow.
"Dear apricot tree," I said, "you cannot know

"How cruel my husband has become. My bed
Is cold and unmade, and my world is dead."

The tree announced, as it began to rain,
"Old friend, eat my six fruit and don't complain."

VIII The Face

Her face looked from a mirror in a tree.
We rode up. Leaves were all there was to see.

Our horses halted at a riverbank.
The same face gazing up through water sank

And vanished, with her long, black trailing hair.
My friend unsaddled in the fading air.

"I'm tired of ghosts," he joked. We drank that night.
Seeking her face, I rode off at first light.

Loaded with sticks, an old hag trudged through rain.
Men sang, carrying a corpse across the plain.

For years I journeyed. I forgot the face,
And then one evening by a watering place

I found her waiting, womanly and strong,
Not as I'd thought, and yet I was not wrong.

IX On the Riverbank

The bank sloped steeply where we ate our fill,
Lounging in grass: the afternoon was still.

Our land was sold for food, our last food gone.
Happily picnicking, the river shone

Into our faces, and the drought which broke
Our family was forgotten. No one spoke.

We stood and turned to face the road again,
The aimless families wandering on the plain,

Tasting inside our mouths the vanished bread,
And the new taste of nothing and vague dread.

Perhaps our clothes and sandals could be sold.
Bedding in leaves, the night was clear and cold.

Next day my sister saw our parents eye
Her shawl and blue dress, and began to cry.

X Refugee Camp

The old men sleep, eat fruit, roll cigarettes.
They squint, discussing old, unsettled debts.

The unemployed youths gamble and wear knives.
Because there's nothing else to fill their lives

Young couples breed. The children swarm like flies,
Mobbing the stranger with their raucous cries.

"We own a melon patch." "Our olive oil
Is best." "Our orange grove has marvellous soil."

"Our coffee shop is famous for its cakes."
"Everyone wants the bread my mother bakes."

Their house is big and white, its vines are green.
They boast of places they have never seen,

A garden with a well that's never dry.
It will be theirs again, before they die.

XI In a Foreign Land

We packed and left at dawn. A man lay dead
Beside the road, struck from behind, his head

Smashed by a rock. We did not linger there,
But as we walked our necks could feel the stare

Of eyes that followed us from hats and rags
Draped on the budding fruit trees, and from crags

Above the snowline. Camped beneath a tree
A man had cakes for sale, and boiling tea.

We pressed our convoy on till dusk, then lit
A fire, and dossed down on a narrow spit.

One of the older men sat on the ground,
Took out a flute, wiped it and played. The sound

Was not addressed to us, but to the sky
And lake, staging their moods for no one's eye.

XII The Last Dragon

A fading line of smoke across the sky –
Flapping great tattered wings, he wants to die,

Coughing cinders, the last of all his race.
The future is a strange and silent place.

He remembers other sunsets, his breath rank
From carrion and marsh water that he drank.

He thinks of childhood games by sulphur springs.
Playing with steam, they'd snort and test their wings,

And adults swarmed across the sky at night.
High up, their nostrils were twin points of light.

Once flying through a rocky wilderness
With emerald wings, he and a dragoness

Coupled and roared. And now this orange glow
Above the sea persists and won't let go.

XIII Across the Border

Exchanging quips beneath a summer sky
For hours we ambled. Tussocks were waist-high.

The parcelled fields were gold with ripened wheat,
The houses white, the pastures green and neat.

We stopped beneath a tree, ate cheese and bread,
And talked about the borderland ahead.

Near dusk the chill and mildew in the air
And mounds of rubble told us we were there,

And women in the woods with painted lips
And hungry looks, who waited hands on hips.

Red skirt and turquoise blouse, one gave a stare
Of beckoning and insolent despair.

Two boys with grass seeds sticky on our knees,
We spurred our horses on through darkening trees.

XIV The World

"These song birds flocking in the citron sky
Have always been here," said the passerby.

"Time has no end and time does not begin.
Child, no one made the world that we are in."

Lightly touching my shoulder with his hand
We parted, and he dwindled in a band

Of fading light, swallowed by rising mist.
I spread my blanket on the lichened schist.

The air was bracing and the night sky clear.
At dawn there was a sudden crimson sphere.

I gazed across the plain at distant herds,
Red ancient hills and crevices where birds

Sang and were balancing on bending weeds
And picking among steaming grass and seeds.

EARLIER POEMS

An Image

Lions on a beach at dusk. A strange quality
Is in this image, a quality of sameness.
One can imagine the lions, calm as the sea,
Great and monotonous, padding through the calmness,

Soft paws on the soft sand, soundless as sand,
Or curled on the beach, hides coloured like the beach,
The colour of the beach matched by a band
Of tawny sky, and always out of reach,

Watched by sailors they pace. Sometimes one roars.
The roar is sometimes echoed by the sea,
As slowly a wave breaks on the darkening shores.
Those phantoms of boredom merge in the dusk's ennui

And slowly stretch themselves and drowse off, each
In a warm hollow of sand in the fading light.
The ocean turns in its sleep and breathes on the beach,
The sensitive muzzles breathing through the night.
                                   1957

The Traveller Hasteth Through the Evening

Leaving warm farmers' homes
Behind, on a dim path
He hurries as night comes.

Black hat pressed down and grey
Coat flowing in soft winds
He makes his silent way

Past silent trees and grass.
This slim, swift gentleman
Knows twilight must soon pass,

Eyes like a fox, lips tight,
Hurrying on into nowhere
Through the uncertain light.
                    1958

Emperor Mao and the Sparrows

One morning the Emperor Mao got up and wrote:
"My subjects, do not laugh,
This is my sober proclamation to all
The provinces of China.
I your old Emperor, for seventy years
Have pondered on your woes, and only this morning
The answer came to me in a dream.

"I dreamed of endless fields of ripe rice,
Strangely silent and devoid of sparrows,
Then it struck me that in my threadbare empire
Sparrows are the reason for men starving.
For every arm lifting hay with a three-pronged fork
Fifty young throats are hopping around.
So I decree all sparrows shall be wiped out.
March through the fields, my people,
Hunting the sparrows with brooms and crossbows,
Exploding firecrackers and ringing bells,
Till not one be heard twittering in your crofts.
Such is my proclamation."

Mao summoned chancellor Chou and rolled
The proclamation and handed it to him wordless.
And so the Emperor's many-fingered hand
Reached through the countryside
Bringing death to the cheeping ones,

And in the spring
A million tiny feathered corpses
Flowed down into the Yellow Sea.

The same day, a year later, at daybreak
The Emperor Mao summoned Chou to his bedside,
"Is the last sparrow gone, the very last?"
"Your Highness, the last that I heard of sparrows
Was seven weeks ago,
A report from far off Sinkiang,
Sent by the Governor himself who said
He saw with his own eyes the last sparrow
Fly twittering coldly into the hills …
What bothers you, your Highness?"

"Only this, brother Chou," the Emperor said,
Shaking a face still pale and thick with sleep,
"Only this, that at dewfall, this morning I dreamed
About a hundred thousand sparrows singing."
                                        1958

The Last Campaign

In battle lines across a narrow valley,
This crumbling army stands, dry, mummified,
The cornet raising to his lips the horn
That never sounded, and a thousand hands
Clenching the hilts of swords they never raised,
Ranks of dead cavalry staring into nothing.

Roistering, songs shouted songs around the camp fire,
And frosty mornings marked their setting out.
They bivouacked near streams and ripening orchards,
Were given bread and meat by friendly hands
And men from every village where they passed
Came out to join their ranks. For months they journeyed
Across the sunlit plateau and began

To curse the mild skies and demand a battle,
And every time they saw pale smoke at dusk
Behind a hill, the veterans sniffed with pleasure
And rode around the bend with sabres ready,
But always men in their own uniform
Rode out to join them.

           So this cavalcade
One cloudless noon entered an arid valley,
And saw a haze that did not seem to move,
A distant cloud of dust, sparkling with points,
(Sunlight flashing from weapons?) and discerned
A barely audible thunder (drumming hooves?)
And cheered and galloped at the cloud of dust
Which spread out and became a vast concourse
Of horsemen spurring sweating horses on.
Headlong they rode against the enemy pennants,
Then saw they charged an image of themselves,
Transparent in the sun, their own reflection –

And so this army still stands in the valley,
The gold braid and black ostrich feathers crumbling
Of riders who still hold the fraying reins
Of horses with their hooves raised in mid air.
                              1962–2012

Lines for a Chinese Tear-jar

Back from the wars my lord comes riding.
The ladies of the court have hoarded
Their tears in tear-jars for their lords
Who from the wearying wars come riding.
And if my jar were dry and empty
What a sad look would cross his face,
My lord who from the wars comes riding!
But with a charming servant boy

To share my cares on rugs and bear-skins
What time had I for tears and sighs?
I'll fill my tear-jar, even yet,
Shake tears from rose briars and small herbs,
Adding a pinch of salt perhaps,
And when I hear our dogs all barking
And hoofbeats thudding in the dew
And servants opening all the doors,
I'll run to him with brimming jar.
Why do I dance and softly hum?
Because my lord will soon come riding?
                          1962–2011

Christmas Beetle

From the cool night this glossy stranger came,
Attracted by the candle's yellow flame,
Blundering in jerky flight around our room.
Dazed by the light his bronze wings noisily fanned,
And lest he burn into an odorous fume
I caught and held him prickling in my hand
And threw him back in to his home, the night.
A pebble dropped and then whirred into flight.

An Aristocrat at the Time of the Emperor Julian

Alas! Volcanoes erupting upon all sides
While I would suck melons in my pleasure groves.

Of mornings I relax, a towel draped round
My thighs, and watch my slave girl shaving me,
Quick flash of razor dipped in boiling water.
She is a Christian and has pretty breasts
And hates me.

Of afternoons from honey-coloured cliffs
I watch the wind blow on the azure waters
And darken them. It makes my balls ache coldly.

Sometimes when walking on the beach I see
The sign of a fish
Gouged in the sand by some fierce Christian child
With a stick.
I prise an oyster from a rock
And sadly eat it.

Arguing with friends I cry:
"That prig the Emperor Julian hates the Christians
Because they mangle Homer, and instead
Of Christ he'd have a Neoplatonism
As arid and unsensual.
The ancients would have laughed, for their rules were
A way of life, not a damned monkey puzzle."

Spitting a grape-skin out I growl
"What makes my stomach turn is this one God
The Christians have.
I've gods for all moods, sad and funny gods."
But what I do not say is that I know
The pagan summer with its many voices
Must soon cloud over.
The lion shall lie down with the lamb, but only
After the lamb has eaten the lion up.

I dream about the past,
Tiberius' grotto, bear and leopard skins,
Fragrant wood burning and stuffed mushrooms.
I think of blood-stained sands in great arenas,
Crowds roaring and frank open savagery.
Now viciousness smiles tongue in cheek, conducting
Heresy hunts and violent baptisms.

Alas! to be
A man of impulse in an ideological age.
(Even I've had to theorise
My aimlessness ...)

At dusk I stroll home to my shabby villa
(Now righteous men command the better stipends)
Past melons scattered in the grass
Like miniature setting suns.

Cellini

Let Perseus be my symbol, poised
With winged feet on Medusa's naked body.
Her breast still palpitating,
He holds her head aloft, hacked off.

The dusty squares of Florence, tepid fountains.
I rant and curse, an ageing master
Starved for materials in a stale summer.
A fool, I let my chateau go in France.
Imprisonment and poison,
The plague in which my family perished,
These should have made me sour,
And yet at dawn and dusk men with keen sight
(Or flattering tongues)
Can see a bright light hover over me.

The bitter smell of metal on my hands.
I see small masks carved in great silver plates,
Gold mythological figures, bright enamels.
Bending at night over my burning kiln
I laugh and think of Perseus.
Dew on his sandals' softly beating wings
Into the dawn above pale coasts and pine-groves
He flies, invisible in his dark helmet.
Look in that massive polished shield of his

And see shapes of pure horror
Strangely transfigured into things of wonder!

I lay my tools down and devour a salad.

Pope Alexander VI

It's good, my child, you often wash your hair
So it retains its gold – my favourite colour.
Your soft young lobe pierced by a golden ear-ring.
I feel so old.
On seaside holidays
I stand at dusk upon a crumbling headland
And watch the darkening surf.
But ah! tonight
The Tiber will throw back the steady blaze
Of lights around the Vatican.
Flutes and bass-viols will sound across the waters,
There will be drunken splashes,
Young nobles falling from the balcony.
I shall throw nuts and watch
As harlots dancing naked
Bend down to pick them up.

Rome is the great test of our faith,
Imperial city built upon a sewer.
The drowsy gold eyes of a gilded virgin,
Gold flaking off from gold and underneath
Plaster deteriorating into dust.
And clever men have seen her and despaired.
Wise men expecting nothing have survived.

My lips, though they absolve
A thousand souls, may yet themselves be damned.
Supreme hierarchy and democracy,
And I the head of this great organism,
Not a dead logical system but a being

Sordid and stupid yet magnificent,
A mother to all men.

Listen to my choirs, augmented
To drown the ribald shrieks from my suite.
In the midst of pillow fights we hear
The majestic swelling of the *Dies Irae*.
Only the corrupt can be truly humble.

A prayer-book glued with arsenic,
Sodomy in vestries,
Bribery in basilicas – these are
The dirty vestments of the Holy Spirit.

Though I may burn,
Remember my polluted hands
Are a link in the apostolic line,
And that I am God's glory manifested.

Gently Lucrezia, do not bite.

Pope Alexander Farewells his Daughter

Eager and flushed you came to me at night
And pulled your knees up with your tiny hands
And laughing spread your thighs out.
Ah little cat! A strange heat grazed me,
Almost too much for an old man. And now
I watch you riding with your latest husband
Young Don Alfonso and a train of nobles,
Your gold hair prim and silk clothes gently jolted
As your small horse ornate with bells and ribbons
Bears you across the bridge to leave me doting
Alone upon Saint Angelo's cold ramparts.
The air is pungent with the smell of lemons.
Each day without you is an emptiness.
Good luck to you my child and God be with you!

MEDITATIONS FOR MARCUS FURIUS CAMILLUS, GOVERNOR OF AFRICA (1962–65)

1. The Dolphins

I
My personal slave in Africa first told me
Of how they play with men and rub against one
(Though barnacles upon their backs may cause
Abrasions, even death)
And how they dive for bubbles and bright objects,
And mimic us with duck-like noises.

This slave once on a journey called to me.
I had my litter lowered, stepped out and followed him.
He ran down goat-tracks to a rocky cove
And whistled and a dolphin danced towards us
Across the flat grey sea. The slave
Threw off his tunic and his rope-soled sandals,
Swam to the dolphin with outlandish shouts,
Hugged it and bit it with a laugh.
Almost intelligible it clicked and whistled.

Months later, at the noon siesta,
He came to me distraught and led me wordless
Past bodies snoring in cool hallways
And over sand dunes to a beach.
A dolphin lay there, puffed with death, eyes squinting.
Making a sign to ward off evil spirits
He split the skull in with a flint. The brain
Lay large and lustrous, bigger than a man's,
A silvery pulp, marbled with tiny veins.
He pointed to it briefly, muttered hoarsely,
Then threw sand on the body.

That night he seized my arm and talked
Of dolphins and their songs and odysseys,
And how their minds excelled our own

And they would contact us one day and bring
Peace to the world.
The palm-leaves clashed,
As breezes fanned the peristyle.
Rubbing ash on his face he moaned
For the dead dolphin he had loved,
And spoke about the language they had shared,
The high-pitched music that its blow-hole uttered,
Inaudible to him, but causing dogs
To freeze and listen, muscles trembling.

He talked of dolphins until dawn,
Their laws and second sight,
And history dating back before our gods.

Reclining on a couch my head drooped.

Soon afterwards he vanished. Fishermen
Told stories of him swimming out to sea
One dusk, a strange light in his salt-wet hair.

II
My home at dusk. Now to forget the triumph
I led through Rome today past roaring crowds.
A slave girl singing to me of Arion,
The lutanist, who sailing home
With trophies from a contest
Was almost murdered by the envious sailors,
But singing on the deck
So the sea came alive with listening dolphins
He jumped upon a music lover's back
And fled to safety through the foam.

A shower of spray becomes a trumpet blast,
Chained Nubians looking puzzled, silver eagles,
Processions carrying pictures of my conquests,
Of plains and date-palms, hills and rivers
(In fact the plains are dry, the rivers brackish).

Men call me happy, but the Emperor's praise
Was tempered to chill rivals to his greatness.

Should I row out to sea with picnic basket
And throw fish to the dolphins,
And make weird noises trying to converse?

And if I found them stupid, what despair
To know that no minds could excel our own.
And if their minds excelled ours ... then what envy!

Safer for me to quietly age in Rome
Amongst familiar unrealities.

III
A lute hurled on a deck and still vibrating,
Sunlight and anger in those sailors' eyes,
And their gesticulating, empty hands.
And is it they that have undone us,
Our hands that covet, make and take,
And if we had no hands ...
Those gentle flippers,
Those heaving seas and that inaudible music!

IV
Walking one evening by the sea I heard
Laughter and splashing and strange voices,
And in an inlet came upon nine dolphins
Leaping and frisking in the stillness,
With moonlight gleaming dully on their bodies.
I listened to their comic mimicry
Of human voices, high-pitched and distorted,
And thought I picked out
Snatches of words from various languages.
They mimicked tones and quirks of speech.
The voices threatened, laughed, were sad or boastful.

Lying face down upon a ledge
I yearned to stand and say, "I am a man.
And you are dolphins, let us love each other."

I stayed concealed. With dwindling voices
They headed out to sea still gossiping.

2 The Lions

I
Dusk. We have set the lion traps. With luck
We'll hear them later in the night,
Baffled in pits, roaring with amazement.
Ochre hills across the lake shine in pink haze,
Grass slopes of lion's pelt, gentle paws of rock
And sleepy shoulders, fading granite brow.
Glimpsed through ravines
All afternoon the lake has haunted us.
Close up we see its edge is a white rind,
And wade bemused through warm mush ankle-deep
Barefoot because the mud sucks off our sandals,
Seeking a deep clear patch to swim in.

This lofty German savage with blond hair
The natives are convinced
Is my athletic bed-mate.
I never touch her. Once I tried,
But she wriggled from my grip
With cool self-possession.
Sometimes she cowers for days in palace cupboards,
Then comes out fragrant from darkness
And shyly follows me like a shadow
With child-like laughter.
Beside me now, still as the lake, she stands
Holding my sandals.

II
Alone I stand in a night of blue charcoal
(Alive or dead?)
In tepid water up to my calves,
Feet sinking into ooze.
The blue-black water reaches without end
From rim to rim of the horizon.
Trudging for miles through water never creeping
Above my knees, my vagueness turns to terror,
Looking for somewhere to rest my body.
This harmless water slopping around my shins
Will drown me if I close my eyes and fall.
Dying again I shall wake in this lake
Standing where I have fallen.

A rush of flames across my face.
Someone holding a torch in the roaring night
Is shaking me awake.
We stumble blindly to the pit and watch
Men hauling up a net
Convulsed by a savage ochre shape.

III
My skin has a yellow pallor,
My tanned legs have pink scars from tropical sores.
The African bearer in the rear is panting,
But my German slave-girl strides ahead to the wharves
Firmly gripping my lurching litter,
And sometimes turns and laughs,
Enjoying a man's job and the shock she causes.
The only blue eyes in a swarm of black.
The natives wave their lions goodbye,
Guessing perhaps their shabby deaths in arenas,
Big charming cats mangled and moaning weakly
Lying in their own blood.
In wooden cages on the decks the lions
Roar and pace in the sun,

And huge oars hit the sea in unison,
Voices chanting in time
As the great ships put out from port.

IV
Skinny legs are running, wind-blown robes flapping
As an escaped lion swims towards the shore.
Panic becomes arrows.
We have cleaned the hills out of lions.
The villagers are happy to be free
From curious sniffing at night around their doorsteps,
But resent our administration.
Their nightmares are less interesting.
The hills are just sun-beaten rock
And no longer contain the death-bringers
Patrolling like dusty shadows.
Patient we build roads,
Exact taxes, erect bath-houses.
The lions will be back in a few years
And we shall once more prepare our nets.

3 Winter Piece from Africa

Sour winds darken the cold-grained sea.
The days are bright and cold, the sun
An icy hive.
I get up late, sit in my sunlit courtyard
And browse through books, wind rattling at the paper.
I hate being shaved. The water chills too quickly.

In summer I laughed at her,
White sweating collapsed flower,
Heat-puffed, pining for German forests,
And yet how easily she stroked
Hair trailing after her through summer waters,
Like a true child of Africa,
Or sang on lazy evenings to herself.

But now she pads from room to room sniffing,
Eyes strained, rubbing her hands and shivering,
Too cold to toy with her hair and stare
In the small metal mirror which she stole.

In rooms not built for the cold she shrinks
By fires heatless as painted flames.
Ho ... she moans, Ho ... bunching her lips
Into a hole she sadly blows through,
Breath mournfully grazing her vocal cords.

We shiver in blue cubes of cold,
In morning sunlight of frozen honey.
Sometimes she beats her knuckles on a wall
For hours on end, grunting with half-shut eyes.

In summer rocks give off heat,
Streets are empty at noon,
And we wait in courtyards
For night with its people and lights and smells.
But the mild winter here subtly cramps our style,
Jolts bodies flabby and sweet from summer sweat,
Shocks and punishes our excesses.
This winter has no snow, no dramas,
Invisible and mean, absence not presence.
Sandhills cast cold blue pools of shadow,
People sing less and go to bed early.

Night comes with whistling emptinesses, doors slam,
Time for a new life, new campaigns,
The palm tree announces rattling in my courtyard.
Ho ... a voice moans from distant rooms,
Hugging itself for warmth in bed,
Congealed in sorrow, legs and toes curled up.
Smiling I sit by my flickering lamp.

4 A Voyage of Lions

Sea-water stained with lion's blood.
Our arrows caught a lion
Escaping in the foam.
The crowds edged cautiously back to the quay,
And so our convoy with its lions set out
For Rome and arenas foul with blood.

At night we sleep in snatches.
In lulls a sudden roar will go
From lion to lion and ship to ship.
They smell each other in the night-wind.
Anchored in a bay we heard
A lion's voice from the hills,
And the darkness resounded with every lion
Roaring for freedom and Africa.

We are dogged by fear and guilt on our voyage,
Imagining the death in the arena
Of these amiable friends
Who happily take raw meat we throw them.
Gently and casually a male
Lays a paw upon his female and looks about,
Snarling at any threat.

Having mastered the lions, we find
The lions have mastered us.
Our clothes are musty from lion hair and dung,
And some nights we dance and sing songs by torchlight,
Watched by lions, their whiskers sensing the air.
Asleep we dream of cages for ourselves
From which we stare out at lions
Freely roaming on deck and sniffing the sea.

5 *In Old Age*

Near Syracuse I called in at the villa
Of a man who was said to keep tame dolphins.
His villa was ornate and tasteless.
A big, self-made ex-sailor,
He wiped snot on his toga.

He showed me through his olive groves and vineyards,
And boasted of their annual yield,
While crickets sang in the dry heat.
We looked out over miles of coastline,
And at the bottom of a cliff I saw
His dolphin pen, hewn from the rock.
Black bodies flashed in a sunlit pool
And dived in foam that surged across a sea-wall.
By a steep path we climbed down to the shore,
I leaning on my ivory-handled stick.

He clapped his hands and shouted
And all the dolphins swam towards us,
Watching us with their small weak eyes,
And did the antics that he ordered,
Leapt in the air,
Swam in formation, wheeling as a group,
And when he stripped and joined them,
Roaring with boisterous laughter,
They fussed around him with affectionate noises.

That night we ate well and he told me,
Chewing vigorously, that he thought
Dogs had a greater intellect than dolphins.
Who'd use a fish to guard his treasure?
But (he confided in a whisper)
Was I aware that dolphins never slept?
Train them, and they'd make perfect watchdogs!

This struck a spark in my old veins,
And at the banquet table all that night,
Reclining on a couch,
I thought of those pure minds
Roaming the sea life-long, by night and day.

At night a slave girl reads me books
About the sea,
And soon I hear strange voices
Calling to me from honey-coloured breakers,
Those voyagers of love
Who do not sleep or dream.

The Emperor Claudius

I sometimes wonder if I am a man
Or a good-natured shadow. People think
I do not care that ex-slaves run my empire.
Such things in fact cause me much guilt and worry.
I often brood when in my bath, but mostly
What worries me is that I do not worry.

Some weeks ago, though, when they told me
That Silius and my wife had just got married,
Mind you, with public contract, feast and all,
And that imperial treasures holus bolus
Were used as decorations in his household,
Well that was just too much – even for me!

A glorious gust of anger filled me. Yes!
I raged! My face flushed darkly and I shook –
Or so they tell me – then my fury vanished
After a pleasant dinner and some wine.

Ah, could I feel again that beautiful anger!
I crave some unimaginable infamy
Or foulness, some unspeakable disaster,
So that my rage might last a week or fortnight!

The Pigs

For Chris Koch

My grey-eyed father kept pigs on his farm
In Tuscany. Like troubled bowels all night
They muttered in my childhood dreams, and grumbled
Slovenly in moonlight, sprawled in night-slush,
While chill winds dried the mud upon their hides.
I lay in the faint glow of oil-lamps,
In a musk-scented stillness,
And from the icy paddocks heard the pigs.

My thoughts were haunted by pig-greed, how pigs
Surge to their food-troughs, trample on each other,
And grunt and clamber swilling themselves full.
Often we emptied food on top of them,
So that they swam in muck. And then one day
When the wind splattered us with dust, my father
Heard a pig squealing, crushed beneath the press,
And we began to stone the pigs, and drew
Blood with our stones, but they just shook their buttocks,
And grunted and still tore at cabbage leaves.

Passing a dozing boar one summer morning
My father pointed at two deadpan eyes
Which rolled up quizzing me (and yet its head
And snout snoozed motionless, and flies
Fed and hopped undisturbed among the bristles).
Only a pig, my father now explained,
Could glance out of the corner of its eye.

I watched two bead-eyes turn and show
Their whites like death-flesh.

One dusk a huge old boar escaped
And chased me through an olive-grove.
Dumpy, it thundered after me,
With murder in its eyes, like someone damned,
A glow of Hades perfuming the air.

That night my father took me in his arms
And told me that of all the animals
Only pigs knew of death
And understood we fattened them for slaughter.
Puddles of hatred against man, they wallowed
In greed, despair and viciousness,
Careless of clinging slops and vegetable scraps,
And the sows even eating their own young,
The knowledge of death made pigs into pigs.

Later that year the old boar ate
A peasant woman's baby and was burned
Alive one night by public ceremony.
My father stood there by my side,
His toga billowing in the rush of heat,
But in the flames my child-eyes saw
Not a pig, but myself,
Writhing with stump-legs and with envious eyes
Watching the men who calmly watched my death.

My Father

Often I think that life is in all things,
And even stones and streams have an awareness,
And life did not miraculously begin.
Perhaps the molecule, perhaps the atom
Has a pure being more rabid than our own –

In Walker Street North Sydney an old house
Of rotten weatherboard with rusty roof
And crumbling fence (a death-trap for stray drunks –
Collapsing fences are the family trademark)
Is hidden by a screen of dense tall trees.
Moss-covered steps of ancient bricks ascend
To a side door, and here my father
Was born and bred on crusts, left school aged twelve,
Became a carpenter, worked his own launch
The *Liberty*, built houses, mended watches,
Nurtured a paunch on beer, for two years courted
My mother, asked her age by chance one day,
Looked shocked to hear that she was thirty-eight
(He had been "Waiting till she'd got some sense")
And promptly married her.
      Rumbustious bear
In hairy brown-gold dressing gown and slippers,
Maundering about the house unshaven, cranky,
Debating the economy of matches,
And bringing home ingenious lighting gadgets,
Generally rusty and impracticable,
Working out betting systems, losing money,
("If I'd kept to the system I'd have won.")
Wearing second-hand double-breasted suits,
Sometimes announcing he would sell his assets
And go around the world ("Son, you can't take
Your money when you cross the other side")
Expressing fearlessness at atom bombs
("Why I'll be dead and buried when they fall!")
A devotee of castor oil and rhubarb,
His master dishes oxtail soup and porridge –
"Porridge puts a hot poultice on the stomach!"
Dubbing those whom he did not like
As "mongrels" or as "stinking little farts"
Hacking down trees and proud that he possessed
"The house where the poet Henry Kendall lived"
Himself no lover though of pretty rhymes
Except "The Boy Stood on the Burning Deck"

Yet leaving on my bed old poetry books
Scavenged from auction rooms he loved to haunt,
Posed family photographs, rows of stiff smiles,
(The intricacies of focus and exposure
And not the subjects occupied his mind)
Five cellars in his large house by the harbour
Crammed full of planks, nails, rusting downpipes, saws,
A kiln, machines for stringing tennis racquets,
Old radios, pressure gauges and a trombone.
(A tiny subterranean rivulet
Red with iron oxide runs through the five cellars,
And when you enter large brown moths flap past.)

These are some fragments, rubbings from my father:
I'm improvising discords on the piano,
The ravings of my adolescent angst
He comes in smirking, lifts a leg and farts
With the precision of a ballet dancer,
Then makes an exit chuckling to himself ...
I'm in his cellar, chattering, five years old,
His circular saw's whining hurts my ears.
I watch him with a diamond scratching glass
Then pulling it apart bare-handed,
And sharpening chisels on his emery wheel –
Torrents of sparks that vanish in the air ...
He's drinking in a bar with workmen friends
And sets me, six years old, upon a stool,
Says "Drink this", laughing at the face I make ...
Saturday shopping. I'm his child-companion,
My flat feet aching to sink through the footpath –
He stares for hours at tools in shopfront windows,
Stillsons, electric drills, and motor mowers,
Makes up his mind, and buys a dozen screws ...
I'm seven and it's Christmas by the sea.
He roars and wallows; shark-like grabs my legs
And wonders why I'm timid in the water.

Yet in him elemental beauties flash.
One dusk gazing out through our kitchen window
At gum-trees, black against a dim blue sky,
He says "Look at the detail of those tree-tops,
As fine as a photograph negative!"
And I remember as a child at Manly
Watching the breakers rolling in at sunset
My father filled with geological movements
(Himself like stone) pointed to cliffs and hollows,
Explained how they were shaped by wind and waves,
And said surveying the isthmus with its pines,
"Son, all of this came up out of the sea."
                              1962–2013

Pieces for My Father

I

My father did not like the Swedish vases
Of purple glass with long thin necks I bought
For the bare mantlepiece above his couch.
"Rubbish", he said and took them down, and chuckling
Set up a row of wine and whisky bottles,
Topped by a sherry bottle on a clock,
To phosphoresce and permeate his dreams
With cobwebbed cellars, great vats, musty barrels ...
Slumped on his couch on summer afternoons.

II

It's spring and children in their billycarts
Roar down the hill, chalk dirty words on footpaths
And birds perched on electric wires are trilling,
And moored yachts point upwind. Ka-dell! Ka-dell!
The ice-cream man drives slowly past and rings
His bell. But in his tool-room my old father
Rummaging in wood boxes thick with sawdust
Extracts an ancient bell with tinny tone
And hurries out into his yard and rings it.

Ka-dell! Ka-dell! And so bell answers bell.
"Ha! Ha! He thinks that he's got competition,"
My father proudly laughs. "See, now he's going."
It's spring and children in their billycarts
Are shouting while a child of seventy
With balding pate is ringing an old bell.

III
Silence of night and only possums scuttling.
The house asleep but for my studious self
And my old father with his eyeglass peering
Into his twinkling galaxies of watches.
Rising he takes his eyeglass out and comes
Across to me. An old man's heavy breathing.
Shyly he lifts his frayed and faded shirt.
"D'you see it son? A tick." Sweet smell of sweat
And flabby, freckled back. A patch of red,
A small black kicking head for which I probe
With tweezers. A sharp jerk. My father winces.
I go back to my book and now my father
Tinkers once more with tiny springs and gears,
The spinning stardust of their ticking wheels.

IV
On his sore ageing legs my father rubs
Rowes' Embrocation from an old brown bottle,
And the hot dusk and sticky scent bring back
Childhood vacations, warm nights, citronella,
Queensland and steam trains crawling over bridges
And jerking us past moonlit canefields,
A cat leaping at brown-cream butterflies,
My sunburned legs itching from sandfly scabs,
My father laughing as I run from wasps
And photographing island scenes and us
Swimming in waves like shimmering insect wings.

Rowes' Embrocation and its swarming scent,
And I would hold my father here against
The window blue with dusk for ever.
Night folds us in and stings us with her stars.

For William Rainer My Grandfather

I

Eidsvold, hard, tropical former mining town
Where green tomatoes left upon a fence
In a few hours would all be brilliant red,
And children drank down raspberry wine at noon
While butter turned to liquid on verandas.
The milkman's house had a high wall of stone
And courtyard thick with shimmering vines and fruit trees.
The children thought the garden was like Eden,
But their elders hired love from the milkman's wife.
Eidsvold, where disused goldmines filled with water
And on hot night the hills lit up with bushfires.
Enter into this town with three hotels,
Just as the light begins to fail near seven,
Amongst a cloud of dust and yapping dogs
A coach with William Rainer and his family.

II

The morning sun outside my grandfather's surgery
Shimmers dully on the banana palms.
In a quiet moment sucking at his pipe
He browses through a faded medical textbook,
Battered memento of his student days
In Edinburgh, wild and untrammelled days
Before he wed dear, proud and silly Belle
With mahogany-red hair and hasty tongue.
He gambled, boxed and drank with college friends,
And once he slept out in the snow all night,
Waking next morning with pneumonia,
So that he won a bet and lost a lung.

III

My mother stands one hot and starlit dusk
Outside his surgery window, unobserved,
And looks in with uncomprehending eyes.
His sleeve is rolled up and his forearm bare.
He goes in and announces to his wife,
"Belle, I am turning over a new leaf."
And talks for half an hour of projects
And plans, excited as he always is,
Then lies down and turns over the new leaf
Of death. The autopsy shows morphine.

IV

That night the black men ride down from the hills
And hitch their horses up, and there are squeals
From all the little white girls dancing naked
Around a hose except my bashful mother.
Walking alone she hears a whimpering dog,
Watches for falling stars and ponders how
Each star means someone's birth and someone's death,
And looks in through her father's surgery window.

V

Fleeing back to the cool south with five small children
Belle will abandon him without a headstone
In red volcanic clay, a pauper's grave.
She'll move from house to house, skipping the rent,
Seventy houses in three years or so,
But will not flee her past, pursued by memory,
Evenings in Wales, and William running down
The street and throwing pennies to the children –
"The doctor's drunk. He went down by the river."
From town to town they moved, would briefly stay
Until his blight caught up with him again,
The Queensland backblocks their last stopping place.
One night of lightning (so she hung up sheets
Across the windows in the children's bedrooms)
He had to harness up his horse and buggy,

To drive out to a distant cattle station
And bury a corpse foul and rank from cancer.
Back later in the week, in a good mood,
He promised Belle he'd get some gifts in town,
But staggered home at dusk with empty hands.
There were raised voices and he left the room,
Came back, "I've taken morphine, but don't worry.
It's not a lot, I've often had as much."
And they made up and ate and drank,
And she went off to bed a little tipsy.
In white silk suit he slumped upon a couch
And fell asleep and never woke again.

VI

My mother on the morning of his death
Slips quietly in to see him on the couch,
Handsome in white silk suit as if asleep,
Opens his eyes for one last look,
Opens his mouth to see his beautiful teeth
And smells a smell of onions. Day outside
Has men in dim bars sweating, drinking beer,
Banana palms rotting back into pulp.
Even her grief she cannot keep whole, pure,
This cold moment she would stretch through all time.

VII

My mother as a serious child of ten
Sun-dazed looks through her father's surgery window
The house is empty since her father died
And she has come to look for butter beans
With pinkish-purple skins in a hemp sack
And sees amongst the glimmering medicine bottles
A black man rummaging, a thief, and runs
And hugs this to herself, a lonely secret.

VIII

Once, William Wilson Farquhar late of Eidsvold,
You put a concert on to benefit
The family of my dead lamented grandfather.
Dying, a bachelor, thirty years later
You left a will directing that your house
And contents were to be destroyed by fire.
An old brown cutting says you had few friends,
All fire insurance policies had been cancelled,
And you could not abide the thought of strangers
Living in what was once your family home.
I greet you down the years, incendiary ghost,
The relic of a formal bygone age
When men at cattle stations dressed for dinner
And grand pianos tinkled in the wild,
And see you tall, genteel, with a moustache,
Advancing through a cloud of dust and dogs
In white silk suit to help a lady down
From a coach just arrived at dusk at Eidsvold.

New Guinea Episode

(June to December 1891)

I

The year was eighteen ninety one, their mission
To build a church on a malarial coast.
I have a small black book. Its pages, edged
With gold, record in broken English day
By day their hard, slow work and illnesses.
Those who quit early, lived. The clergyman
And carpenter who stayed both died, but left
A half-built mission house and "native chapel",
Whose corner pole, still green, became a tree.

II

Johann Ernst Lehmann, Saxon carpenter,
I see you in an ancient photograph
Outside your house in Walker Street, North Sydney
With bowler hat and long black shovel beard,
A small and comical man, slightly forlorn,
(Your beard and trousers look too big for you)
With three of your small children caught for ever
In the brown haze of a forgotten summer.
I imagine shimmering trees, heat and cicadas.
A camera clicks and freezes you in sepia
Amongst your children on a happy day
Far from the flying fish and the blue waters
That wash the deadly beaches of New Guinea.

III

Arrangements for departure to the tropics:
Maclaren stumps around the countryside
Preaching and raising money for the mission,
(His self-description: "energetic beggar")
While Lehmann, as the foreman, gets supplies,
Purchasing timber, down pipes, powder, shot,
The bits and pieces for a mission station,
A horse and dray to carry heavy loads,
And hires the carpenters, Carroll and Brady.
A letter from his friend, A. Stradler, warns
Against the trip. He frowns and tugs his beard.
Perhaps he's made some terrible mistake,
Carried away by pious enthusiasm.
Annie's subdued. She left a dairy farm
In Wales to emigrate from poverty.
But he's signed up, and business has been slow.
And so the *Grace Lynn* sails from Double Bay
With my pale grandfather and his gear and workmen,
And a blue page of water closes on him.

IV
There was a Farewell Service at St Andrew's
With rousing hymns the night before he left.
Their children's cheeks were burning with the cold,
Annie leaning her shoulder close to his.
Arriving home by dray the naked branches
Of figs and mulberries glimmered in the dark.

V
Three arduous weeks. He sends a telegram
From Cooktown: "Arrived safe". And writes to Annie
About the poor black women in the street.
After a five days' stop they leave the wharf,
To anchor under tropical stars becalmed,
Hoping to catch the early morning breezes.
A voice calls from a passing government schooner,
"Is Mr Maclaren on board?" and wakes the priests
Fitfully dozing in their hot, cramped cabin.
The Reverend Chalmers is a welcome sight,
The "Dr Livingstone" of Melanesia,
Who comes on board and talks till they nod off –
And ten years later he is killed and eaten.

VI
A whale is blowing as they start at dawn
And sail the inside channel's dangerous calm,
Criss-crossed with coral reefs and tidal raceways,
A maze of underwater hanging gardens,
Of tinted spines that mangle ships and sailors.
They pick up speed and head out through Lark Passage,
Passing the Barrier Reef at noon, relieved
To hit the surging open sea. The priests
Sit palely on the deck, both sick. "Thy way
Is in the sea, Thy paths in the great waters."

VII
Rain leaks into the cabins, bunks are soaked.
The *Grace Lynn* was not built for tropical service,
A collier schooner wallowing in high seas.
Maclaren confesses he's no judge of ships,
And should have stuck with being a fisher of men.
His tenor voice charms Copland King, singing
Continually, "There is a blessed Home."
Sails thunder and spray crashes on the deck.
Vacantly watching the stinging crinolines
Of passing jellyfish, my grandfather hears
A sudden shout. Men scramble up the hatchways,
Maclaren's peering through a telescope,
Even the drunken mate has roused himself.
The sea has calmed, the ship's no longer pitching.
After six days of water – there is land,
A distant line of mountains, their first sight,
Magnetic and inscrutable, New Guinea,
A long thin strip of green on the horizon.

VIII
Windless and miles from shore, canoes arrive,
"Fuzzy heads" trading coconuts for tobacco.
At night the camp fires blink from distant beaches.
And next day smiling faces clamber up
With armfuls of green fodder for the horse.

IX
The mission: two quite disparate Anglican priests,
Albert Maclaren leading Copland King,
Whom he recruited on a train to Tamworth;
Three contract carpenters, who are not "church" –
These men, a letter from Maclaren says,
Are "decent fellows", but they're always grumbling –
A cook and, joining them at Samarai,
A short, wry chief, Abrahama, who worked
The Queensland canefields, their interpreter.

X

Outside Chad's Bay, no wind and very hot,
And Brady has to shoot a sun-struck dog.
The last leg of the voyage from Chad's Bay –
Slow rollers break on beaches at the foot
Of high, steep hills glinting with waterfalls
And burnished trees, and green with rank, tall grass.
A German staircase-maker gazes up,
Transfixed, and fails to hear an anchor drop.

XI

Maclaren's trained and waited all his life
To hear an anchor drop in Bartle Bay.
The serious business of converting souls –
Fishing for men – can start, five happy months
Before the wet sets in and death arrives.
He badgers – it is four o'clock already –
His plan to get the whale boat through the breakers
And buy the mission site that afternoon.
The priests and carpenters row for the shore,
With Abrahama calling from their boat:
"We're friends, and we have come to dwell with you."
Men watch them from the beach. Some run away.
The elders are debating: shall we kill them?
And a boy throwing stones will be a priest
(As will his son and grandson after him).

XII

The whale boat's hauled up on the coral sand.
Maclaren tries to read the tattooed faces,
And Abrahama leads him to the headman.
A crowd of chattering men and boys (one woman)
Watches Maclaren fasten a sarong
Of turkey red around the headman's waist,
And Abrahama takes the priest's umbrella,
And stands beneath it in a long harangue:
They've come, he says, to make a house and gardens;

Then prompts his hearers, shaking the umbrella,
To chorus "Dewa Dewa" – very good.
As dusk comes on, the mission site is bought
With tomahawks, tobacco, shirts and knives,
A high and grassy plateau called "Dogura".
And Abrahama, unknown to the priests,
(Who've paid him well with turkey red and beads)
Has claimed the lion's share of the purchase price.

XIII

Standing on deck that night and saying grace
The mission party sees the Southern Cross
Glitter above Wedau, a happy omen.
Fires twinkle from the beach, where natives led
By Abrahama serenade the ship.
The village and dark gardens on the shore,
Dogura with its backdrop of high ridges
Promise and threaten, as clouds cross the moon.
The singers pause. Six weeks from Walker Street
And in this sultry air it seems like years.

XIV

The *Grace Lynn* rides the early morning swell,
Rising and falling imperceptibly.
On deck a group of native carpenters
Sit on their haunches staring in deep silence
As men in straw hats measure and saw planks
And hammer loudly – and a raft takes shape.
So many tools, so many tricks for us
To learn, the brown eyes wordlessly explain.
Brown hands and white, both fondle work that's fine.
My grandfather, dying of malaria,
Months later will take home a long black oar,
With intricate inlay of mother-of-pearl.

XV

Without a wharf, how did they disembark
The horse? My grandfather's diary doesn't say.
It swims, guided by slack reins from a dinghy
And trots out on the sand and shakes its head.
Nervous legs run to hide, then reappear.
Brown fingers point and mouths are white with laughter,
They chatter. "Big Pig" is the monster's name.

XVI

Maclaren's tropical Stations of the Cross:
Digging drains, hammering with his carpenters,
Cajoling native workmen with tobacco,
Treating the sick and even barbering.
Dipping his cut-throat into boiling water,
He carves a layer of foam from round his chin,
And Abrahama points: you shave me too?
Standing in his pith helmet on the beach,
He watches oiled and brown-skinned teams of men:
In single file more than a hundred backs
Loaded with poles and palm leaves climb Dogura.
They've beaten down the grass and cleared the ground,
And twenty architects are arguing loudly,
Building the "native house" with crooked walls
And wayward measurements. They work
In energetic bursts, then squat and rest.

XVII

The rains slow work down, make things soft and clammy.
Week after week, unloading the *Grace Lynn*,
Lowering veranda posts, bags of cement,
Ladders and laundry tubs, and towing the raft,
Maclaren's old faithful, the *Tasmania* –
His whale boat named in honour of the donors,
Four hundred yards to shore, then back again.
Firewood is short, the Samoan cook is ill.

At dusk, the heat does not let up. They sit
On boxes eating lukewarm meat from tins,
And yearn for linen that is white, not grey.

XVIII

"Gelaruru" the shout goes up – a smudge
Of something on a wave, a trick of light.
My grandfather pegging out the mission site
Looks out to sea: and on a blaze of light
Small dots, canoes, their sun-baked owners trawling
And searching for the spawn of flying fish,
Mariners with no chart or sextant, reading
The wind upon their cheeks, watching the swell,
They can survive for days away from land,
Water in gourds, pounded tubers in leaves.
There's meaning in a flock of small white terns.
They know a hundred stars by name, their colours
And brilliance, an essential text at night.
In daylight guided by the sun, they see
Reflected in the underside of clouds
The light of a lagoon past the horizon.

XIX

"These people have their gods. Planting the gospel
Will not be easy for us, Mr King.
The influx of the whiteman could be tragic."
After eight o'clock Evensong the priests
Are talking in the native house (just built),
Candlelight wavering from a coconut.
Maclaren is high church, and King is low,
Both bookish, and surprisingly good friends.

XX

Alone at night with only insect noises,
Worried that somewhere there is something wrong,
Lehmann, the foreman, checks his small black diary,
Lists of materials and the dimensions
Of the church that he is about to build,

(A church upon a hill to catch the sunrise)
And enters what he does from day to day ...
Work on the cart 2 hours ... first native service ...
Pegging out ground 1 hour ... finished the punt.
(The cover of his diary's creased with sweat
From lodging in a flannel shirt's breast pocket.)
His carthorse, pinched and patted by the natives,
Can't pull a load of timber up Dogura –
("Horse not ben strong enough to do the work".)
John Carroll, one of the hired carpenters
On the ninth of September swore and struck him
(The diary notes "Carroll used upseen languige")
And left and caught the Grace Lynn back to Sydney.
(So Carroll lived and did not die of fever
And when he went past Annie in the street
His eyes would always stare down at the gutter.)
A distant coughing in the hot still air.
Writing alone at night, the world becomes
Mosquito, burning oil-lamp, moonlit sea.

XXI
Halting at noon upon the sand, a horse
And cart, and a man listening to the sea,
A German carpenter with long black beard.
Waves roll with sleepy thunder on the beach
And strange birds call and whistle from the mountains.

XXII
Many have skin diseases and the old
Are pockmarked from an ancient epidemic.
Showing them black dolls, looking glasses, pictures,
Maclaren says hello by pinching noses.
Amau Alaberta – Father Albert –
Is how he styles himself – the guttural Scots
Of his tongue-twisting family name defies
Wedaun phonetics. Pre-empting low church carping
He pleads as fact his papish title "Father" –
They *are* his children. But he has no words

And goes among them, when his time is free,
And leaps the gap with mime, with bird and frog calls,
And horseplay (but he lets them test his strength).
They sing two native hymns that he's composed
To "Daily, Daily" and a litany tune.
(The words are nonsense, King will later find,
Returning, staying on for thirty years.)

XXIII
The church-site, "level as a bowling green"
Is pegged out and the sun has just come up,
Lighting a shimmering sea from cape to cape.
(They start work in the early morning cool)
Rainwater pools, bare earth, and sawdust smells.
A crowd of women ("they ar very disent"),
Working apart, are digging holes with sticks
(The mission needs a grove of coconuts).
My grandfather in his flannel shirt is driving
A pile into the ground. Last night a ship
Arrived, and letters. Annie is expecting.
(The child that Annie carries is my father.)
She writes: "You may expect something next year."
May's hair's been shaved, she has to pay for doctors,
The weeds have grown, and it's Flower Service day.
Agnes was sent with roses to the church.
Her postscript: Otto (who is two) keeps saying,
"Daddy is gone" and pointing down the street.
A letter from his hardware merchant, Felton,
Asks, "Whatever possessed you … to go so far …
May God in His Great Mercy … bring you back".

XXIV
At night he picks the speargrass from his trousers,
And cannot sleep, listening to rats and lizards;
Turning and tossing under just a sheet,
In the worst heat of all, heat without light.

The darkness loosens, frays to bony paleness,
And the light spreads across the water, shines
Upon the faintly stirring tops of trees.
Yawn and roll from your hammock, wash and drink
The sweet and woody milk of coconuts,
Skim curlicues of wood off with your plane,
Position nails, and drive them in,
And watch your spirit level's sliding bubble.
Translate the Word into your daily acts,
Blood of the Lamb into coconut milk,
World without end, the whanging of a saw.

XXV
Each dusk they swim in a fresh-water river,
Described as "large" and "splendid" in his letters.
He tells his wife about the church they've started,
Ninety feet wide and twice as long, a tower
And cross and belfry high up on a hill.
He cannot bear the blanket on at night,
And looking through a square space in the wall –
He's quartered in a native house – he sees
A moonlit skeleton of beams and posts,
A building that he will not live to finish,
And lies back in his hammock, sweats and tosses
Dreaming about his children and the bridge
Above the small stream running through his garden.
And always outside his mosquito net
A thousand small shrill voices sing and drone,
The "worthless ones" who breed in sago swamps.
A speck of singing silver sometimes drifts
Across the moonlight coming through the window.
By day it is brown cobweb, oily fluff.
And one day a soft breeze will fan his neck,
And lightly settle there and itch and kill.

XXVI
"Unwell …" the diary entries say, "Unwell …"
The mission house has taken months of work,
Is still unfinished, and he's on the roof
Crouched over, screwing the ridge-capping down.
Heat beats up from the iron sheets, and the tree-tops
Spread out below break into spots of light,
And spin, and sweating he climbs down a ladder.
A native girl with sores, wearing a string
Of dying butterflies, watches him touch
And sit down weakly on veranda boards,
And take his straw hat off, resting in shade.

XXVII
Bearers and other building parts are missing.
The monsoon will be on them and Maclaren,
Shaking with rage, sun beating on pith helmet,
Castigates Lehmann, then apologises.
My grandfather's diary has an entry: "Better".
But King is sick, and building at a standstill,
And so King and the carpenters start packing.
A modest ceremony for their departure –
Maclaren, vexed by boils and bouts of fever,
Says prayers for them in the small native chapel
(His pride and joy, with its thatched palm-leaf walls
And altar – and a lopped modawa post
Still green, will grow, and the modawa leaf
Will be the sign of a transplanted faith
On Anglican letterheads and tracts and pamphlets).
After the prayers, there is the long walk down,
Maclaren helping King downhill and then
Across the beach, and shaking Lehmann's hand.
Their hands unclasp, both men about to die.
Maclaren's death will devastate the Church.
A workman's death will be a quiet affair,
A "decent fellow" mourned by wife and children,
Who'll get no help – his wages have been paid.

XXVIII

I have the letter still, a century late,
In which King asks a Brisbane architect
For his report on faulty timber samples.
The letter's not delivered by my grandfather,
Suddenly ill upon the *Aramac*.
He's taken from the ship for medical treatment,
And worsens – blackwater fever has set in.
Delirious in Brisbane Hospital
He staggers from his bed to travel home,
A four or five day voyage down the coast,
A desperate chance, racing against his death –
No telegrams to say he's coming home,
His family thinks he's still at Bartle Bay.
Crammed in a bunk, the fever comes and goes.
Eating a biscuit, drinking some weak tea –
His four small children, who'll look after them?
The boys – Otto and Carl – and his two girls –
Agnes, the eldest, with her serious stare
And long face won't forget him – he is sure.
And there's the unborn child without a name –
Nine months and one day from the Farewell Service
Small lungs will cry out in a widow's house.

XXIX

December 1891. The grapes
Are small green bullets on the vines he planted,
The roses and the mulberries almost finished.
Annie is at her tub, plunging her arms
In suds and cranking wet clothes through a mangle,
Dour, practical, not fanciful like him.
The boys are playing with marbles in the dirt,
And Carl (aged six) is lecturing Otto (two).
Two days from now her life will change for ever,
Staring at twenty years of penury
And sleeping in a double bed alone,
She'll call his name, and stroke his brow, her arms
Grasping the spirit living in his body,

Grim and tenacious she won't let him go.
And when he's gone, eyes closed, the struggle over,
The doctor will rebuke her: "Mrs Lehmann,
You have prolonged his life. It wasn't right."
No inkling of her coming widowhood,
Stocky, hair in a bun, pegs in her mouth,
She hangs her children's clothes out on the line.

XXX
The day that he arrives back from New Guinea,
His urine black, dying and coughing blood,
The steamship slowly moving through the Heads,
The harbour opens in a blaze of sails and water,
With islands and green foreshores filing past.
But lying in his cabin, on his side,
He's not aware of this and doesn't care –
Some crumbs, an empty plate beside his bunk,
A dirty porthole's pale and sickly light.
He vaguely hears feet tramping overhead,
Tropical birds, tattooed faces singing hymns.
At the same moment to be coming home
And going away upon a longer journey …
Portmanteaus bump up stairways, creaking doors,
Someone is knocking, he must rouse himself.
Somehow he manages to disembark,
And take his tool-trunk with him and his things.
And he sits quiet and lonely on the wharf
Now merely half a man, a living ghost,
Until a stranger notices he's ill,
And gets a dray and helps him into it.

XXXI
In Walker Street a child plays in a garden,
Aunt Agnes, with blond pigtails, eight years old,
Looks up and sees a strange man in a dray
That rattles to a halt before their house,
A strange man with a face brown as a penny,
And wonders why a black man's stopping here,

And then she sees a trunk, her father's trunk,
And knows this silent stooped man is her father.
The wife runs out and clasps a blackened ghost
Who is too weak to lift his tool trunk down,
Or his grass dresses, painted shields and spears.
And now he greets his children by their names,
Turning from child to child and speaking slowly,
As if to show he still remembers them,
But strangeness hangs around him like a wind
And his tongue stumbles on the name of Agnes.
His fig and mulberry trees have all shot up,
And Annie has swelled out, three months to go.
Children, stand back from him with silent faces
And watch him slowly mount the front door steps –
And Annie, clutch his hand with all your strength,
Then straighten out his bed with desperate love,
For by tomorrow night he will be dead.
                        1962–2010

Two Photographs

My sister took two slides with yellow filter,
Of father tinkering with a radio
Glittering with tiny lights upon a table.
Wrapped in a hairy old brown dressing-gown
In heavy yellow light he sits and listens
To ancient earphones plugged into the set,
And in the next he has the earphones off,
And sits, a puzzled frown upon his forehead,
A man of seventy with kindly lines
Upon his weathered face, a youngster trying
To probe the age-old whistling of the ether,
The moans and crackles of the distant stars.
How young your face, old man, how young the hand
Of love that made the camera shutter click.

The Song of the House

Blue gas-rings burning in the darkened kitchen.
As figures move in doorways, shadows cross
Rectangles of light flung on lawns. Floors creak.
My mother reads in bed, spectacles on nose
(A brief glimpse through some double glass-paned doors),
And on a couch, lights on, my father dozes,
Hands clasped, face baked with the red glaze of age,
Deeply inert features of fired porcelain.
My desk-lamp spotlights foliage, cricket songs wobble,
Air shifts through windows, barely perceptible,
And an autumn coolness prowls around the house.
This is a song of love for childhood's house,
Galvanised roof crouched low beneath the night
Of bright stars flashing rapid messages,
Dim plankton of remoter galaxies,
Leaves of black glass and yellow juicy moons.

My Father and his Landlady at Young

"Emma," she said, "my daughter with the vineyard.
Emma, my daughter in Victoria.
I haven't seen her for ten years or more."
Night after night the name of Emma crossed
The table cloth and mingled with the clink
Of knives and forks, the lamplight, steam from soup
And the blue evening through the fly-wire door.
Emma, the name became engrained like smoke
Into the kitchen's draughty wooden walls,
And in the back rooms of my father's mind,
Then just a lad from Sydney in the bush.
He and his brother idling out one night
Noticed a train arrive, and coming back
To Mrs Cranfield's place in Wombat Street
My father whispered through her bedroom window,

"Are you awake, mum? Emma's coming. I saw
 Her waving a hurricane lantern from the train."
"Get off to bed," she said, "You're only kidding."
But an hour later Emma in a coach
Bringing two casks of wine came from the railway.
"Emma! But where's your hurricane lantern?"
And all that night they stayed up drinking wine,
Marvelling that my father was a spook,
Sitting around the table in pyjamas.

Kerosene lights the dead, and they're still talking
Before my birth, in the house where my father is young.

The Poisoned Hand

I
Your swelling hand caused sleepless nights and bowls
Of boiling water, liniment and drugs.
The day I drove you to the hospital
Arm in a sling you blubbered like a baby.

II
One afternoon of unrelenting heat
My mother watched you plod uphill, nursing
Your sick hand like a child, face strained and creased.
You weakly tried to hail a passing taxi,
The desperate gambler's last extravagant bid.
The taxi did not stop. Nor did the sun.
My mother from the door watched you continue,
Seventy years of slowly moving pain
In baggy suit that vanished at the crest.

III
Back from the hospital, gloved hand held high
To drain away the remnants of infection,
We toured your empty, run-down tenements.

Motioning me to grab a length of wood
(A weapon I did not intend to use)
You stuck a length of hose upon a stick
And then like Jupiter stamped through a hallway
Cracking your rubber whip upon the tiles,
Giving legs to a pack of dogs who squealed
And raced ears back, paws skittering on the floor.
One hurtled from the first floor balcony
Over a cast-iron railing into the garden.
Laughing you ran, your left hand raised in blessing,
Your good hand hurling thunder on the floor.

IV
Fumbling one night along our dark veranda
I felt a soft limp thing brush past my nose,
The old brown woollen glove for your left hand,
Hung up to dry, damp in the eucalypt dark.

Somewhere Near

A Racecourse Episode

"Here's something you might use," my father said,
"Today I saw a poor wretch on the way
To Canterbury, poor old bugger, a real tryer,
He had a club foot, see, and here he was
Trying to get this hot dog stand up on
The bus and juice was dribbling down his leg.
I helped him heave it up and handed him
Two bob. Ha, he was worth it. *I complained
Until I met a man who had no feet.*"
My father sits down at the kitchen table
And reads a poem I wrote about his father.
I laugh and say, "It's no good, is it, Dad?"
He nods and grudgingly mutters, "Somewhere near."

My father reads a poem about himself
Upon the plate glass of the kitchen table.
My father when he cuts his hair with clippers
Stands in between two battered flaking mirrors
And his reflections cut each other's hair.

The Human Element

My father, an old-timer, in the sun
Waiting in queues to bet upon the tote
Defeated by "the human element.
That always beats me. Sometimes I miss out
Or read a number wrong or hear the fellow
Ahead of me laying bets upon a horse
And then I think haha! and change my plans.
I lose because I can't keep to my system.
My system's always right. I make mistakes.
Look, here it is in black and white, the horses
That I've got marked to back and yet I didn't."
My father stands straw-hatted in the queue
And makes mistakes. On paper, though, his system
Revolves like clockwork stars and horses win
Predicted by his pencil notes in form-guides,
Their glittering tracks as regular as comets.
Defeated by "the human element"
Not losing much or winning much my father
In shabby suit waits hopeful in the sun.

Night Pavan

Between the mother's bedroom and the son's
Was a veranda where dead leaves would skitter.
Her bedroom had a double glass-paned door.

A glow upon her ceiling showed the son
Was home, and she would prop herself in bed
And see beneath his door a crack of light.
What woman's sleeping body had he come from?
Shoes dropped upon his floor, the light went out
And she would lie back worrying the darkness.
Our fears and loves are leaves that whisper faintly
Waiting in bedrooms lit by a stone moon.

The House

In these first waters, eyes of sleep, stars formed ...
My father, Aries, me-first, blustering ram,
Jostling my mother, criticising her cooking.
"What do I care about the bomb?" he says,
"I've had my life." My mother Cancer, crab
That broods in darkness under rocks, worried
By all the starving people in the world.
My sister Diana, Sagittarius,
The Archer, straight high nose, direct and honest.
Another Crab – myself. Joined in one house
Amongst the intimacies of linen, soap,
Clothes draped upon a chair, trees in a mirror,
Papers upon a table, varnished timber,
These signs, archer, two crabs and fiery ram.

Winter Piece

My father had to clear some undergrowth –
A council notice had declared it a fire hazard.
Despite ill health and seventy-four years,
He cleared an acre back to chocolate earth
With vengeance over just a week or so
And piled the brushwood in a monstrous heap
And one day set his *auto da fe* alight,
A day when gulls scattered on harbour winds.

Just as a neighbour put the last white licks
Of paint upon an upturned boat a wind
Blew ashes from my father's fire and turned
A white hull piebald, and the neighbour, angry,
Shouted against the wind, "You silly old fool."
My father's comment later was, "He sold
His parents' flats for just four thousand quid!
Silly old fool. Huh! Who's the silly old fool?"
Framed at the edge of life by cold blue sky,
My father stands, burning and filthying the wind
On the brown dirt he loves because he owns it.

Out After Dark

Out driving after dusk my headlights fumble
Through dust and trees, undulate over tarred roads.
My father somewhere in the night is plodding
Dark hills he cannot understand, loose earth,
My father innocent, frail as worn silk,
Mild at the end, not knowing he has cancer,
But knowing that he's finished, gentle, silent
So selling bit by bit his watches, silver,
The crumbling mansion with its vast verandas,
Its palms and cedar doors with cut-glass handles
Hiving the light in honey-coloured facets,
House where we never lived, our lives unlived.
My headlights brush moths, scrub, and scan and wander,
But what I'm looking for is past not present,
A hot night twenty years ago, myself
A child reading *The Moonstone*, all of us waiting
In canvas chairs for trains eternally late,
Bells ringing as we lumber luggage aboard,
Pineapple fields lit by our passing carriage.
Reflected in the glass, our figures seated
Beneath a lamp travel dark fields and rivers.
Loving, transitory, we never existed.

Alone in the Afternoon

Something slumped on a footpath chars my mind.
There is a childhood of burned photographs,
A space I cannot name, a name which has
No use again, a common word gone dead.
There is an old man dozing in a room
Amongst his rusting clocks and unwashed tea-things.
Immense light beats up from the bay. A man
Becomes a speck in a decaying room
High over harbour blazing through glass doors.
On such an afternoon the burning comes
And haste for help, the street – and spectacles
Left on a page of print read only air.
There is a childhood of burned trees, a house
I cannot enter, burning, nothing there.

1968

Last Meal

The meal no one came home to, chop and peas
Screwed up in paper for the garbage bin,
Cry out, are bleeding glass, are fluttering hands,
The meal he was to eat, private and dreadful.

For My Aunt Agnes of Walker Street, North Sydney

"Where is the Milky Way gone?" asks my aunt
In her decayed house among high office buildings,
House that her father built, with its dense garden.
"The man at the lecture must have thought me silly –
Or mad – asking him questions such as that –
But where's it gone? The air's so thick these days.
When I was young it was full of stars at night.
And there was wild boronia next door.
The springs were clean, we showered beneath a ledge.

I'd go out picking flowers. One day, some boys
Were frightening horses in a field. I worried
They'd shy and break their legs against the fence.
'Now stop it, boys,' I said. But they just laughed,
And carried on, terrifying the horses.
I stood there holding onto my bunch of flowers,
Squeezing the stems – *and let those rascals have it.*
I screamed and shouted at them till they stopped.
That night we went along to a clairvoyant.
Each of us brought some flowers for her to feel.
She shut her eyes and touched the stems like this –"
(My aunt, with half-closed eyelids trembling, strokes
And feels the air) "and when she came to mine
She stopped and said, 'My word, this one can *rouse!*'"
I'm still conversing with my aunt, now dead:
"Agnes, the Milky Way is in your garden.
The Milky Way's our galaxy. It's here."

Summer Night

Gardenias scent the blue-black sky which glows
Over grey lawns – blurred glimmering lakes of space.
Leaves patter with the fine spray of a hose.
A woman with a watchful, downturned face
Shining a pocket torch walks through the night,
And on the ground a circle of weak light
Hovers, dancing before her as she goes.
                    1964

For J. A. R. McKellar

Gods, men in straw hats, girls in calico
Wave from the buntinged ferry of your rhyme,
And the festoons of forty years ago
Are dwindling down the hurrying tide of time.

The hours, the sea, Rome and a scattered rose,
And Newton in a cosmos that made sense,
A cricket field ... all through your verse there blows
A gracious, clean, colonial innocence.

What pleasure to browse through your sweet, rare yield,
And quicken at the name of Jove or Mars,
And hear balls crack across a fading field
As flannelled ghosts bowl under the first stars.

After the Examinations Chinese-style

For Don Kirby

So we had passed!
The evening sky was hot and starlit
And static lightning flickered on and off,
Silent and meaningless.
We must get drunk, I cried, in the brothel quarter.

Yes, I suppose we must, my friend replied.
But listen to the crickets' endless singsong.
Now we have passed,
We have before us everything and nothing,
Wives, children, service to the Emperor,
Another fifty years to choose exactly
Which sword to fall upon.
Look at our footprints in the dust.
They only lead to us.
We wear our feet out just to reach ourselves.

But look, old boy, I said,
The moon is wine, the night is jasmine scented,
I can see lights from under doorways.
I can hear flutes and women in silk dresses.

Kiev Waiting for the Mongol Hordes

For Steve Wilson

The wind across the steppes
First told us of their coming.
Three days and nights a murmur on the wind
Of horses, rumbling cartwheels, iron and voices,
Has kept us tossing in our beds.
How many thousands, hundred thousands are there?
Three days, three nights the wind has warned us,
And still there is no sign of them,
Only odd spots of distant haze.
We have stocked up provisions,
Strengthened our walls and stationed boulders.
Most of us hardly sleep
And when we do we yell and wake up sweating.
Peering out from our wall with haggard eyes
We watch wind patterns in the grass
And hate the happily flitting sparrows.
We hate the sweet cold dew of summer mornings
Crawling down stalks.
At night we envy
The clear cold waters of the stars
Mocking us in our sleepless watching.
How can we succeed
Against a hundred thousand butchers?
Our hearts pound with the pounding in the wind.

The Trip to Bunyah: A Letter for Les Murray

Our Land-rover jolting and banging over country roads
In a night of mist and stillness, fields of maize,
Foliage ripped past, our lonely headlights fumbling
Through moonlight, white dust, gum-trees, Hawkesbury country
(Sleep snatched, head shaken against drumming metal),
So by crumbling, forgotten roads we travelled through valleys.

Night hills passing were shifting dream perspectives.
Then the bitumen-smooth coastal highway, shallow undulations
Through emptier landscape, dead trees, salt-grey scrub
Brought us at last to the wrench, the bumpy turn-off
Into the Murray country, gentle valleys
Of sheltered creeks, grass tussocks, rain-scoured rocks,
A cup of tea at midnight, your dad Cecil
Barking out greetings, fixing up the bedding.
Darkness shovelled heavy loam in our heads,
Digging three young men into paddocks of sleep.

Next day you opened up the book of your childhood
And led us through pages stained with streams and horses,
Fields which we ran through scattering burning matches,
(Striplings with spotty complexions, grown-up boys)
Scrub shrieking into flames, birds in the rush
Of fluttering ash and brown haze to the sky
Darting on life that scurried from burning fissures.
Fresh greenness would come from burning off, you said,
Reading the fine-grained lines of your country's hand,
Explaining how hawks patrol the hill-tops on thermals,
Nesting among the high and windy places,
How cows are man-shy, foxes cough at night,
And land requires three generations to tame it,
And become a dreaming place for people, man-scape.
And on this sleeping breast of hills and grasslands,
Darkening and brightening with the moods of clouds,
Rosellas dropped like fruit before your rifle.
(We were pink-skinned youths, abhorrent to girls.)

"Quiet! Merlin sleeps in this wood!" you commanded,
Standing in a soundproofed grove of paperbarks,
A hundred trunks of dead skin, tattered, feathery,
Rags of bark fallen on the ground like kapok.
Tearing a strip of muslin from a trunk
I found a monstrous centipede and ran.

We climbed and ranged amongst your childhood hills,
Vast soft things with their eerie wind-picked summits,
Brief plateaus caked with chunks of cow-dung hardening
In winter sunlight into khaki rocks.
We gazed at your forefathers' country far below,
Land gambled off to strangers, vanished homesteads,
A pine, a crumbling tennis court in a paddock,
And a fenced-off granite war memorial.
(We'd not escaped childhood and the British Empire.)
And then when darkness snapped its frosty fingers
In night air fresh from the hills we heard the stories
Of country dances, broken violins,
And voices countrymen can hear that speak
Of distant loved ones' illnesses or deaths –
Your father has the gift, he hears the voices –
Memories licked into shape like cigarette papers,
Rubbed in the hand beneath the lens of night,
Blowing up the chimney, smoke amongst the stars.
Years late, I send this note about our journey,
Water I have stored in a cool place in my mind.
                    1965–2010

Rural Life in the Great Depression

"Wot's this?" asks Cecil Murray with bull lungs
In thick scrub on a narrow track confronting
A brown, black, white and speckled monster, winding
Its way through whisky grass, a dingo bitch
And pups – startled, as much put out as Cecil.

Student Love

For Livija Strauts

I
Journeys, highways, railway stations, nights
Of blue glass, high flying birds and stars and sheoaks,
Two months of journeys each week-end to meet
Love aching from three hundred miles away.
Think of those windy trains bumping, their wheels
Singing in gusts, racketing over plains.
You read and looked out thinking spindrift thoughts,
Then stepped into air hot as fresh baked bread.
Heat-flushed, she stood among dry weeds at noon.
Think of her grasping daisies over fences,
Plaiting them self-willed in her hair's gold river,
And country nights plunging in coolness, clouds
Fractured by moonlight, darkness pricked by stars,
Walking past silver birches hand in hand,
Beds and crisp linen and the milk of sleep,
That first ridiculous night when you made love
In a seaside hotel, laughing yet solemn,
So different from your final night together
When she shrank from you tortured and your shoulder
Suddenly felt her grief's first silent water.
Think about love's first wind, slowly undressing,
Her fingernails in your back, the cry of night,
Remember grass like honey, journeys, birches.

II
Lights burn in hallways fragrant with floor-polish.
Sweat in his hair, turning away from her
To sleep, the boy dreams in the seaside hotel.
"We lie on a brass bedstead, lax, not touching.
Down a blue street three negro sailors walk,
Footsteps resounding, hands in their hip pockets.
You watch them come with interest in your eyes.
I get up from the bed and leave you waiting."

Beside the sleeping boy, the girl sleeps also,
Heavy and naked on damp furrowed sheets.
Pink porphyry her silent body speaks.
"I am knifed by the moon and past mistakes,
That afternoon I babbled, led you on,
And then you kissed me, our first kiss. I shrank,
Blushed purple, hid inside the railway shed,
And only when the train left came out waving.
I wish to own you, but I do not want you.
I am consumed, burned by the penetration,
Yet reach no climax, only toss and strain.
Those desperate minutes act out my whole failure.
I fall in love and then my feelings vanish.
You know at least that you feel love and pain,
But I have nothing, only the power to hurt.
You'll call me cold, but you're the cause of that.
Somehow your passion is too cold and conscious.
When I make love I see someone so clearly
That he lies open and exposed before me.
I have a splinter of glass in my heart."
Some of her golden hairs cling to a brush
Which rests upon a varnished dressing-table
Before a mirror forming sepia shadows.
Her ghost wanders an empty railway station,
Stabbed by the moon, waving to vanished trains.
Morning with sea-lights flashing on the wall
Arrives and waking they make love like children,
Forgetting what their bodies said in sleep.

III
Dust scuffed up by their halt. Car doors swung open,
Then slammed. Grasshoppers crouched and clicked away
Before their legs pushing through dusty grass.
Near dusk, a river, pebbles, misty trees.
She showed the spot where she had almost drowned
Losing her childhood's gold and amber cross
In ghosts of sand that rose up in the current
From feet brushing across the river bottom.

The air went chill. Rambling amongst willows,
Bushes and spiky grass, somehow he sensed
That she, hurrying always a step ahead,
Was wanting to escape like running water.
He pushed after her unkempt, beautiful body,
Her thick legs leading him on, sandals flapping,
Branches whipping back, leaves slicing his face,
And knew instinctively that he had lost her
Amongst the splattering leaves, in the green maze.
That moment clear as a snapped twig he felt
Their love begin to shift beneath his feet.

IV
He leaves by train, a train that won't come back.
Behind him in a dusty town a girl
Stares in a mirror, dreaming about pine-trees.
She combs her waist-long, straw-gold hair for hours
Her pulpy silk flesh melting in the heat,
And waits for strangers, a wind in the mirror.
The afternoon drags on, interminable stops
At small, tired stations, then the wheels jolt forward
Through a dull land, only half finished, waiting
For roads and signposts, softer vegetation.
Men smoke and pace the jerking corridors.
His mind relives her warmth, her sudden coldness,
Which shocked them both, her shrill self-justifications,
Painfully imagines the night which meant the end,
His best friend switching off her bedroom light.
Something outside him smiles and knows this pain
Is giving cliffs and rivers to the mind
Of a half-formed youth with blown hair in a train.
The coast and city come frost-hard at dusk,
And over red tile roofs the moon is rising,
Over slow-motion breakers whose dull thunder
On a bare beach is heard by lovers lying
On laundered sheets in a dark hotel room.
A trembling hand lifts a glass jug of water.

Night Flower

Sussex Street sleeps in mists of nickel moonlight
And echoes ghostly music, but the sound
Inside is crushing, voices, drums, stars jerked
From electric guitars, and swaying, shaking bodies:
Young, beautiful and cruel my friends are dancing.
Night in your cold vase hold this crumbling flower,
Stung smiles, dark corridors where bodies push
To a white stately room of bare feet stamping
A gritty floor, figures dissolving in shadows,
The dance, this great, sad, bitter swaying thing
Which burns and moves and kisses us with salt.

Elegy for Jan

For Janet Campbell Muirhead ("Jan Miller")

I
From the bloodhouses of my youth, vagrant hotels, I see your face
Dead girl (dear Jan!) in smoke-filled rooms glass-littered slimy floors.
Out of those brine-cold years, derelict houses with cracked lino
And crumbling ceilings, poems and obscenities scribbled on the walls,
A humid wind blows from that night we met and loved as strangers,
The first night that I slept with anyone – you blushed and laughed
About the red scars on your wrists from self-inflicted wounds,
And the deep scar on your abdomen from which the child
You loved, but gave away, had come, and then you folded me
Into a darkness better than I had dreamed, yet terrifying.
Night wind, fumble amongst the rusting cast-iron balconies,
Dank dishes in a sink and bodies on soiled mattresses,
But in a downstairs room lit by a naked globe a girl
In a red night-dress stands before a nervous, garrulous boy.
She is the night. With pale, translucent face, dark liquid eyes,
Black hair and almost oriental dignity she stands,
Says "Tuck me into bed" and leads him into a small room.

Remember after the scalding seed, sleeping in love's sour milk
In a cramped single bed, your black hair on my naked shoulder,
Pain in our bones, a flimsy sheet across our tangled bodies,
Your breathing's sea-sound in my ears, bird-noises in your throat.
But in the silent dawn the wind stops, and I wake to hear
You grind your teeth in anguished sleep, your mind lost in cold rooms.

II
May 1963, eleven o'clock,
One windless autumn night
Of floodlit streamers and tooting horns
With friends you stand
At Circular Quay in Sydney
Farewelling an overseas liner.
A hundred miles away
I pace a country railway station.
The ship is leaving,
The ship you could not catch to Europe
For lack of money.
Aged twenty-two,
Drunk, high on pills,
Light-headed
(You had not eaten for eight days)
To get a better view,
You climb the railing, overbalance
And fall through thirty feet of air
Onto the concrete.

III
The laundry grumbles, eats its girls.
At morning mass she faints from weakness,
Is dragged outside, hit on the face.
Frost and the older girls' cruel eyes.
Potatoes, mash and bread for meals.
The laundry hisses, thumps all day.
Nine hours each day amongst the steam
Kneeling she sweats and works for Christ
And calluses form on her knees.

Her mother gets the widow's pension,
But sends the nuns her board each week,
And once two extra pounds for shoes.
They get her men's shoes second-hand.
The laundry eats her mother's money.
On summer nights a hundred girls
Lie in a huge bare dormitory
And hear waves breaking on the beach.
Couples a hundred feet away
Make love, drink beer and splash each other.
The girls watch shadows on the ceiling.
They sweat and toss. The iron beds creak.
Only the laundry sleeps at night.
"I was thirteen when I was there.
They called the place a girls' reform school,
And I'm the only girl from there
Who didn't land up on the streets …
The only old-girl who made good …"

IV
A cheap cream fountain pen
With Chinese characters
Engraved in blue and brown,
Some old black slacks,
A couple of woollen jumpers,
A battered suitcase,
A gold watch for her twenty-first,
A scarlet night-dress,
Some photos of herself when drunk,
A small address book
Are left without an owner.

V
From old brick lavatories lit by a wavering candle flame, drab parties,
Songs of doomed protest drunkenly shouted to a strident guitar,
Cold nights of driving rain, the hastily swallowed pills, couples on floors,
Your face shines sadly, purely, and you sit all night inscribing
Black circles on a page until at dawn the page is black,

Or in a bar you sit inventing little games and laughing,
Describing a hospital tour with childish relish (and bitterness)
A funny old wooden model womb, and the white pillow pushed
In unwed mothers' faces when they take the child at birth,
Or you sit in a restaurant happily playing noughts and crosses
(I shudder as your pencil gaily disfigures the tablecloth),
Outside you climb my crouching shoulders for a piggyback,
But when I stand you fall and knock your head upon the pavement.
I still bend helplessly over your bruised and curled-up body
And mutter ineffectual comfort under the glaring street-lamps –
And two years later on an autumn night you fall and die.
(The noisily waving crowds are hushed, floodlit in sudden silence,)
Out of those tangled nights, backyards of stunted weeds and cinders,
Damp walls, rain spitting through an open window, blowing curtains,
Dear Jan I see you so the whole world radiates around you,
Compassionate for all living things, forgetting your own body,
In bare and draughty rooms undressing slowly to the night
To hold us whimsically and tenderly upon dank beds.

                                                Easter 1966

Philosopher and Poet

John Anderson, philosopher, stooped, brooding,
Bored with philosophers approached Lex Banning,
Poet and sceptic who had cerebral palsy:
"I wonder can I join you Mr Banning?"
Rolling his words out with his rich Scots accent.
Coming back with his coffee, Anderson
Gazed at a table crowded with his students:
"I wonder if my whole life work has failed.
Look at my students who are critical
Of everything except being critical."
Lex loved to quote this, grimacing with laughter.

A Poem for Maurice O'Shea

For Garry Shead

It is wine-harvest, summer, the year's heart.
At night the vines bend on their wires, old sheds
Of whitewashed galvanised iron bake in the moon,
And Maurice's cats sidle in the wind.

"Gypsum takes away harshness ... clarify
With albumen ..." Love failed and has become
A vineyard, carbon dioxide in dark vats
Which prickles when you thrust your arm in wine.

But through the vineyards a ghost woman walks,
Whose failure honed his art, sharpened that nose,
That long thin delicate nose which peers and sniffs
Into a long-necked glass, then passes on.

The moonlit water-tank gobbles, rumbling briefly.
A possum thumps upon the roof but Maurice
In hock-pale light is sitting at a desk
Writing in vine-scrawl of the wine he loves,

Myopic eyes given a quizzical look
By thick-lensed, rimless, gold-framed spectacles,
And always ready for a laugh, whisking
Up culinary marvels on a kerosene stove,

And once a bandicoot cooked in red wine
Greeted by ignorant cries of "Bravo Maurice!
A champion dish!" as bits of bandicoot
Dissolved with herbs and leeks inside his guests.

"I do not like machines. We use the hand-press."
Men grunt and push a handle slowly turning
Upon a metal thread, and the great press
Squeezes the grapes till Maurice calls, "Enough!"

Feeling inside his chest (which cancer eats
Like secret phylloxera through his body)
The texture, substance, weight of grapes, that moment
The first juice breaks and floods – and it's just right.

But wine is more than art, or the fine mind
Sniffing at mathematical purities,
Or testing acidity levels in a lab;
Wine is a man inside a darkened cask,

Hunched in that primal gloom, scouring out filth,
The terror as he crawls in through the bung-hole,
And when they haul him by his helpless arms
Back through that hole, reborn into the world.

Wine is an ancient Catholic God, whose sun
Beats on Pokolbin earth, demanding faith,
And also works, the hand, weary from turning
The soil and dropping grapes in metal buckets.

And wine is also wisdom, which announces
As Maurice does, we should drink common wine
As well, for too much fine wine spoils the palate.
And he is quiet and shy behind his fame.

In khaki shirt and shorts, with battered hat
Maurice at vintage time stumps through his vineyard,
Dust on his forehead, sweat beneath his arms,
Retires inside the whitewashed galvanised shack

And sits and smokes, drinking a cup of coffee
Poured from an elegant metal percolator,
A taste rare then, but student days in France
And his French mother gave him a Gallic flair.

He smokes. Ah yes! But don't smoke near the cellars!
He'll cut your arm off if you smoke near there!
Those purple bubbles, maroon foam must breathe only
From polished concrete vats, cool stone, good oak.

Now Maurice sits tonight alone and humble
In summer's heart and gets up from his desk,
And pours some red, savouring it like a baby.
Night and wine, his face wavering on the glass.

The Last Winter – Maurice O'Shea

Coming – coming down on the Flyer – the last journey,
Sitting with hands in overcoat pockets and eyes half-shut,
Engine smoke trailing a running shadow on the ground,
The winter voice of the train – hissing and grunting in sidings –

And grass bends double beneath the weight of rolling casks.
The cold months blow down the valley and mottle the leaves with bad blood
And tilt and blow them free and strip the vineyards to matchsticks.
The cats mope, chasing wind-shadows in winter sunlight,
A cabbage moth flutters to rest against a water tank,
At night winds murmur around iron roofing and empty down-pipes.
They prepare us well for death, the old gods of the vineyard.
As the vine ages, so does the mind and has its ration
Of beauty then dies back to a blackened puddle.
The cellars are cold and absent, your wines live after you.

Coming – coming down on the Flyer – the last journey.
The winter landscape burns briefly beyond the dusty window.
You silently reach without hands to fields turning suddenly cold.

Night Soliloquy – Maurice O'Shea

For Bryan Gandevia

A canvas stretcher
A grey pillow –
You turn in after
A night of – so to speak – study.
Coffee grains
In an enamel mug.
Simple, bachelor pleasures.
A sugar ant quests
Across the earth floor.
Lights out except
The wireless valves,
Lighting the wall behind dimly.
Handel's Messiah.
Hand limp by the bed
Trails a cigarette.
Angel of nicotine
And wine.
Over Christmas
The vineyard sweats by day,
Acres of light,
Heat which the slopes
Lose at night.
My personal things
In a mess.
But the cats don't mind.
That ant's gone mad –
(Like cicadas singing at night).
What's he looking for?
But Handel and grapes
Know what they're at.
The white ants are flying
In thousands tonight
Rustling like leaves
Towards every lamp in the district.

I can smell them in the dark.
Acrid.
Thank God I don't give a rap
If the place falls down.
But amazing how fond you become
Of a broken fountain pen
Or old wine press.
How fond you become
(As the young are not)
Of being with yourself.
Content with your death,
Smoking a cigarette
At night,
The two of us.
Myself and myself.

Fall of a Greek City

From a theme of E.M. Root

Running and running through the dust and heat,
The city waits in silence for this man,
A speck of light moving on silent feet.

The lines began to crumble and retreat,
Swords flashed. He watched and noted and began
Running and running through the dust and heat.

Through granite passes where harsh sunlight beat
And water dripped in shade with pain he ran,
A speck of light moving on silent feet.

How long he trained to make his limbs complete
These bitter honours never in the plan,
Running and running through the dust and heat.

The city waits for what he will repeat,
Mothers will mourn tonight in every clan
A speck of light moving on silent feet.

To fall down on his knees and gasp defeat,
He knows that he must do this, and he can,
Running and running through the dust and heat,
A speck of light moving on silent feet.

The Kerosene Lamp

From an idea of Sally McInerney

The kerosene lamp hisses and sings with light,
With the voice of planets singing, a constant blowing
Subtly unnoticed, merging with the mind's hum.
But the silence of the kerosene lamp is deafening
When the light is out and we are cupped in darkness.
Foxes cough in the distance, cattle talk,
And through frost-rubbed panes night lights palely assert,
Blackberry stars and the dark spaces of trees.

Colosseum

They did not wait for this, the crowds:
Two men with a wheelbarrow in the dusk
Collecting the mess.
The muscles of a lion not quite dead
Contract as if shuddering in sleep.
The last life stops on a gently inserted knife.
Patiently, courteously the two workmen
Lift each body into the barrow
And wheel it away.
They rake the gore into the sand
And talk in undertones,
Not of Europe's vanished fauna,

The mountains which have no lions,
Birds twittering in grass amongst the empty lairs,
Africa ransacked for elephants.
They do not talk of this,
But of women and the high price of food.
And they dump the bodies
In the foul, rancid pits in the foundations,
So foul that workmen digging two thousand years later
Sickened by the smell will lay down their spades.

Plants die cleanly
In stationary impersonal conflicts
For light and water.
But the death of animals appals.
They grow legs to run from death
And death as quickly grows legs to hunt them down.
The manure of grass eaters is mild,
But the shit of man and the carnivores is corrupt,
For what they eat resents being eaten,
And when man and the animals die
The stench of the carcass
Is our last silent protest at death.

But they are not talking of this,
No, certainly not of this, our two workmen
As they come out from their underworld
Of monstrous corpses decaying in half-light.
Perhaps they wish that the pleasure seekers
Should have to go down there with them,
The frivolous children of serious fathers,
Gaudy with expensive gold and more expensive silks
Women admiring themselves in metal mirrors,
Eating sweetmeats amongst cushions on stone tiers,
While death-yells drown in the roar of the crowd
And the florid music of hydraulic organs.

But now in the dusk as the last blood is soaked up,
There is even a kind of peace here
With the lonely rumble of an iron wheel
Across the empty arena.

The Painter in Italy: For Lloyd Rees

Morning, a sound of scratching and a hat
Of French design, capacious, black, is hanging
Deep in mid air in thought before a pencil
Tracing a carbon line of pearly blackness

Over rice paper tacked to a drawing board
Roughened with sand set into P.V.A.
To grain and break the line with living texture
Behind the paper, mind behind the pencil.

The easel imperceptibly creaks to feel
A motionless dance of hills, stone walls, ripe frost,
The architecture of man in his landscape
Sketched in, all Tuscany floating in air.

To stroll down olive groves through cross-hatched sunlight
And find you, "Signor Rees", an early riser
In a grey dust-coat, splattered, rumpled, always
A messer – but the painting comes out pure –

A rare, rejoicing old man, a Welsh Australian
At San Gimignano in late summer,
Standing in shade and sketching with black hat
Slung down across the eyes to stop the glare,

White ruffled wisps of hair, old sheep's wool stuck
Upon the worn tough boulder of your head
Which marches firmly on a broad square trunk
(What glacier brought your head to rest so surely?).

Now to pour watercolour on the sketch.
The test. A sudden rainbow bursts and scuttles
Across the paper, quick as fragments
Of vision breaking behind the eye's sun.

How strange you should have come so late and far
To Tuscany with face of soft-rubbed sandstone,
Eyes of blue watercolour clearly watching
The hillside slowly turn in sunbaked sleep,

Trees with inching cucumber cool shadows,
Bel canto hills singing of line and space,
Fields with low walls, the classic ground which man
Has made a work of art, a woman's body.

Returning to your source, where landscape started,
An old man with an easel in the olives.
It is the new world come to drink old fountains,
The eloquent dancing waters of our tradition.

(And still Australia calls you back, that dream
Of trees as sculpture with some remnant leaves,
The soft geometry of ancient hills
And light that dazzles from a heart of quartz.)

The lunch bell's sounding and you pack your easel.
Fresh bread and wine and veal ... Doze on the terrace
Watched by aged towers the townsfolk volubly love.
Are soldiers calling from that tower – or children?

Last night there was a frost, a glide of owls,
A woman danced among the darkened groves.
The hearth leapt warm with burning olive branches.
Who cut his wrists beneath the mulberry tree?

Last night there was a stream which chilled our heads
With second sight, Minerva's ghostly weaving.
Nodding, she moaned and muttered with grey lips.
And now you startle, blink yourself awake,

As sunlight moves away and shadows lengthen,
Finding your richest harvest at the end
Of distant outlines, smoky orchards, villas,
Time that remembers, landscape which is man.

Standing this afternoon upon the terrace
Before the country's shimmering silk you watch
An old man in the distance of the morning,
Yourself with easel, and you wave and laugh.

Five Days Late

Late, five days late. At night in sleep they fumble
To feel the cool gold ring which is not there,
The space beside them which is sometimes man.
The wind-chimes stir. From their high rented rooms
The city is a wave of black stars breaking
In violet abysses, clouds of gasoline.
Pads of rouge, scent bottles, eyelash brushes
Are mummified in the dressing-table mirror.
They travel nightmare elevators up
And down with flimsy shifts fanned by ozone,
In empty buildings, buttons pressed by no one,
And ghosts of children crawl in moonlit playpens,
Clamber and strain for milk from dormant breasts,
That crave the press of life, the tug of lips,
Anguished wombs twisting, curving to be filled
With Baby and his big blind head of bread,
The bawling horror spilling porridge on floors.
In rented rooms the coffee cups are cold,
And single girls toss in their night of doubt.
When morning wakes with blood, they weep, are safe.

At Bulga

To walk by moonlight down a mountainside
By steep clay-gravel tracks past shaggy tussocks
Through moth-swarms, fern-crackle and the constant burst
And boil of sea thumping the beach below,
Anthracite cattle cropping salt-warm grass,
Geometry of blackberries, palms, lantana
And shelving paddocks crumbling in the Pacific –
To walk and trust the moonlight on such nights
Is to live by wind shuttling clouds like lantern slides.
We walk into a gap and sudden darkness.
We stumble down no path, walk on air pockets,
Squeeze from cattle hooves trampling close, totter
On cliff edges, lost beyond all hope of the house
Beside the beach with candles, love, clean sheets,
Until the hillside breaks out in moonlight again –
The shadow and light of headlands' receding sculpture.

Colosseum at a Distance

High above the city, stretched on his pallet
He is getting drunk,
The collector of carcasses.
In the attic of a block of concrete flats
In a city of immigrants
He is drinking wine by himself.
At night the supplies rumble in,
The cartloads of cucumbers, melons
And jars of wine, cured meats,
The night of sudden conflagrations,
The brazier tipped on the floor
And feet thumping down unlit stairways –

High above the city,
Semitic and stolid, not given to talking,
His shoulders toughened
From wrestling dead hippopotami,
Levering them onto wagons.
Below in the alley invisible voices argue,
Their carts jammed in the dark.
High above the city where hills
Stand against a zone of fading dusk,
He is drinking wine on his straw pallet.
He does not smile with the crowds
When elephants trace the signs of the zodiac
In sand with their trunks.
Undisturbed in the tumult of grief
He watches a popular gladiator die.
He makes no judgment
About the viscera he shovels up.
In a city of imaginary fear
Where Christian zealots and astrologers wrangle
And every stranger is a threat to the state
(Dogma demands scapegoats)
He blames no one for his loneliness.
Stacking bodies in the cool pits,
The age has no soap to cleanse
The musk of blood which haunts him.
In his rented space he drinks wine
And sees no conspiracies or subversion,
Just a blind metropolis,
Slums in the sky rotting and collapsing,
The intersection of forces no one can cope with.
There is a chamber-pot on his floor,
And a mallet to strike the head of a twitching cheetah,
And neatly folded
The theatrical costume of Charon he wears
When he slips with his spade into the roaring arena.

Pear Days in Queensland

Based on comments of Judith Wright and an article of James Wansfell

Days of pear-murder, nights of pear-madness we spent
Digging and burning the prickly pear,
Poisoning, crushing with rollers drawn by bullocks,
Standing in pubs and swapping pear yarns,
Scraping the spines off with knives,
Sponging our thorn wounds with mustard,
Scratched brown and purple with Condy's and gentian violet,
While beyond the pressure lamp's wavering circle
The pear massed its nightmare armies by moonlight
And peered with balloon green faces over pub railings.

We hacked, we poisoned, we crushed, but the pads
Just split and sprouted again.
A tree grew from a burned green ear.
Eating the yellow flowers and soft red fruit
A wandering cow scattered the seeds in her stools.
The pear flew in the stomachs of birds,
Breathed on the fur of bees,
A pad lived for three years hung in a room.

How could we fight what stuck to our boots and travelled
The red volcanic soil on our clothes and horses?
We sweated, were smeared with pear.
Pear cities covered millions and millions of acres,
Our horses galloped,
Pear leaves flying in all directions,
The roads just narrow green tunnels.
We climbed up trees to spot the heads
Of cattle amongst the plazas of cactus.
Our horses jumped and crashed in the pear,
As we tried to muster
A strange new race of small, dodging beasts
With horny palates and nimble gait.

We bred and we hacked in the great pear-loneliness,
Close neighbours cut off by walls of thorns
That buried wire fences and boundaries,
Creeks and even hills lost,
No one quite knew where.
We walked the moonlit track to the privy
Striking with sticks at slits in the moonlight,
The small death-adders who swarmed among the cactus.
We cut and we slept,
Afraid of losing our one track out,
And stared at night from our verandas
Looking for neighbours' lights.

But we learned to live with these miles
Of green intestine digesting the world into pear.
We mashed the pads for feed,
Fermented them into alcohol
And extracted second grade dyes and oils.
We used the big yellow thorns for gramophone needles
And heard Enrico Caruso husky and faint
Sing from a thorn as we boiled in hot pear nights.

Then a moth came and Troy fell overnight.
The cactoblastis chewed through green cities,
And the arcades of pear collapsed.
We blinked at the sky
And a hemisphere of grassland tilting to the sea.
Our houses stood unpainted and rusty
In acres of pear-slime and melting branches.
And we waded through the slush
To shake the hands of forgotten neighbours.
Now the hillside is a honeycomb crumbling with fire
As in winter we burn the sugarcane
In blue indigo twilights blowing with orange smoke.
Our rivers and country daze us with largeness.

But at night we doze in mosquito nets
And smell ghost armies of cactus
In the heart of the rain forest,
New resistant strains sending out clouds of pollen.

Garden Piece

For Douglas Annand

Somebody's mother runs one summer morning
Through air with Edwardian overtones of thunder
Clenching a silver dish cover for a tail
Dodging elusive as a Chopin etude.

A flicking briar announces judgment has passed.
The shadow of the dish cover runs
Held by a bodice bursting with opinions
Descends on zinnias but no rabbit kitten.

The rabbit's feet disturb the friable beds,
Pulsing and running out of sight through shrubs.
The sun is a flash on a silver dish cover,
A brooch and a white hair drop in the leaves.

Through gardens quickly changing into houses
Past vanished rose beds nobody is running.

Snow

Snow – that day for the first time you saw snow.
We woke in your parents' house dazed by the sound
Of thrushes, magpies singing for miles around.
All night by the fire the kettle constantly talked,
The kitchen sang with the pressure lamp's greenish glow,
And in the yard the shadows of wattles walked.

Around the ramshackle timber house the vine
Of the cherokee rose leaned in the winter moon
And liquid stars inched their snail trails in the sky.
We woke and drove through cold air fresh with pine,
Tyres humming with a distant insistent tune,
Urging past trucks, racing through miles of trees,
The winding road gripping us with unease.
And then past Lithgow you caught sight of snow.
"Let's stop," you said, drenched in the sudden flow
Of dazzling purity. But I said "No".
And you had the light of first snow in your eye,
While with an arid snow my mind was cold.
Too late I give this snow you cannot hold.

Plot with Camera on Back of Dog

(From an 1890 engraving)

See, through this landscape master and his dog
Pace at an amicable jog
Across the setting sun, in tweeds, sedate.
Clippers full-sail scud on the bay.
Ladies in bustles free of care
Ride penny-farthings through the fading air.
Then master blows an eery whistle, Tricks
Wags tail, pulls cord, a shutter clicks.
The landscape vanishes through the lens, is gone.
Trapped in a box upon a dim glass plate
Motionless ladies will never ride away
Out of those fields, that amber-tinted day.
Their dinners will grow cold,
Their mothers scold
And wait and wait,
And fathers search where fields once shone.

Elegy for Sonnets

"The sonnet is a house that's been destroyed."
And more than sonnets: marriages, real houses:
These days have seen whole countrysides destroyed,
Growers of food who have no mouths to feed.
Renounce the frontiers, give them back to silence.
We irrigate until our soil turns sour,
So all the systems turn to marsh and salt ...
More than stone houses, vines and lyrics finished:
A structure in our cells is breaking down.
What can the private person say or feel?
Go loose, rejoice that walls are falling, teach
The heart again – the heart which will not learn
And yet we must: give ourselves to change,
When marriages and countrysides break down,
To live on air, to seek no house or answer.

Roses

For Charles and Barbara Blackman

I
We left our bodies and we dreamed of roses,
But woke to shrapnel whining over the tundra,
Faces drained in the time of great bombardments,
Staggering through gas and mud, eating from tins.

Clutching a crumbling edge, our deafened minds
Reached for the tiny bursts and pops of space.
Then the guns fell silent, men climbed from their holes,
We laboured back along exhausted roads

To find the house and village of our birth,
Veterans of all denominations, ranks
Erased, the convoys thundering back at sunset
To a place of weeds, cattle munching wild peaches.

The lily pond and garden beds were gone,
And gates were chained and windows boarded up.
The simple climbing roses, the shy cousins,
With trunks like trees were thick with flowers and insects.

In rooms of fading brick on dusty floorboards
We dreamed of children's voices in a treehouse
And girls in silk shawls and their mothers' clothes,
Who hated boys and played with coloured drinks.

An old sun-weathered ghost stood by our heads,
An earth-stained mattock glittering in his hands.
"The windlass by the well needs a new rope.
This is the childhood house you never left."

II
The mercy of the rose is simply asking.
The soldier scoops up water from the fountain.
Returning from the war they sing in trucks
To unkempt shining fields and passing hills.

His wife and child are painted ghosts, are toys.
He doubts the green new skins of orchard harvests
Ripening in rain-wet leaves to smoky purple,
That glistened like some distant bitter story.

His family looks up at neglected stars,
A group of strangers in their altered bodies.
A large, slow sugar ant will cross his floor,
Insects like jewels will cluster on the wall.

III
In an empty house we sleep by a wicker chair.
Our boots are mudcaked, mattresses are musty.
Acres of roses scent the night, at dawn
Their pink wax stems grow almost visibly,

Out of a tangle of dead wood and weeds,
The hairy pink moss and striped Rosa Mundi,
Thorny survivors of a dead man's dream,
Obscure and refined, wild and commonplace.

Stepping through broken windows into fields
We find beside a spring bubbling from ironstone
A jug upon an old white-painted table.
Pink and grey parrots fly up from some pines.

IV
The planes flew low and strafed a line of trucks
Piled high with looted furniture and clothes.
A boy was standing barefoot in the snow,
A woman giving birth among the rocks.

Watching the sky for death, starved by anger
The soldier turns his back on pulverised hills
And burned-out trees, the field of infinite wars.
He wills himself to pardon viciousness,

Wash out his blood-stained garments and discard
The crutch of hatred, so that he can walk
Not judging through a landscape scoured of noise.
Only amongst some distant carob trees

In limestone hills, an old man, sunburned, digging,
Is turning over dull earth, hardly noticed.
And near the trees with hanging pods are flowers,
The Changing Rose with its five flimsy petals,

And in this aimless landscape is a house,
House of no argument, of sun-dried bricks,
No doors or furniture, the traveller watching
His clothes dry on a rock, birds in a bush.

V
There is no absolute rose, there are the names
And differences, the roses of a night.
The musk, the green rose, the extraordinary mosses,
Where do these strangers come from with their gifts?

Tangled in snow, the shapes, the names, the families,
No mind, no system can contain the rose.
A rose in a glass of water waits by a bed.
A child with a pencil draws a singing bird.

VI
A man is coming back along the roads
Of crumbling bitumen, thistles in potholes,
Wading a river where a bridge has fallen,
Dossing at night by trees, in empty barns,

A man whose papers have been burned is coming,
Mud-stained, baked to the colour of the country,
Coming through passes, crossing plains and borders –
But all the guards are gone, the gates collapsed.

He briefly smiles at strangers as they pass.
Walking past blackened villages, his eyes
Look straight ahead, and still with bandaged feet
He seeks a hearth he knows, a weatherboard house

Amongst the medlar apples, airy verandas
With currants hanging from a trellis, insects
Drifting like dust, air bitter with roses.
At night on the ground beside him, stirring faintly

A woman sleeps in a silk camisole,
Cattle stare from the orchards of his seeking,
Eggs nestle in the seat of a rusting truck.
He wakes alone, walks on month after month.

VII

The briar rose with its apple smell means somewhere
Their families meet, where two old roads join up,
As plants and beasts meet at an earlier place.
The hand with its five petals holds a rose,

The body with its head and hands and feet,
Five pointed star, five petalled rose, the fives
Are spinning from the darkness, flowers and bodies
Flung from the die in their allotted shapes.

VIII

The harvest moon above the thistle forests,
The cattle snuffling follow at a distance,
Dust rising from their hocks, browsing in briars.
Boots that have marched and now must learn to walk

Are hesitant to leave the road and find
Mint under foot, fresh roses in a glass,
A lantern flickering on a pine veranda,
And fingers darning clothes torn on a journey.

IX

At winter sundown following warmth up slopes,
The tracks of cattle are a thermal map
Of an abandoned mountain valley.
Through raspberries and wild chillies brown sheep skelter.

Children have taken to the roads, the children
From ruined cities and bombed tenements,
Living on fruit and game, sleeping on earth,
Finding again the land their parents lost,

Finding among the green of bunya pines
A roofless house with feather mattresses
And frugal oranges in waist-high grass.
They fill old kettles from a gravel creek.

Who left a ladder weathering against a tree,
A rusting bath which cattle sleep beside?
The children call the animals by name
And come in from the dark to share our fires.

X
At night an old man on an island waits,
His lamp reflected in the window pane,
For the brown girl, last of his mistresses,
Who stole the boy he cherished as his son,

His coffee drained, the polished chronicler
Of love and hate, the aquiline nose, pale eyes
Asleep across a page on which he finds
All pain redeemed, all lovers reconciled.

Xl
The characters, their history, who remembers?
The plots and scripts are interchangeable.
Who knows who threw what spear or fired which rifle?
The earliest cottages are under clay.

What matters is a rose grew in wild places
And that all space is immanent with roses,
And strangers, who had little, cared to bring
The grafts and cuttings to a southern climate,

Who suffered, cared for roses as a notion
Of excellence in rugged, lonely places,
Damask and hybrid tea, rambler and moss,
The precious amber hips wrapped in brown paper.

There was no comfort in the heath and sandstone,
But still they built their huts and brought their plants
To scatter fragrance by cold bays and mountains
Growing roots from the centre of the world.

XII
Girls check themselves in mirrors, mothers fuss.
Welcoming fires are burning in the hills.
Tonight your sons will come back from the war,
Crowded in trucks, lights filing through the dust.

Women are reading letters from the dead,
Will dim their lights and lie in bed alone,
But there's a band of welcome, couples embracing,
The soldiers see their wives reflect the light

Of wheat-fields, faces given shape by hardship.
They find each other quickly in the dark.
The voices of the dead touch sleeping foreheads,
And when they wake they will not be consoled.

Old earth, moss-rose, rambler rose in space,
Pinching between your polar caps this garden,
These fleecy blues and greens, this fist of life,
This whorl of petals where we meet and part.
                              1969–2000

A Girl Reading a Book in a Country Village

The shop is closed, there is a single street.
Only a girl at dusk sits in a chair
And reads a book before her parents' house,
While trees hiss with the rush of passing traffic.

The yard in which she reads is small and bare,
The house is weathered brick, a workman's cottage,
But the town has ancient pepper trees and gums
For the green mind of a girl pleasing herself.

She smiles into her book while strangers pass,
Eyes cast down in her public reverie,
Is friendly in a light which has no shadows,
Facing the road and gazing at her page.

NERO'S POEMS

TRANSLATIONS FROM THE PUBLIC AND PRIVATE POEMS OF THE EMPEROR NERO

(1970–2002)

FOR SALVATORE ZOFREA

Proem

I'll drink with my best wine
to aristocracy's decline.
Tyrian purple's out,
and personal luxury.
In hectic verse I'll sing
of an oyster woman's son
with curly hair – that's me –
and embrace my girl-friend – the nation.

Aqueducts

I
The moon. An aqueduct,
water power for our mills.
But Rome is miles from here.
In this brown field, beside
the road my urine spills.
Steam rises from dead grass.

II
While young men touch themselves
in lodging rooms and thieves
hide in your stripes of shadow,
and voyeurs watch behind
a screen of trembling leaves,
this utilitarian dream

on arches high above
the city never stops –
it regulates itself,

on humid days when meat
and cheese are rank in shops
a torrent cold as ferns.

While children fret and bang
the table with a spoon,
and wives strain to hear footsteps,
and lonely migrants pace
beneath our Roman moon
your concrete channel brings

coolness to sultry courtyards,
flowers and bean leaves lift
beneath a tilting bucket.
Our people comatose
on pallets take your gift
of water under pressure.

Stumbling up darkened stairs
without thanks we accept
what makes life possible,
carried in jugs from public
fountains which are kept
constant and clear as springs

by water in its gentle,
calculated fall
from mountain clay and gravels,
and through a family tree
of pipes and tanks to all
our city's mouths and bodies.

Our urbs a body which
attends to its own needs;
the volume is so vast,
careless of what it wastes
our city drinks and feeds
us with impersonal love.

Children on grass-slopes
where you tunnel through a hill,
shout down inspection shafts.
Your massive shadows dwindle
across a plain to fill
a basin or arena,

and water siphoned over
valleys through the care
and skill of engineers
is piped to barbers' shops
with muralled walls (as hair
peels on a hot wet razor).

In public toilets broad
hammed on a marble seat
(framed by a pair of dolphins)
exchanging dinner dates
and gossip we excrete,
water sluicing through channels.

We sit in solemn semi-
circle, grunts and farts
surveyed by sculpted heroes.
Finished we wash and dry
(still talking) wrap our parts
and go home light and free.

From market ponds fishmongers
hoist their thrashing trout
(toddlers dab at the edge).
Around the water-filled
arena thousands shout
as crocodiles scent blood.

But most of all we worship
water which you bring
our monumental baths.

Our Roman's simple dream
of heaven is to fling
his clothes into a niche

and wallow with his friends –
to rub-down, freeze and boil.
We rise from our siesta,
file through the streets, each with
a towel and flask of oil,
to bathe our innocent fat,

the cripple in his litter,
lovers who come late,
this naked congregation
of bodies washing off
their dirt who celebrate
a common love of water.

Public Baths

The baths after sunset.
Statues grapple in half-light.
My whisper sounds enormous.
There are no female wrestlers
or bladder balls slapping
from hand to hand,
no iron hoop rolling
over the mosaic.
Marble's warm to my touch.
Steam hisses somewhere
in a pipe.
I walk through the musk
of the thousand bodies
who cleansed themselves past noon
and have vanished.
Our water culture
depends on an ant's nest of plumbing,

the pipes feeding
even in our sleep.
Slowly as the gods
formed the heavens
we construct our cities of water.

Lady Wrestlers

I've fallen in love with two lady wrestlers.
After they've slapped their peasant bodies
with oil and wax,
and they're all shining and supple,
they coat themselves with dust.
"Pull your head in Gert."
"Rosa you shouldn't have let your husband
get up you this morning."
That says they're ready.
Shifting from foot to foot, they clinch
and sway, a glimpse
of dark cunt, shuddering muscle.
Rosa's thrown and rolls, is up again.
This is true music and philosophy.
Some fingers nip a buttock.
Bravo Rosa! Foul play worthy of our senate!

For Verritus, a Jockey

I
Permanently aged twenty-two!
Five pregnant girl-friends claim your body.
What will the balding praetor do?

Half a million Romans grieve.
Our city grandly mourns its jockeys.
I saw (but just could not believe)

the distant blond spot of your head
trampled in the crushed mineral sands,
that quick whip, joking style go dead,

your green outfit and motionless back
(with knife to cut the reins unused)
face down and bleeding on the track.

II
Horse fever, gossip never stops,
in bed, at meals. Passing we see
your portrait with black crepe in shops.

Girls crowd to snatch a lock of hair,
hostesses never cease discussing
the death of our young millionaire.

Every boy loves a ribboned horse,
the silver panels carved with wings
of chariots flashing round the course.

Horse mania in the young who play
with ivory chariots on a board,
horse mania in the old and grey!

III
Blanketed horses in cold light
at dawn in stalls are blowing steam:
the blue and red, the green and white.

Stable boys, grooms and saddlers fuss.
Floured pastry-cooks arrange their stands.
Trainers in undertones discuss

their mounts, tails held tight in the air,
manes starred with pearls and amulets.
Jockeys lean with a confident stare,

their leggings swathed round calf and thigh,
helmet on head and whip in hand,
the focal point of every eye.

IV
Under the bleachers and arcades
of concrete faced with marble, vintners
whores and astrologers cry their trades.

The race course is a passionate stage.
Starters and judges play their parts,
and gamblers shout with hope and rage.

Mathematics, the calculated line
of chariots as they skim the post
and turn, while coins change hands, define

this world – clean numbers, healthy greed.
These drivers who harass each other
live by one test: fail or succeed.

V
Phoebus Apollo knew no shame
when he was jockey of the sun.
Why shouldn't emperors do the same –

so drivers of the state can feel
real leather pulling in their hands,
sand fly beneath the spinning wheel!

The sudden fall or murderer's knife,
jockeys and emperors are alike,
their death as public as their life.

Crowds watch quick flames and crackling run
along the funeral logs and see
with grief your smoke rise in the sun.

Acte, an Ex-slave

Keep your nose out of Acte, mother.
She's by Special Appointment,
so eager, she wets
if I just look at her.

Build the temple of Venus outside the city,
(they say)
so her rites won't corrupt
young men and matrons!
A working-class fuck is more
than the love you've known, mother.
Murderer and wife of your uncle,
watch out, or I'll build
an altar to Venus right here in our senate!

Civilization

Travelling through pretty scenery,
orchards and valleys and so on,
we find a place that is brown
and barren with fifty pigs
lolling in the sun.
Stop everybody!
This is the landscape for me,
devastated by pigs
who've chewed up the last twig
and hosed out every gully with their urine,
a pasture for gourmets
who lick their plate clean.
Here a man can feel at home.

Rufus

At Sulla's house the other night
you raced in, dressed up as a sausage salesman
with four days' stubble and sandals
dragged through dog-turd.
People looked away as you set up your stall
and shouted, "Sausages for sale!"

Then at Clodius' dinner party
you brought your two favourite dogs along,
insisting they stretch out on your couch.
Later you crawled around on all fours barking.

I know your angle, Rufus.
You think your fool's mask conceals
the determined cunning of an Augustus,
and hope – by sheer persistent foolishness –
to become a celebrity.
"Tiresome and feeble" is the general verdict.
For you this means making an impact.

Pull yourself together, Rufus.
If you keep on boring the pants off us,
you'll find your wife and servant boys
have eloped with your dogs.

Claudia

Claudia, the wife of Rubellius,
she-devil and angel.
Devil at night when Rubellius and the boys
come hand-standing home,
but the front door is locked from inside.
"Claudia! Claudia!"
Her household is stubborn silence and darkness.
"Claudia, I'll smash the door down!"

But her door won't budge.
"Claudia, I'll kill you in the morning!"
But Claudia does not exist.

So Rubellius and the boys
go upstairs to his empty flat.
(No one will rent it for long
because of the uproar downstairs.)
Then the boys play whoopee
(some croaking out of windows)
as the flat devastates.

Claudia, angel of the morning.
She sweeps in, dolled-up in her long gown
with a rustle of perfume,
and gives the punished bodies breakfast
with cool hands.
I've slept under a table.
I say, "Rub my back please." She does.

The Gracchiad

Poor old Gracchus,
he's so wrapped up in dead books,
he celebrates Virgil's birthday
and forgets his own,
always leaving cakes
on the grave of "the master",
and pouring his best Falernian down the libation pipe.
Bring yourself up-to-date, Gracchus.
Don't pour good wine down old plug-holes.
Celebrate some of our modern gods,
myself for instance.

The Death of Virgil

I'm writing judgements and a ghost
appears – the face
of Virgil in an oil lamp flame.

"Nero, a favour, clear my name,"
he says,
"Burn every copy of my epic.
I had to write that awful phrase
'godly Aeneas' so many times,
and then the ultimate disgrace –
that crass anachronism –
how did I let Actium,
your great-grandfather's famous victory,
become the centre panel of Aeneas's shield?
When the death rattle came, the game was up.
I called out from my death-bed:
'Burn my epic.' But Octavian's guards
patrolled the house, no-one dared move.
Nero, I beg you as another poet …"

"Publius Vergilius Maro," I reply,
"I know your game.
You kept your epic under wraps –
and read a passage here and there,
with courtier's smile implying a likeness
between your hero and your greedy listener
to tease the gold from his imperial purse.
And when he died you'd change the lines,
the monument for which he'd paid
would vanish, phrase by phrase. No-one would know.
Virgil, you got it wrong.
His greed for life and fame outlasted yours."

Acte Again

Our classiest Roman matrons are famous
for yelling half a dozen names
before they hit on the right one.
By then it's time for iced drinks.
"Nero ... oh Nero ..."
Too late.
But Acte, my backstreet brat,
gets my name every time.

When she's whipped off her flashy clothes and jewels
there's more taste
in the fold of her buttocks
than all the fan-parties of senators' wives,
and her eyes close
as she kisses my mouth from side to side.

If our Roman bakers baked bread
as fresh as her cunt
I'd eat bread all day.

Roads and Markets

I
Two men squat by their mule and cart,
eating dry bread and cheese, then rise
stiffly and take their picks and start

to hack and trim the sweating load
of ice they'll lift with leather gloves,
and ease down the sheer mountain road

to Rome. Gasping they do not think
of summer nights on terraces,
the conversations as we drink

their ice; they only see the snow
lapsing to water as spring comes,
the valley system where they'll go.

II
At dawn farmers light small wood fires,
drink wine, fix prices and expect
the jostling sandals of the buyers.

A parsnip man with currant eyes
and toothpick arms and legs is perched
on heaped pears. "Cheap," the fruiterer cries

and curses as a copper coin
disappears in a crate of apples.
Today we'll sing of roads that join

market and farm, inspectors of weight,
fish dripping on a marble slab,
the detailed glory of our state.

III
Legions and wheels pass and re-pass.
We govern through a line of stones
cutting across provinces of grass,

our net of roads, law on a map –
riders bringing sealed despatches.
But our imperium is a trap.

I see past villas, soldiers' farms,
plateaux denuded by sordid goats,
men from the outposts carrying arms,

horsemen splashing across a ford,
miles of fast road, and at their head,
a stranger with my personal sword.

For My Goddess Given by an Unknown Admirer

I place before your snow water glance
some winter cyclamens,

my painted wooden statuette
with necklace of red shells.

I could sit in a room all day with you,
my child without a name.

I'll have the senate pass a law:
This world's just a bunch of flowers.

Instructions for a Murder

Write nothing down,
tell them in person.
Choose your elite guards,
and at your mother's seaside villa
their authority will not be questioned.
You may vacillate about killing
a defenceless woman.
When they leave your room
give them fast horses.

Mother

My ears scream,
my eyes drown,
your dead body on a wave breaks over me.

I am a child again,
swimming with you.
Your white shadow with black hair
swims under me
and you surface laughing at my side,
the daughter of generals.

We go fishing, lightly clothed,
mother and son.
You pile up brushwood,
pluck wild rosemary
and grill our catch on the rocks.
Your feet like leather,
your skin tanned as an oyster-woman,
I watch you peel squid,
watched by their black intelligent eyes.
Tossing your clothes off,
you touch my boyish parts with a smile
and head for the water.
As you frolic
your dark hair glistens.

But, mother, on the beach
they've hastily stacked up driftwood for your pyre,
they're cremating your body on a dining couch.
Your lies and manipulations are burning away,
your self-love dressed as mother love,
your talk at dinner parties of your baby.
"He rarely cried, because he lacked the voice.
That's why he'll never make a singer."
They're burning the smell of you mother,
the sexless marriage which you forced on me,
your claims to every dress
in the imperial wardrobe,
your jumping up on the dais
to share my throne.

Memories of you are drifting ash:
in a closed litter at noon
the two of us play games.
"Get your hands off me," I tease.
"And you too," you reply.
We scandalise the street.
Men are irrelevant,
you tell me, for your pleasure.
Even when lovers pant on top of you,
you despatch yourself with your hand.
You laugh: "Be careful of such women."

The daughter of generals,
they are burning you on a dining couch,
but you have left your powerful body.
Disdaining ferries
you swim across the Styx.
There are lights and crowds on the beach
and dead men wading out to see you.
Uncle Claudius whom you married and poisoned
for me, gets your first kiss,
then Lepidus, your old lover,
and brother Caligula
who shared your bed and talked with statues,
all of the men you loved
only for love of power.
You are welcomed by our imperial line.
On the dim bank they swarm.
Our dead who married cousins
and killed other cousins,
flutter and clutch at you for news.
"My boy has killed me," you announce,
"but I'm an emperor's mother!
I carry on my breasts his farewell kisses
and in my trunk the knife-wounds which he sent."

Rome welcomes and forgets your death,
only a son remembers
and leaves your grave unmade and raw
beneath the heights where Julius Caesar's mansion
looks out to sea.

Why do you show yourself naked,
your black bush flecked white?

I don't forget the debt,
but Nero leaves you drowning, mother,
not your boy.

Sweet Suite

Every big wooden beam has a beetle inside it,
the rankest desires lurk under the most conservative togas.
How sweet it is to rob some finely-dressed Roman matron
(out after dark in her carriage)
and find she's some well-known senator.
Sweet is the moment when angry husbands tear off the bedclothes
and you run through cool gardens pursued by diminishing curses
(while guards wait in the shadows of shrubs).

It's sweet after a night of burgling to auction the proceeds,
dirty books from the houses of famous puritans,
in gold-leaf cylinders with prettily painted red and blue knobs.
It's a gay and responsive collection of bidders
as I auction the toga (purple stripe of course)
of an angry someone whose cognomen starts with P,
stripped naked in an alley last night (I relate)
but his parts were so wrinkled and small I gave back his loincloth.

On hot afternoons when actors are bored and jealous
it's sweet to sit incognito in a wig
and applaud in the half-empty theatre as they scrap.
"Kick him in the balls, Fulvius. Scratch his eyes out, Brassius."

I've roared myself hoarse when our actors get going.
A broken chair leg in the face is politeness for them.
And it's nice when some Scythian lady's gyrating her navel
to run up on stage and join in the fan dance.

There's a ton of loving in our city when nights are warm,
as old Rosa rolls off old Marcus like an apple from a tree.
In the night of love the vegetable carts rumble in.

Charred sausages, sweet cinders ...

On the Beat

Down on the beachfront at night
savage hands drag
me into the shadows.
Each time I ask
do they bring joy or a knife?
The savage hands
make me lean against the brickwork gasping.
They could strip me, rob me, stab me,
I wouldn't care.
But I know they feel as I do.
We know each other by signals,
fingers clicking.
On the beachfront at night
I go to meet my black god
who holds my life in his hands.

The Night of the Wedding

Flinging my clothes on the floor,
about to be deflowered
the maiden emperor of the Romans!

Suddenly I was
my mother, little gelded Sporus,
every girl and widow,
the Ladies' Brigade
of bleeding and suffering ghosts –
my hymen – just a commodity
as fake blood was splashed on the sheets.

The Morning After the Wedding

Waking with you at my side
in the smell of melting ices and stale wine,
my bridal veil flung on the floor,
Servants with mops move through the palace.
It's morning. I can never be deflowered
again, weeping as I was pierced,
and glad, the full bit,
like any poor young thing.
Husband, you do funny things to me.
I gave up all my girlish toys
for you.
But even a simple girl has her tricks.
(My fingers prowl beneath the sheets.)
You can't beat a woman in bed.

Ode to the Beauty of the World

I dedicate myself to beauty.
My life shall be wine and roses.

Uomo universale – here I come!
For party tricks
head down and roaring like a lion
let's bound across the salons
of well-bred hostesses
and burrow into your garments, ladies and gentlemen

to chew your mucus.
Here I come,
a couple of black hairs curled in my teeth,
the spirit of universal love
ready to lick your ugly parts
that smell like an open latrine in midsummer.
My ear-rings jingling,
nothing can resist my encyclopaedic compassion.
I am man and woman,
poet and wrestler,
imperator and thief on the run.

With my face on your coins
I'll buy you a bag of onions
or a pretty boy.
I'm the pin-up boy in every whorehouse.
They want pictures of me
done in metal,
heaps of them with curly hair and dimpled chin.

This is what I bring:
happiness without morals
and order with a sparse seasoning of rules.
Let me sing, Romans,
now the days of your glory have come
of my common peace
which builds bath houses in Croatia
and loves you right down to your scrotum.

The New Academy

Education,
not entertainment for the masses
is the answer!
I say, send back the hippopotami.

(Already I see lions and elephants
strolling off decks
into the foothills of Africa,
amazed.)
Close down the gladiatorial schools.
It's finis to mass spectacles of blood.
(As the crowds roared,
I'd watch for the odd man bent over
vomiting with shock
and send him a bag of coins.)

It's my decree
there shall be education,
music schools and play readings
in the arenas,
the rhetorician's paradox will hover
where the lion's paw swiped,
doctorates will spread like an epidemic.
We'll study pond-insects,
sewerage systems
and the basket weaving of the Etruscans.
No subject will be too minute.
Your garbage man will address you
in a dead language,
barbers' razors will describe
a philosophical point with a quick flick.

How will we keep the unemployed employed?
With instruction, not games,
with books, not blood, I say.
Like aqueducts the new academies will stand
piping knowledge into our slums,
and will never end.

Aqueducts II

With tourist necks we see
ferns sprouting from cracked mortar
and lichen-spotted arches.
As sheep graze by the piers
a colonnade of water
transports its mountain coolness

to the mud-settling tanks
and water towers of Rome,
feeding by gravity
amongst the high-rise suburbs
for men to carry home
in jars from public fountains.

Water commissioners
are plagued by water fraud,
unauthorised pipes to brothels
or courtyards of the rich,
and loss from channels flawed
by age and settlement cracks.

Driving past farms we see
illegal tombs and trees
trespass on the arcades,
paddocks suspiciously green,
our Roman do-as-you-please
with public rights and easements.

Limestone deposits show
leaks which we cannot cure,
imperfect, dripping on
our heads, while we abuse
yet venerate this pure
and neutral flow of water.

Epithalamium

I
Double divorce, double disgrace
the matrons mutter. My Poppaea,
one glance of sunlight from your face

leaves them for dead. When we undress
stepping out from our clothes
we blow no lights out on our nakedness.

Your gaze meets mine, frank, indiscreet
(my wife, your husband in the shadows),
hand touches buttock, our lips meet.

We hurt to love, life devours life.
Your nipple hardens touched by tongue.
Hymen's ring makes adultress wife.

II
We exchange passionate billets doux,
wild gifts if we're apart. "Nero
this cat …" "Poppaea, goose eggs for you …"

After a fight or chariot race,
my head dissolving in your lap
I lie and gaze up at your face.

In crowds you subtly lean, hands twine …
Some nights your lust is fierce and sudden.
Rotten with wine, your thighs ride mine.

Each glance, each kiss is contraband.
"Fancy it's you again," we laugh
and every night's a one-night-stand.

III
Divorce, abortion – anarchy!
the stoics mutter. But the young
see dancing bodies who are free.

A million different skins – there's joy
displayed in every public baths;
beauty steams from each girl and boy.

Our bodies teach us what is true –
this bowl of cyclamens, this bed
prepared for love (as we undo

our clothes), not theories are what's real.
I bite your arching back and breasts.
We touch and know how gods must feel.

IV
Roma, Amor reversed. The heart
of empire is our happy bed.
Rome splits when we're one hour apart.

Our rule is love. With naked skin
and naked minds we lie. I touch
your crevices, you take me in.

We screw until we're bruised and red.
Darling, we're nuts. We wish to die,
we say, together in one bed.

Still moist with love, love on each face,
your cold hand clenched around my prick,
the pyre shall burn our last embrace.

Notes for a New Civilisation

I
Our youth shall bury the obscene
and bloody gladiatorial swords.
We'll wrestle, we'll be Greek and clean.

II
Our poets will write of moss and grime
on fading stucco, broken toys
and channels green with weeds and slime.

III
Palm trees and poplars in the street
will calm the blood lust of arenas,
and leaves will civilise the heat.

IV
We won't exclude the common man,
our palaces shall have no courtyards,
space will be freed, an open plan.

V
This world is all that we require,
and touching you, Poppaea,
I touch not shadow, but a living fire.

A happy bed's a happy home,
unprudish naked ease and grace.
Our love becomes our love of Rome.

VI
We swim on lapis lazuli days
and pick at melons on a terrace,
and hearing poetry and plays

our pax Romana hangs, the white
plume of Mount Aetna over groves
by day, and a red fire at night.

Gardens

Because she coveted his garden
my mother had a man accused.
Stroll through our costly real estate
with me, Poppaea, our guilt excused
by daisies growing from cracked stonework.

But as we walk, fine drifts of spray
blow on your dress and make us run
like children down a cypress walk
through intervals of shade and sun.
You break a gilded sandal strap.

Our eyes adjust to sudden gloom
as on a grotto's marble seat
we pause. You drop your sandals off
and brush the gravel from your feet.
Barefoot you're off again, bending

to pick a small rose for your hair
and raging when you find I've set
the water-trap, surrounding you
with walls of water, jet on jet
crashing and bubbling on mosaic.

Panting and drenched we slowly thaw.
A bee vibrates a rose, we hear
girls on a distant handball court.
We can pull down our walls of fear.
An unwalled city's open space

with vineyards by our blocks of flats
will halt our spectacles of blood.
Our unemployed will raise their hens
and lettuces from city mud.
Great parks will liberate our poor.

Grasshoppers click across ploughed fields
as we advance, hands linked, and talk.
Courtyard gardens hide and enclose.
Exposed to sun and wind we walk
and look back at our Golden House,

the colonnades of a long stage,
where we are gods on public view.
Gardeners will spell in topiaried box
your name and mine, my love for you
as obvious as this bank of poppies.

At theatres we kiss open-mouthed.
Livia was chaste, Augustus said
upon a million threepenny bits.
Our coins will say you're good in bed
and love a landscape architect.

At noon we rest in a pavilion.
Facing the constant northern light
with brush and paint, I sketch the scene,
a Venus blotched with shade, the flight
of dragon-flies past iris pools,

ponderous birds snapping unripe cherries;
but worlds of sound escape my brush,
from pines the parrot's tearing cry,
the stir and quarrel, splash and rush
of concrete channels painted blue.

When cornflowers flop in summer doldrums,
like hope, a thread of water quivers
into a rust-marked marble basin,
and everywhere small man-made rivers
feed ponds or race down water-stairways.

But Terpnos' lyre, as we munch quinces,
tonight will flash through shadows, wait
by sunlit porticos, then plunge
through complications and create
in sound the waters of our gardens.

For winter by this wall I've planned
a windless alcove for the sun.
Naked we'll lie and soak up heat.
But look! The sky's changed, shivers run
through myrtles, swollen clouds are poised.

Over brooding acanthus beds
there's purple lightning, a neat crash
as close as snapping timber followed
by dull reports. As rain squalls lash
and pit the surface of our lake

men see this theatre in the sky
as the gods' mad and playful acts.
My sun-god is the sceptical
imagination lighting facts,
and, now the rain's gone, steam from urns

trailing violets on balustrades.
A man at sunset blows a horn.
You stand, half veiled to tantalise,
and feed the geese and hares with corn
as they emerge from fading thickets.

All gardens perish with their owners,
and statues need the play of light
and water for their eloquence.
We walk past daisies shut at night
up terraces to lights and friends.

Eating with Friends

Emotions can't be managed, Cupid aims his shanghai blindly,
but for a night we eat and talk in a planned happiness,
lobsters and truffles, apples poached in wine and honey,
course succeeding course, like the serene transitions of a sunset,
my friends, my own academy – artists and engineers,
builders of a new world, inspired and foolish in our cups.

It's midnight in my Golden House. Poppaea, with her veils
awry, mascara smeared, is yawning, rubs herself against me.
I wish to go on talking, democrat with equal friends.
(Parade your vice, and I'll forgive your crimes – even your insults.)
Flambeaux are mirrored in the lake. The scent of moonlit rose beds
invades through windows as we scheme up bacchanals to shock
the senate – prostitutes arranged as living statues, daughters
of knights soliciting from makeshift brothels on the lawns.
The painted stars and moon revolve above our circular room.
With our ideas and art we'll make the world a Golden House.
The surface of my wine's a curve, its centre is the earth's.

I send the shadow at my side, my taster off to bed.
Drinking is now like dancing without clothes – nothing between
the wine and me – nothing between my friends and me – our talk
is naked – we may never meet and talk and eat again.
If gods can visit men, they do – at dinner amongst friends.

Our "Sun-god" at Home with Poppaea

Your fury brushed aside the flowers I picked – late home from the races.
So I kicked you in the stomach – Poppaea, my angel or my harlot?
The dusk is sultry as our workmen pack and hurry home
across the fields and woods I've built replacing slums.
Fabullus in his dowdy toga wipes his brushes clean.
Still wet, his great blue mural dazzles the wall of our dining room.
Tonight I'll strum my zither singing of our Golden House
that's growing marble block by marble block across the lawns,
I'll sing of mornings when mosquitos sink in bedroom corners,
I wake and bite your ear, and through the window men are whistling
and wheeling barrowloads of sand and lime across grass.
Then someone hammering copper nails sets your invective going.
A chisel chips and carves a triton's beard – we're shouting insults.
A crane is hoisting up a gilded cupid – you're in tears.
Why do men love impossibility and tangled bedclothes,
wet eyes and breasts and the mons veneris which crucifies
the man it welcomes? But tonight you stare through slits of hatred,
nursing our feverish two-year-old as though she's yours alone,
flicking your fan, the heart-beat at the centre of an empire.
Outside, crickets are singing in the darkened garden beds.
I pace along unfinished colonnades past builders' rubble,
thinking of bruised carnations – rejecting classical restraint.

By the Sea

I
"Our Golden Age is now,"
Caesar told Cicero,
pacing the beach. "Our verse
and prose have flowered at last."
As they exchanged bons mots
shadows swam out at sea.

"We are an inland race,"
  the barrister replied.
"A river brings us trade.
  Protected by our hills,
  our strength and dogged pride
  are products of this landscape.

"The Greeks as seaside dwellers,
  doomed by disunity
  and their indented coastline,
  hanker for foreign things.
  The presence of the sea
  unsettles and distracts."

"My dear old hedonist,"
  Caesar said with a smile,
"you have your seaside villa.
  Call me corrupt and modern.
  Marble veneer's my style,
  not your republican brick."

II
Poppaea, we'll leave these two
  old cronies on the beach,
  the lawyer flustered by
  young women who can't weave,
  and Caesar whose long reach
  is with us in this room.

There's sand inside our bed.
  Jump up, shake out the sheet –
  We swam then slept, my hand
  prone on your lazy bottom -
  Now with each downward beat
  you flick sand at the sun.

Our Golden Age is now.
As sea-lights undulate
and flicker on the walls,
we lie without desire.
Our bodies radiate
the hours of sun we've shared.

Marble seats where we lounge
and fish and sip our wine,
cypress walks to a beach
and fleets of pleasure boats
are symptoms of decline,
says Cicero, the sea

and sun contaminate.
We swim for miles and sky
and water fill our minds,
the oleandered cliffs
and villas simplify
into a distant line.

We give ourselves to change,
these waves and now the sand
receiving our limp bodies.
A lighthouse flares at dusk.
This marram grass, unplanned,
resists the moralist.

Nero, Hades, Poppaea

Pacing the palace grounds after your death,
I found your gilded sandal strap. I stopped
and heard the girlish intake of your breath,
and recognised a mirror you had dropped.

I saw your footprints fading in the dew
and followed through a half-built portico,
past beds of dried weeds, down an avenue
of oaks and into woods I did not know –

a wilderness that had no birds or sound.
My feet ran down a path to an abyss,
down basalt stairways, over cratered ground,
and halted at the great black gates of Dis.

Cerberus stopped barking at the empty plain,
and the gates opened, as I touched my lyre
and stepped into that featureless terrain,
flickering with pinpoints of volcanic fire.

I queued behind an old crone carrying sticks
and fanned myself – there was a sulphurous smell.
A ferry heaved to on the River Styx.
"Your pennies," Charon cried and rang a bell.

We left the shore, Charon pulled at the oars
and shadows flocked and twittered in the air.
I looked for some small thing I knew was yours –
a trace of rouge or scent, a strand of hair.

The painted lips of faded Jezebels
hissed in my ear: "Good times. No clothes. Get pissed."
"My cockleshells, where are my cockleshells?"
a voice – Caligula's – called in the mist.

Some friendly hands reached out, a garrulous stammer:
"Dear s-stepson, what a j-joy to m-meet you here –
I'm still at work on my Etruscan grammar,
but when I write, the w-words just d-disappear!"

The childless god sat on his granite throne,
frowned at my golden lyre and scowled at me.
He spat and scratched his fleas, morose, alone:
"She's mine. Don't ask for what can never be."

"We gods are blamed for crimes we don't commit,"
I spoke and plucked my lyre. "Hades is great.
He can unravel what the Furies knit."
I paused and watched his face contract with hate.

"Her Abyssinian cat howls by her bed,
her maids bicker and sprawl in summer heat.
I rise at noon, unshaven and eyes red
and pad depressed through the imperial suite.

"I'd paint her with a parasol and screen,
then we would eat and drink, no longer care.
Drunk, with a daisy in her mouth, she'd lean
and breathe on me and ruffle up my hair.

"Release her from the fields of asphodel!
Show you are free, great god. Break all your rules!"
"Vain poet, as you lead her out of Hell
don't look behind, like all the other fools."

My lyre hung from my belt. I stared ahead,
and walked that long road through an endless night
straining to hear your gasps and tentative tread.
Slowly the road curved up towards the light.

"Poppaea," I called, and heard no answer back.
"We're almost there." There was a distant rumble,
the ground began to oscillate and crack.
I thought I heard a cry for help, a stumble.

A trick of Hades took me by surprise.
I turned and saw your bridal veil on fire,
your charred and shrunken face and bloodshot eyes.
Your lips spat: "Curse you Nero and your lyre.

"A normal man would not have looked behind,
I wanted children, a domestic life
and someone unimaginative, kind …"
The flames consumed you and I called, "My wife!"

Lament on the Death of Seneca

My friend (and tutor) Seneca
what a pity you lived in a flat
above a bath house.
When you lectured me
I could hear in your epigrams
the rumble of hot water pipes.
When your heroines declaim on stage
it's the boisterous cries
of large matrons wading in up to the waist.
What a pity you came all the way from Spain
to say those nasty things
and die in a bath.

Potters' Field

Maecanas buried it under a garden.
Fresh soil, twenty-five feet deep
had to be dumped on the rotting bodies and scraps
to satisfy his manicured mind.
I'd have left that cratered landscape
in full view of the city,
an affront,
rotting cabbages,

the stench of battered victims
and drunks that no one claimed
rising up in anger.

When I go to a new city I ask,
"Show me your potters' field."
The Lord Mayor and officials look nonplussed.
I say, "Show me where you throw the bodies
of your murdered whores!"

Armed with smelling salts and my scribe
(and one or two close friends)
we rummage through dead bodies
and vegetable scraps
for small tokens, a child's toy, a broken comb,
or a nicely carved walking stick.
"That donkey's rather high,"
I say to a friend who is squirted
by something rotten he treads on.
"I wouldn't have minded *her*," he says, pointing.

The stench is dreadful.
"Not many lyrics around here today!"
I tell my scribe.
Bitter melons scramble
across ageing piles of refuse.
In the distance old men are poking with sticks.
Birds fly up from the open pits
where the bodies and scrapings have been flung.
Smoke drifts from burning mounds.

The gardens of Maecanas are a fake.
The petty criminals and the poor,
who had no friends to bury them,
cry out under twenty-five feet of soil.

I'll put their bodies in the forum
propped in places of honour
for the sun and wind
to dissolve.
Maecenas and respectable people
dress death in black veils and shrill mourning,
hide it beneath a garden.
I'll pass a law:
"Death is fact,
and after death there is nothing,
and nothing is nothing to fear."

As I was squatting one dusk
in a thistle patch behind a tomb
a smart ghost tapped my shoulder and said,
"I don't exist. We don't exist.
There are no gods,
no heroes waiting in the Elysian fields."
I laughed
at my own unimportance,
with relief as the huge machine
of religion blew away in the grass.

All the milk and wine we pour
into tombs
are a sham.
Why are we frightened of a corpse or a turd?
A man who handles faeces and corpses
has no horror of death,
and lives happy in his flat, with wife and child.
He stacks bodies and refuse on his cart
without contempt or sorrow,
loads and unloads
with the deftness of habit.

Bitch Talk

When it rains, my friend the fuller is sad:
an empty shop won't pay
for his army of serving girls,
indoor fountain
and murals of pomegranate trees.

When it's sunny the parasols
float through his door
like a butterfly plague.
(The air clots
with the powder from fluttering wings.)

You don't need to sell to women, he says.
His hand touches
a slightly faded spot on a matron's garment.
"Tsk," he sucks his palate
with sympathy,
or pats a bulge madam thought
was hidden.
Such compassion.
The wretched woman goes to water,
she'll sell her soul
for a dress with a slim look
or colour for her blotchy face.
"You've no idea," he says,
"what they spend on themselves."

You don't sell, you guide them
into bath salts, silver combs, special perfumes –
all for the love
of some gladiator who's murdered
five hyaenas and seven men.

The husbands of our town wouldn't know
what our women spend on themselves
or their lovers –
they're too busy on their knees
worshipping the eaters of oats.

My Singing Career

Rules must be observed.
Waiting my turn
standing in the queue,
popping my name in the urn,
whose name is pulled out first?
Your emperor's of course.
then I sing for three hours flat.
I'm sweating. What a tour de force!
When my teacher signals
to rest my voice, I pause.
My Alexandrian sailors
start their antiphonal applause.
What artistry!
Who wins first prize?
Whose face is reflected
in a thousand eyes?

No one else is allowed to sing.
Rules must be observed.

The Grand Tour of Greece

Light bonfires on the seven hills,
heap garlands on my statues.
Today, on my birthday,
I'll write a poem!

I've never been so sharp, so critical, so keen,
the poem flows through me like cold white wine,
but hardly have I started on my tour of Greece,
twining in my hair
wild anenomes from the grass,
than the chorus of horrible poets starts its pursuit.

"Emperor, just let me read one lyric ...
Now that was shorter than I thought,
let's read one more ...
Do you think you could get this published in Rome:
Could you get Petronius Arbiter
to read my epic?"
(As though he mattered more than me!)

We're just unpacking
in a provincial governor's palace
when the deputation of the local poetry society arrives.
A half-shaven youth begins
with an ode for the moon,
then his sister and uncle recite some awful love lyrics.
I announce
that I've slight diarrhoea.
"We'll wait until you've finished," they say.

The worst thing's their funny poems,
the simpering self-congratulation
and deathly smiles as they recite.
At Corinth my diarrhoea was severe,
at Sparta I cracked lightning and thunder non-stop,
but they declaimed all the while
as I was dying on the lavatory.
The nine muses joined forces with the three furies.
Even a nice young screw I found
recited an elegy for his grandfather,
before we could get down to business.

Poets, I've decided
are as hardy as warts or thistles.
We're a race as common
as ticks in dry scrubland,
and our bite persists as long.
Inspect a ruined temple
in a desert place,
and the voice of a mummified poet
will drag you
into his sarcophagus.

Unpaid, we write
for friends who shun our work,
and the glory of our Empire.

In Praise of Tourism

At the end of summer Greece
is a land of the dead.
Burned plants and mountain slopes
linger through winter,
then heal with a fortnight of spring.
Anemones and white sheets of camomile
lacquer the plains and gullies.
Flowers are lapis lazuli in the grass,
painted moths and beetles
inhabit the scrublands.

Mercury, God of Tourists,
lend me your winged sandals,
show me the roads I've known,
days of jolting in midsummer
over cobblestones
through plains of dried grass thick with dust –
and the relief at dusk,
the country house with fragrant wine and rissoles
served by a peasant girl,

and next day a theatre
where I sing again in triumph,
new houses and new people,
friendships and cliques,
then we move on.

The journey becomes a passion,
as the caravan of imperial culture
trundles from city to city.
Day succeeds day,
the lion we meet on the road,
the old man's face tattooed with birds,
the grasshopper on my pillow.
Sweating on horseback or in my carriage,
smacking insects from my face,
I am driven by hunger for new places
through heat and cold,
ravines and hot springs.

At night a sealed despatch arrives,
to toss aside
for others to read.
I'm busy watching
the mosquito-choking smoke
from flambeaux
as frogs are croaking amongst willows.
I piss behind a dusty bush.

The roads were built by our fathers
for trade and war,
but the young are taking them over,
avid for foreign culture.
We cram our lives with faces and places,
lovers of the poppy
whose red petals blow away in the grass.

Advice to Young Poets

Murder your mother,
go to live in a flat
and forget who you were.

Keep away from schools of rhetoric.
With their hyperbole
and unreal situations
they can only train liars for the senate.

Let your school of philosophy
be the streets at night.
Roam with gangs
of disillusioned aristocrats.
Wear a poisonous flower in your hair.

When you've nothing to say
don't write.
Our world has too much poetry.

Celebrate unpopular heroes,
heroes of the bedroom, like Paris.
Revise your inspirations.
From a heap of cancelled tablets
your true thought will emerge.

Do all these things,
and you still won't be a poet.

It's Business as Usual

On these cold mornings I hate
being shaved.
A white cabbage moth floats drowned in a fountain.

Galba does not exist.
There are no revolts in Spain.
Of course all the troops are loyal!
After dusk there are parties,
  non-stop music and dancing,
  but some faces are missing.
"Do something," my friends say. "Do something."
We have drunken water fights
  after midnight in heated baths.

Your Troubadour Emperor

A philosopher or lawyer's a sore arse,
a senator's a sharp attack of piles.
My friend's that ape-like man who wheels a barrow.
I shake his hairy hand. He spits and smiles.
The streets where litters lurch and hawkers shout,
the pumpkin scraps, this is where I belong.
Galba can have my sceptre – I'll survive –
while I can stop the traffic with a song!

Dreams

Ants flying through the night
water running over floors
a door swinging in moonlight
roadside tombs
a voice out of the ground
a lantern carried by no one.

Advice to Emperors

Simplify,
as gardeners say,
pruning their vines.

Cut back your duties,
let your hair grow long.
Ignore rules of dress,
give audience
in slippers and silk dressing gown
embellished with a spotted scarf.

Poke out your tongue at old fogeys.
If an official goddess doesn't work
piss on her image.
Single out
your true from your false wants.

Reserve your judgments.
Get written opinions from the best sources
then write out the verdict yourself
(late at night)
as the unanimous decision of the court.

Don't let advisers drag you back to Rome
when there are singing contests
to win in Greece.
Sculpt and paint,
but not like some timid amateur.
Show them
savage and fantastic landscapes
or street musicians and gladiators
hacked out of the pigment.
Build a palace to astonish the senate
then call it "The Shack".

Go on stage.
The senate will hate you, the people will love you.
Play the role of heroes and villains
or a bereaved mother.
An emperor's an entertainer,
an empire a super-show.

Send people home at dusk and happy
forgetting the knives they wear.

After dark go out on the streets,
become a thief,
bash and be bashed.
Your blood will be blood
which has flowed on the cobble-stones at night.
Let the sores of the humble
speak in your judgments.
Ask questions and more questions.

Fill an arena
with water and crocodiles
then drown all the senate
and your statues will have garlands for ever ...
(if I haven't beaten you to it).

Steal other men's ideas.
History acclaims leaders
who are unoriginal.
Our republic is an elephant
you can lead, but not push.
Don't worry about your extremities;
a province or two may fall
to an Asian or British tribe
then revert.

If you fart loudly,
don't apologise.
Your imperial quirk will be praised.
Keep yourself fit with wrestling and riding.
From time to time
let the people cheer you in the arena
tussling with an old lion
whose teeth and claws have been pulled.

If the presentation is right
murder in high places
won't concern the people.
But watch your treasury.
Don't spend fabled wealth in the caves of Africa
until you've seen it.
(That fraud, Philobius!)
When there's no wheat for the plebs
there's worry in the palace
as a shipload of sand arrives
from grain-exporting Egypt.

When generals conspire against you
become a philosopher on a marsh
of white mineral sands,
alone in a miniature world of close-up,
picking through fine grass-tufts
for bird-bones,
yellow daisy discs
and purple snapdragons
the size of a baby's fingernail.

Your genius will inform the age.
Cultivate erudition, expand your tastes,
become like the latest and largest model of water organ,
then play only simple tunes.

Decipher
your own mind.
Official business, urgent matters –
how did I emerge from all those files
and become a man?

At My Tomb

A whore or two, an ageing queen will come
to scatter flowers upon my tomb and say
a world of style and possibility
has shrunk and life is nasty, dull and grey.
Each year they'll look more painted and absurd,
like summer insects when the days turn cold.

Imagined Scenes from the Second Half of My Life

Stripped of my sceptre,
a singing beggar
I sleep in doorways
or under the sky.

Some of the jewelled friends
of my youth
laughing and camping it up
walk past. I hide
in the shadows of an arcade.

Soldiers of the emperor
make an early morning sortie
through frosty estates.
Who's this old corpse
shaving himself amongst the roadside tombs?

I thieve from rubbish tips.

I meet Acte at a public fountain.
We wish to weep because we're old,
and she takes me home to her bed.
But I'm gone before sun-up.

Who's this old beggar
with bandy legs and sun-weathered face
who skips and juggles
and sings lampoons
and can charm a penny from a Jew?

Mother in your white marble tomb
aren't you proud of your son?
My art is my life.

A Vision Addressed to Emperors of the Future

Oh my brothers of the sceptre,
my hair is light blond
and worn in ringlets.
My eyes are dull blue
and acne is a problem,
but my neck is thick
and I get my way.
Oh my brothers of the sceptre
do I see you in a mirror?
Smiling Spaniards, stolid Arabs
with my sceptre and imperial ring –
Rome as a language and a way of life.

Old Italy is dead.
The clans are forgotten.
Grass is growing
on the hearths of our feuds.
Rome has become the world,
our armies have vanished,
sand is blowing across our outlying fortifications
and earth has swallowed
the blackened sticks where our last division
lit their camp fires.
Our soldier settlements are now just farms.

I walk through the moonlit streets
of Necropolis,
plucking my lyre.
There are acres of mortuary marble,
with wheat and cypresses amongst the graves.
I stop at my tomb.
The ghost of Acte still visits my bones.
Some close friends and parasites
rustle out of the fields
to listen as I play and sing
satirical sketches about the new world order
of peace and love.
We drink and spill our wine in the grass.
Then I play some rowdy pieces
on bagpipes and water organ.
Some of us dance and stub our toes
on bits of broken marble.
A silver eagle flies over
heading towards the unrisen sun
as we sink back into the earth.

SPRING FOREST

(1970–2010)

FOR ROSS MCINERNEY (1918–2010) THROUGH WHOSE
VOICE THESE POEMS ARE SPOKEN

Getting Started

When we first came our house
was two weatherboard rooms
in a bare paddock.

I was just back from a war.
There were no trees
and I chose the name "Spring Forest".

It was dark when we drove up
and lit our pressure lamps and unpacked.
Our children found potatoes sprouting
on a wire mattress of a large iron bed.
What were they doing there?
my daughter kept asking.

We burned iron bark
in the old brick fireplace,
rubbing etherised hands into warmth.

At dawn Sally and Peter were out
calling in the frost, exploring.
A long icicle hung from the tank.
That day five cars passed on the road,
and the children ran out every time.

Photographs

My wife's the daughter of a professor
and married the winner
of the brick holding competition

at the Cucumgilliga School picnic.
Sally, aged twelve, photographed us men
in various postures of expiry
tilted over backwards, or bent forward
holding a brick in each hand in the heat.
But there I am bolt upright, holding
my bricks out to the sun.

My wife born in a large house has come
to our two rooms of aged weatherboard
and an added one of iron.
You can see cracks of sky through the ceiling –
and there's no power,
so our evening conversations take place
by the greenish-yellow light of pressure lamps –
and there's no water laid on,
so my wife washes up in a plastic dish.

Olive, do you regret your life
of photographing country weddings,
and recording local children in silver bromide?
Do you regret the calf born at three in the morning
when I tramp out into the frost?
Or our two children
playing with rocks and broken glass
out in the hot scrublands,
running and calling
to imaginary playmates?
Their garden of jonquils
withered in the first week of summer.
Olive at Christmas wrapping gifts,
inserting notes:
in a book, "Ross with love from Snotty" (the cow),
"Sally with love from Marco Polo
and the guinea pigs" on a box of chocolates.
A pocket knife for Peter given by the geese.

Hunger and Fear

My laboratory
is the dust where I stand,
the sulphur smells of the farmyard.

Your tests show fear
is stronger than hunger.
Maybe true of a laboratory animal,
bred so he's easy to handle.
But try the same trick with farm pigs –
too big and difficult for white-coated technicians.

When their own grass is shrinking,
and the next door paddock is green,
pigs will gather
away from the electric fence, and scream –
in their minds they are already burning.
Then they charge.
Small ones slip under, and big ones,
tangled in wire,
wriggle through – screaming as it crackles.

We are like farm pigs, half feral,
and the fences can't cope
with our numbers.

Ex AIF (Australian Imperial Force)

An invitation to poverty –
soldier settlement farms.
We were back from a war.
Our government said: the young men
saved the country,
they shall farm the country.

There was a stone office building –
I don't know which city –
and a fan was revolving
from a high ceiling
and someone drew a line on a map.
This line became my five hundred acres
and a standard form letter
inviting me to poverty.

No one added up how many acres make a living,
and I mortgaged my life
to a low interest loan
with a thirty-year term.
But my eyes were open. I signed.

The large properties, broken up
mourn their lost parts.
They will never be whole again.
Small fibro houses
have grown on the fragments
like mould on bread
and dream tenaciously
under the stars of the antarctic night.

We do not starve. We trade favours.
I go away to earn.
You water my animals.
You go away. I water yours.
A countryside of absentee peasants.
But we return to our mortgaged acres,
our lives of scratching to pay bills,
my life I cannot reject
of squatting on this veranda
as a rainbow lorikeet pecks my finger
taking bread from my hand.

The Old Rifle

In the long school holidays in summer
I'd be out in the orchard
with an old rifle Mr Long fixed up,
shooting at rosellas
that were raiding fruit.
As each bird fell I'd watch
where the blue and red flickered down,
then I'd drop the rifle and run.
That way I stocked my aviary
with broken-winged rosellas.
And somewhere in my childhood
I dropped and forgot that rifle.

A year of grass grew over it.
Men were working in the orchard one day,
and my brother, the dentist, four years old,
was playing in the grass and found the rifle,
rusted all over – a wreck –
as though it had lain there for years.
My brother knew how to hold a gun
and pointing it at Jim Long, said,
"I'll shoot you Mr Long."
He said, "Oh don't shoot me, Barry –
shoot Bill over there."
Barry pointed the gun at Bill.
"I'll shoot you Uncle Bill."
"Don't shoot me, Barry," Bill said,
"Shoot Ted here." And Ted said,
"Why not shoot Jip?"

Jip was a good sort of dog,
my black and white fox terrier cross,
who was racing around the orchard,
looking for rabbits.
Barry dropped to one knee and squinting took aim.
Jip dropped dead on the spot.

They buried him, telling no one,
but in their haste made the hole too shallow,
and a few days later the story came out
when the fowls scratched him up.

"You know, Barry's quite a fair shot,"
Mr Long said,
out in the bush with Barry and me.
"My word I am," said Barry.
"I can hit anything."
"Can you, Barry, well – see what you can do."
Barry took the rifle,
went down on one knee
and aimed at Mr Long's billy hanging
from a distant branch.
He fired,
and a stream of brown tea came spurting out.

Tools

Man's tools
are the last stronghold
of something ancient.
You can fool the consumer
but not the workman.
He'll make use
of a newer, more powerful tool,
but the brace-and-bit doesn't change.

In department stores
with their wilderness
of veneers, synthetic wood and plastic brass
give me a counter
of hammers with real wood handles
or spirit levels of solid wood and brass –
or my cattle cane,

its handle plaited with hide
hanging on the veranda
among my rifles.

I spray my tree
with a long thin pump of brass
that can reach among the branches,
elegantly,
a design that's not changed for years.
On a hot day
the metal chills your hand
as the spray flows through.

The tools are tenacious.
My spanners will be able to take
the nuts off spacecraft.

Poverty Ridge

"Poverty Ridge," Mr Long labelled it,
"the loneliest camp in the district."
A time of drought and bailiffs,
a red MG with a loud muffler
patrolling the hills,
my brothers hiding under portable bushes
in a paddock after dark,
a lavatory seat banged down as a signal –
a time so dusty
my wife took to brushing the dogs with a broom.

Sally at the windy end of winter
would rub the wattle buds
(just on the brink of blooming)
so the yellow whiskers popped out
while we went looking for lost sheep
in the dry, cold paddocks.

My sister rabbit trapping.
Her children carry the corpses tenderly,
except Kellie, who bangs them on trees and rocks
holding an ear in each hand,
twirling the corpse over on itself,
like a grocer with a paper bag.

Rabbit kittens were spared
and taken home to a box,
but the house stank of "currants"
when the rabbits broke out.

Noxious Weeds

Driving through our district in late spring
with my daughter and new son-in-law –
it's not country I would go to look at,
mainly iron bark and box country
broken up with outcrops of granite.
On a bank purple with Paterson's curse
there's an antique sulky
for the tourist who pays a dollar
to see a cow standing in a paddock.

I recite the deaths and accidents
this road has known.
Past Morongla Post Office
I miss that red rambler with the white eye
wiped out by the Shire
in mistake for a blackberry.
"What sort of poison are you using?" I asked.
"They oughtn't to issue you with that."
The man from the Shire who was spraying
screwed his face up in alarm –
so we still have notified noxious weeds,
our roadside briars
whose leaves in spring smell of apples.

The house is among those trees.
When my son-in-law first came
my brother the dentist with toothbrush moustache
asked, How does he find the toilet facilities?
meaning either down the creek
or over the hill.
Now my brother asks, "Does he call you Dad?"

A marriage on my wife's birthday –
we're all born and married on the same day.

Down at Hickey's

You can't hear it in the house,
the wind in the upper air.
But out in the paddock
with just the sky-travelling moon
and your shadow on white grass
it sounds like a distant express train,
gusts of huge pressure,
while on the ground
the ears of phalaris are barely stirring.

My bed has a cover
of red calico striped pink.
On these cold autumn nights
grass is turning into milk,
and on the veranda where I sleep
iron bark seedlings in metal tubes
are pushing out slender blue leaves,
while down among the poplars
on a rusting mattress
the ghost of Mr Hickey sleeps.

My postal address is "Spring Forest",
but we still talk of
"down at Hickey's".

I wish I had the teams
of school pupils he used
to weed his vegetable garden
sixty years ago.
Slave labour for country schoolmasters.

The pressure lamp hisses in the kitchen,
and hot cocoa faintly steams.
A green lacewing lands on the board table.
Several times a night
Joe wakes me with her nose
to make sure I'm not dead.

The leaves of my poplars drop
into Mr Hickey's open mouth.

Sparrows

I don't mind if silver-eyes eat my grapes
but sparrows –
aggressive foreigners –
are the plague of my life.
I built a bird bath
and sparrows came,
the miniature thunder of a hundred wings,
and drove the natives away.
But I'm forcing them out
of my silver poplar grove,
poking their scruffy nests down from the branches
leaving the neat circular nests
of blue wrens and other natives,
setting traps for them on the ground,
a war of attrition on sparrows.

I've no time for birds
with no limit to their breeding
and slovenly nests – like some people.

Jack

I've given up drink for good,
by natural evolution.
Alcohol is for the young,
out of love, in love,
young men chasing the same woman,
urinating by night among camellia bushes,
ramming trees with their cars.
Somewhere there is music playing,
glasses are breaking;
they cover themselves with grass seeds
and mud, teased by girls.

Now I've enough mental furniture
to shift around in my mind to keep it busy,
something the soft minds of the young
cannot understand
who see middle age as a shrivelling,
not a storing away of energy.
So drink is strangely irrelevant;
I say "strangely", because unplanned.

My house is dry except for the grapevine
that loops around the veranda.
Jack would have said what a dullard I've become.
"Come on Ross," – his ghost standing
between the grapevine and me –
"What about a booze-up? Olive
and the children don't want you to martyr yourself."

Jack and his friend Higgins,
as medical students,
swaying on the doorstep of a hostess
before a dinner invitation,
and Jack persuading Higgins, full of beer,
that a pot plant would soak up the lot
without trace.

The pot plant stood in a saucer
that was filling with tepid water
as Jack rang the bell.

Jack crash-landed in the sea
off Vanimo,
helped free his two friends from the cockpit
as the plane submerged,
and drowned himself.

Jack became a small part of history,
a pioneer doctor
bringing civilisation
with a stethoscope and syringe
to the dark people who mourned him.
I was Jack's audience,
the younger farming brother.
Jack,
fatal for girls, fatal for himself,
my mentor and guardian in the city
of wartime parties, floating populations.

The roof garden of Packie's Club
with potted palms, outlines of office blocks –
this is *my city*, a wartime city,
railway stations where we sang
and people smiled at the drunken soldiers;
but now it's gone, the T & G building,
Packie's in the starlight,
my city exists only in my mind.

But Jack bitter, unreconciled,
chasing a glimmer of phosphorus on the horizon,
stands between my grapevine and me:
the hundred possibilities as I stepped
from the train at Central Station.

Chrysanthemums

This is something
about late starters – chrysanthemums.
I suppose we humans
start slowly. The baby
playing with his food, dropping it
even when hungry
is no match for a twelve-month squirrel.

Shortening of days sets off a time switch
for chrysanthemum buds to form.
Dull, intricate weeds,
through spring and summer
they've nothing to say.
But in autumn they burst
in motionless fireworks around the homesteads,
yellow and vinous red and russet,
sagging by wire fences,
dusty by galvanised sheds.
They bivouac in the long dry grass
beside the spacious verandas
as lucerne is baled in paddocks
and basket willows turn yellow.
Unlike the irises and jockey's caps
of summer, living for hours,
or hibiscuses quickly crumpling,
the chrysanthemums select a time
when the sun will not exhaust them
to speak out acrid and dry.
Their blaze persists,
saved up, parsimonious, calculated,
like the last burst of a marathon runner,
as the sun shrinks
giving back all the light they've known,
dazzling as they totter.

What a way to die!

I'm not saying chrysanthemums
are best.
Perhaps I am fonder of the flowers
of spring – the soft scents,
expanding with the warmth.
But I like the way chrysanthemums
answer the cold
with remembered light.

The Future of the Past

Talking in a tent during the war
I heard a stranger in the dark
shout from another tent,
"Hello! Jack, you old bastard!"
(Jack and I had the same voice.)
Lately my daughter woke at dusk
and heard the radio saying,
"A plane has crash-landed in the sea
off Vanimo and the pilot has drowned."
Not Jack, but his double fifteen years later.
Ageing I speak with the ageing voice
of Jack that was never heard.

Uncle Pat

What despair or contrariness
persuaded Auntie Bridge
to marry Pat?
Old Pat driving his car –
"She houlds the road well," he would say,
letting go the wheel to prove it.
"Ouh!" he would grab the wheel again in a panic,
yet the steering hadn't shifted an inch.

Auntie Bridge and Pat –
I felt like chasing the old blighter
and ducking his head
in one of his cowshed buckets
when he gave my children some holy medals
and said, "'Ere, take these.
They'll keep people orff yer."

Pat believed in Adam and Eve,
the snake and the rib-bone, that made sense.
He had no objection to the chariot of fire
and the dead rising from their graves,
that was something he was looking forward to himself,
Pat rising out of red Cowra earth
from a patch of skeleton weed
and not letting Jesus' hand go –
No, old Pat would be taking no risks
in his riding boots, "houlding" on grimly.

There was only one Bible story
he couldn't quite fathom.
How did Noah
fit all them animals into that ark?
It was hard enough getting cows
into a milking shed or sheep
across a road. How did he round up
an elephant couple,
or even worse, all the moths and midges,
snakes and ants?
Did they have termite mounds on the ark?
How did they stop all the animals
biting and poisoning each other?
Pat's mind ran around in circles,
worried that this one gap in his faith
might keep him cooking in Purgatory,
scratching his head for a million years.

A Pat in 2050 won't be so incredulous
about rounding up
all the species that are left.

We're herding them into our arks
of concrete and chain wire,
the last of our friends, the beasts
who travelled with us through time –
herding them into our zoos and game reserves
before they're engulfed by the Flood –
and the Flood is us.

The man from the Shire
talked me into laying baits,
carrots dipped in tasteless liquid.
And we got a few rabbits –
and half a dozen wallabies with them,
prone in the dust among small native pines.
Next time I'll dig the rabbits out.

The condor going and half
of the animal world with it –

Each species we destroy
is a plane lost off Vanimo.

Tommie

A girlfriend's Mercedes
is parked in the shade of a Cootamundra wattle.
Inside, Tommie (my mother) is doling
out gossip and tea,
quietly proud of her position on the ridge,
looking out over miles of country
but hating the six gates
between house and road.
The cars are gathered for a bridge party,

a thousand feet above sea-level,
among the lichen of high places,
encrusted rocks and rotted fence posts.

Tommie (the ladylike spelling was Mother's)
née Miss Thompson,
married into a family of police-hating Irish,
what did your father do?
Don't mention it to those cars parked on the ridge,
as a fly settles on a tinted windscreen.
My father's nickname for her,
"Criminal Investigation Bureau" –
too close for comfort.

Oh Tommie, the Bush lie detector laying traps,
even for granddaughters.
"Sally, don't you think Barry's legs
are awfully thick?" No answer.
"Now Ross," she'd say later in Barry's hearing,
"Sally says Barry's got legs
like tree trunks."

Tommie being driven down
Mount Tomah, eyes shut, huddled forward,
face in her hands.
"Oh Godfather, Barry, we'll all be killed."

"Dan," she once said to my father,
"There's two dead mice under your bed,
one in each drawer."

Tommie
privately licking the cream from the egg beater,
then emerging to join her ladies at bridge –
but now they're going, it's dusk,
the cars winding down the hill,
stopping and starting at each of the six gates,
red taillights winking

through mist rising from stagnant ground.
And there are sounds from the kitchen of "smashing up"
as Father calls it,
who arrives with the tea-towel of peace.

Mother Church

I came into this century a Catholic
and shall leave it with no belief,
like a hundred million others.
Faith like mineral salts
is leaching out of the soil.
A Pope was afraid to speak out
against blackshirts and murderers
and did nothing
as the world drifted into war.
A later Pope, lost in his own dogma,
was too craven to speak the word
that would release the unconceived
from a birth without future.

Transubstantiation, free will –
mouthfuls of nothing.
Mother Church
when our earth cried out
you had nothing to say.

Where is your "life after death"?
What about the life now?
"Infallible" – 1870.

How silly it all sounds to our ears.
I can only laugh and cry.

Yet if outsiders attack you
I'll strike them down.

"Menindee"

At thirty-three my brother-in-law
is dying
of a hatband that chafed a mole.
With seven children –
three his own,
four others the children of a dead man –
he won't give in.
Married at last to the woman he battled for,
still begetting children,
after the brandmark showed,
he insists that unwilling surgeons
cut as each secondary appears;
excoriated and scarred
in a one-man cosmic war
against death.
In the last year he has built a dam,
purchased a capacious deep freeze,
set the fences in order
and the women are saying their prayers.
My sister is in a state of collapse.
This year with spring
cruelly lush and wet
his false lucerne tree flowered profusely.
The lilac he planted,
and other costly trees and shrubs
are just coming on,
but my sister, the horse rider,
is a ghost of her beauty,
lined and haggard with his war.
The children she knitted and sewed for
are growing like weeds,
and the house
the cream wooden cottage on the flat
tucked away in an elbow of creek
among pepper trees and haystacks

is an empty shell hole
where they subsist
in the lushest summer for years.

There are spiders on the fibro veranda
and cats germinating under the boards.
Clothes are scattered on the laundry floor.
Two summers ago newly married
they would lie there, idly joking,
soaking up coolness from the concrete slab,
gazing at the ceiling, dim green
from the garden's glare.

This is chronic country,
terminal perhaps for some.
After ten years of drought and waiting,
the lush seasons have come
and wool has collapsed –

Terminal for the big establishments
with big mortgages
building up their flocks for years
and borrowing, and now
they're selling prize rams for carcases.

We are sheep farmers
and nobody wants us –
driving at night through paddocks
the eyes of sheep in our headlights
are green incandescent jelly,
shaking and moving away as our tyres bite through gravel.
Men reject the soft wool
which comforted us in the Ark,
preferring the loveless synthetics,
false economics.

But beware, your children
will curse you for letting dodos die,
half of the natural world perish,
and when our flocks are dwindled
you may not entice us back.

This planet which tries to house
half of the men who have ever lived
wants no one in particular.
It does not want you, either –

We are all sheep farmers.

Myself I wage no cosmic wars,
I travel light
with my five hundred acres,
half of it uncleared, kangaroo country
because no one wants
what it would grow.
With my bees and yellow jonquils
and journeys with a carload of calves,
trading in a small way,
I survive.

My sister still desperately beautiful
rides the boundaries of their big establishment.
One of her children sleeps with his eyes open.

At the Gate

At a time of dying
and barely managing,
my sister's children are at a gate.
Their faces express the coming doom.
A horse is grazing just behind them.

The girls have cotton frocks,
sprigged floral patterns with puffed sleeves,
Peter Pan collars
and sashes tied in a bow at the back.
Bill, in white socks, well-polished shoes
and hand knitted jumper,
(his mother can knit, eyes closed,
and not miss a stitch)
is collecting letters from the mail box.
The children have a single mind,
a child mind
like a flock of birds.
My car travels across damp gravel
and they are gone.

Bird-watching with Mr Long

"What's that bird, Mr Long?"
"That's a chipper."
"What's that small bird over there?"
"That's a fly-bird."

There's a forest I'll never see again
where birds with exotic names
whistle to each other,
flashing blue and scarlet
as they dart and fan their wings.

"What will you have for breakfast, Mr Long?"
asked my father.
"I could eat the leg of the Holy Ghost,"
replied Mr Long (meaning toast).
"I would *not* have expected that of *you!*"
said my father with ice.
But Mr Long was rarely put out.

On a wooden chair by my bed
there's hot cocoa I'll drain fast
because these autumn nights
are taking the warmth out of things
as they loosen the poplars' yellow leaves.

Then I'm going on that journey
Mr Long always promised
through the spinifex
with a covered wagon and cockatoo,
cooking fish on river stones,
to Palm Valley and its wild blacks.
"What's that bird, Mr Long?"
"That's a parson bird with the white collar."
"And that one over there?"
"That's a grey hopper."

Walking all day
out on the western plains, Mr Long
could sustain himself
with a line of trees on the horizon.

Hens in the Saltbush

If he was a man of spirit
you ate your enemy after fighting him.

But the flesh we eat now is insipid,
blind, force-fed calves,
and mass-produced hens
with their egg yolks the colour of custard.

My egg yolks are rich yellow,
so deeply yellow they're almost bloody
and city people get squeamish.

Mind you, my hens eat everything!
Dirt and dung and wattle seed.
They roost in the shells of rusting trucks
or on a low branch of saltbush.
(I introduced it – Spring Forest's not desert country yet.)
And my dogs sometimes eat hens
and so do foxes.

That's bad for the profit and loss accounts.

I've been a great hater in my time –
battery-raised hens and plastic wood,
cities destroying the landscape –
but now I rein my hatreds in.
The crusaders
wear themselves out hating,
and what matters – their own minds,
where it all begins and ends –
is forgotten, they're so busy hating.

Plant the Spring Forest,
to start with, in your mind.

The Light on the Ridge

Throwing stones in the creek forty feet below,
careless in those remote hills,
my brothers and I heard a rock
not thrown by us hit the creekbed.
We threw more, and paused.
Again a ghost rock
knocked on the pebbles.

We peered over the boulder's brink.
There was Father,
sitting on an unreachable ledge,
smoking his pipe.

Medical science preserves our bodies for a ripe old age
in the men's home.
My father, eighty-seven, rides a horse
and tells me of a home for the aged
where they are locked in their rooms at night.

I watch for his light on the ridge
five miles away,
living by himself now Mother's gone.
Peace, heavenly peace, he used to call it,
while Mother was away,
and now the heavenly peace is permanent,
and peach trees have grown to obscure the light.

My father, the grandfather of many,
takes no sides, commits himself carefully
to no one,
white-haired diplomat, peace-maker.

At night investigating moths in his pressure lamp –
white with orange stripes, that deserves a prize!

A master of courteous truisms –
but why did he keep peacocks and a monkey?

Like underground water,
that I struck last week, three hundred feet down,
dissolving in and out of landscapes –
Father.

Lines

A vertical line through our roof
would intersect
with stars somewhere in space.
(There are other Spring Forests in the sky
and children crying. The stars
are a million mirrors of the earth.)
Closer to home this line
might bisect the moon's molten core,
and pass through
radiation belts,
the ozone filtering out the ultraviolet,
a tawny frogmouth flying
with a moth in its beak,
frost on our galvanised roof,
a kerosene pressure lamp perched on a book,
various texts on animal husbandry,
some short stories
and a cherrywood pipe
I have lost and not yet found
(that's wishful thinking –
I probably lost it in some paddock
and a tussock has grown over it)
down through pine floorboards,
a ginger and black guinea-pig asleep
beneath the house
and into red Koorawatha earth,
earth with only one need –
water for the green life chains.

If I tired of vertical lines
I could draw a horizontal line
through this fire of iron bark logs
(with its two sounds –
the billowing and beating
of rushing blue-red air,

and the dry cindering and splitting
of timber)
a line extending through the curl
of steam from the iron kettle
warming on the flagstones,
through my moleskin trousers,
as I sit on an old car seat from the Morris
(my favourite low-level armchair)
just missing Olive's legs
busily gathering tea-things,
on through the bedroom with its black piano
carved with flowers and mandolins
(how the steel strings and sounding-board
wince in our draconian ranges of temperature –
the felt hammers decayed
when my wife the musician
married me and a farm)
through the weatherboards
and a stand of red geraniums,
on past the trunk of a giant dead wattle
(I don't remove old friends,
as birds like to perch in bare branches)
through the chicken-wire enclosure
I keep around the house and garden,
past some dogs and a fruiting fig-tree,
past the cough of a fox.
I jump up with a gun and that's where that line ends.
But it's no use. Try shooting ghosts.
I come back inside.

Drinking a cup of cocoa
I draw a circle around the house
starting with the metal windmill
and the creek where the ducks paddle,
but that's too wide.

I'll start my circle in closer
among some grass. It collects a hen
in a crater of dust, continues
through the bee-boxes with their new white paint
on past my antique steamroller
"the slumbering giant"
and then I fetch up against that fox again –
or is it my mind?

We have cosmic rays and cow manure,
flowers and a rusting dry-cleaner's van,
but there's no line around here
that will intersect with a decent toilet or bathroom.

Through the dimensions I do not understand
I move
a column of living water.

Weather Report

My father's a still day
smoke rising vertically in the calm
from a distant horizon.
There are high cirrus clouds,
mare's tails, thin streaks of ice crystals
combed across the sky.

My sister's light air,
smoke drift, a faint breeze
you can feel on your face,
and leaves rustling under
a deep peach sky at sunset.

Mr Long is one of those small clouds
that sit on top of mountains,
a wry companion,
scud that rushes across the sky in a storm.

My mother is cumulus cloud,
brilliant white and puffy in fine weather,
billowing and changing shape with her mood,
while leaves and small twigs are in constant motion.

She starts raising dust and hen feathers,
the wattles around my house begin to sway,
and telegraph wires are whistling,
as mother becomes a gale.
Smoke venturing from the chimney
is shredded into nothing.
Our old white horse (that's me)
canters around the paddock, wondering
why the sky's become so black and blustery,
as branches are breaking off trees.

Then it's sunny again,
and the glistening hillside
is my one-month-old granddaughter's face.

I've thought of all this,
on a summer night, silent
except for frogs which mean water,
smoking by myself on the veranda.
And the sky is lit by static lightning,
violet flashes. Jack.

The Spot

A child was killed crossing a road.
A neighbour, kind and honest in his way,
says, "Ross, do you want to come and look at the Spot?
Ellen and the kids are going to have a look."

When cars crash the traffic slows
to a snail's pace as passing drivers
crane to look at the wreckage.

We are absorbed by scratching our scabs,
or taking a quick look backwards
at our turds.
Making happy noises
babies try to scratch out each other's eyes.

There is part of our nature
where morals and logic are irrelevant,
some marshland of the brain.
In another latitude
Yellow Thunder, an ageing Red Indian,
was beaten up and thrown
with no trousers into a crowded dance hall.
Later he was wandering the streets.
His young tormentors packed him into their boot,
and dumped him at the edge of the town
to die.

In most of us ancient malice
has atrophied into words or thoughts.
Listening to music or holding the hand
of a woman or child you love,
where do these pots of boiling fat belong?
They are not the meaning of our dream
(as some say).
Criticism is useless.
They simply exist.

Shifting Gate Posts

One of the pallbearers said,
"By George that box was light."
Crouching on the veranda edge in riding boots
I press the plug of burning tobacco
with my thumb
and smoke blows away in the night.

I come
as an observer, not mourner.

Against Incendiaries

Clearing and burning off –
from my father's place the fires
on the plain look tiny and remote,
as dusk closes in.

Driving home that night
as we come round a bend
the fires are on us, in close-up,
a huge stump blazing in the dark,
the felled logs burning
in the bulldozed blackness,
deserted and eerie
as a flying-saucer camp.

Tossed on the hearth at home
the empty skin of a persimmon
glows orange as the fire itself.
Paper, cotton, matter that has lived
burn cleanly, leaving a pale
ash ghost.
Plastic, synthetic cloth
bubble, reduced
to fuming chemicals.

I was going to build a fire in my mind
where I could burn
all the trash of our world,
lurid newspaper headlines,
our constant exposure to violence,
machines designed not to last,
advertisers, sterile cities.

I wanted
charred earth, stubble
for a clean start
under stars scrubbed large and new.
But my firesticks got lost somewhere
by an old pear-tree
or behind a tumbledown shed.

I've decided not to burn
for my beliefs.
Heretic and inquisitor
feed on each other's flames.
They'd incinerate our world too.

On the coast they burn off paddocks on a whim.
Our feed is too scarce:
we only burn scrub we're clearing.

Outside hearths and combustion engines
fire is something I suspect.

The Pressure Lamp

With Olive away, the house is in darkness.
My feet fume with the cold.
There is nothing, no room, no house, just freezing darkness
as I rummage
for a match.
I am dead. We all died
on the same day
and are buried by the river
our chins tilted upwards
still sprouting beard.
We are all dead under the rotting leaves
under the trees dying of mildew.
I manage to strike a match
and place a ring of blue fire

around the stem of the pressure lamp.
The smell of methylated spirits.
The mantle (silk charred to white ash)
trembles and smokes with orange heat.
I pump. The lamp and the room
hiss into light,
a resurrection of familiar cupboards,
the violin on the wall, books at all angles,
the straw mat in the middle of the floor.
I have made my own light.

I place paper and kindling twigs
on the hearth – and fire,
my second need, has been established.
I make my own climate
(my domed microclimates
on the icy moon) –
one step further than the warm-blooded animals,
two steps further
than the lizards and insects
who are cold or hot as the day.

I move from light to warmth,
to food and sleep,
the last of my simple needs
of a winter night,
and the house is in darkness, silence,
waiting for the chains of actions
to start again.

Life Chains

Life chains –
a lamp of incandescent silk,
so much light from a small silk net
(see yesterday for an explanation).
Life chains –

sheep farmer, wool scourer and retailer,
the two spirals of the DNA molecule
twisting around each other.
Some ancient mind read its message in our dust
without an electron microscope
and saw the caduceus,
the two snakes writhing around the wand
of commerce.
Life chains –
so tricky to tamper with,
no beginning or end,
stretching beyond the brief flash of our life.
Outside our room of light
are genes we do not understand,
systems too fragile to observe.
Chains in more ways than one,
binding us, hard to break –
the revolutions kill
and do not make us free.
But if the life chains lead to death –
the growth economy
exploding on itself,
half of mankind starving
in darkness with no match and no lamp –
we must break
and rearrange
the life chains
by intelligence, will, perseverance
before they have gutted our planet.

On top of my refrigerator there are some eggs
and a pair of earphones.

Life, the silk mantle that started in a caterpillar's stomach,
incandescent –
(I was going to say burning; but that's not accurate.
It burns only the first time it's lit - for a second.)
Jarred, it disintegrates.

Driving at Night

Driving through thick bush
alone – mist scatters in my headlights.
The death of a parent.
The earth loses its heat
by long wave radiation at night.
When the sky is clear
the long waves go out into space –
sweltering Christmas dinners with my mother
eating her family with pudding and brandy,
stentorian gossip,
the panic in the bushfire –
are leaving the earth
and shall not come back.

The earth loses its childhoods,
wood houses with their hearths and willows
flow away into the sky,
fathers and their horses,
mothers with iron pots
are going, and wives
who were warm
when dew formed on tin roofs
leave a crater of coldness in their beds.

There are no clouds to stop them.
The long waves leave us
feeling nothing.
Movement of air in the hills
turns dew into mist.
On the plains it's dead still
getting colder and colder.
A frost for my mother.

Questions for My Horse

Music is unevennesses
of pressure on the ear-drum.
Sight is the vibration
of rods in the eye.
My dog's called Joe.
Meaning to ask for Ock her son
I asked Mrs Wearne
"Where's Olly?" (her dead husband).
"You tell me," she said.
Waking in winter –
a big bush cat was sitting in the starlight
scratching at green parrots in a cardboard box.
And where was Olly?
You tell me.

Outdoors at Night

It's surprising
that the universe is able
to look at itself, from end to end,
the near fires and remote fires
burning in a clear vacuum.
I stand under the grey antlered limbs
of my dead box tree at night
and watch the stars
signalling to each other.

As light a million years old glimmers on me
I ponder, among my white bee boxes,
how much more likely
that space should be opaque
an obscurantist's delight, a vast sponge to be lost in.

No ... the stars announce
their presence over huge distances
to my yellow tractor, a beetle and myself.

While Fetching Wood

Galaxies receding –
their light shifts to red –
The horn of a train approaching blasts us –
when it's passed, the pitch drops.

My neighbour sent his horse to the knackery
when its working life was over.

The music or person we cease to love
suffers a red shift, a drop in pitch,
but does not change –
only our position.
They go on in time, the objects, the persons,
with no need for our say so.
How cheap to think of their worth
in terms of ourselves – trees,
earthworms, old sheds and a snake
lacing through a stack of logs
I can see into, black against light.
And I don't kill it.

"Good day, old horse,"
I say to my neighbour
on his way to the knackery.

Postcard for the National Rifle Association

They're out shooting again tonight.
Driving past they shine their spotlight
through my naked silver poplars
on to me in bed on the open veranda.
(For a second I'm on stage!)
They're charitable.
Last time I found a dead mangy fox in my mailbox.

Guns are for cowards –
too scared to grapple with their enemy
face to face.
The flabby finger squeezes a trigger,
the eyes look away
as the quarry falls.

There's no mystique about killing sheep,
no sheep slaughtering clubs,
but Hunt Club secretaries tell us
we are squeamish about killing
the meat we eat.

Well, you don't find men in red coats
killing meat for their sausages,
or the Duchess of Buckingham
slaughtering hens
at the chicken processing factory,
while her lady-in-waiting hoses away the blood.

I stopped some fellow shooting
on my property,
took his two hundred dollar rifle
(a very fancy model)
and with bare hands broke it across my knee.

Traveller, do you shoot?

My Daughter

Sally's poem.
"My father seemed so strong
and well able to survive.
But I waited in an agony for my mother
(afraid she might die or get lost)
when she went over the hill.
I climbed up trees to watch for her,
sweating with fear.
At night when father went to bed
I listened to her shoes
scraping the linoleum, her hands
stacking dishes or turning a page.
To hear her every movement
I lay
breathing through my mouth.
(If I breathed through my nose,
air made a rushing sound in my nostrils.)
I kept my head still
so my hair didn't rustle in the pillow.

"One day she had been away so long
from a trip to the bushes
I climbed a silver poplar
and saw some animal larger than a dog,
a brownish-chestnut colour,
in a field of wheat, but no mother.
I couldn't quite see its face.

"But this thing had eaten my mother, this was certain.
Then it was gone.
I came down, an orphan,
and found my mother, a ghost
on the veranda talking to Peter.
There was nothing I could do with my mind."

Music

This house hasn't known much music
except Sally sitting in the dust,
tightening the wire strings of a bee box frame
and plucking them.

At night the trees rush with different sounds
or a bull is restless
and dogs interrupt the darkness,
these are a sort of music –
or sleeping in a travelling car my ear
listens to the change
from bitumen to gravel and back again,
the chassis vibrating.

Young, I needed an occupation,
felt myself going mad without it.
Older,
I find music in anything,
sounds of nature, personal idiom, doing nothing –

Calves

Some musical intervals survive
from when the ice sheets began retreating.
Feet travel over grass.

I'm travelling with a carload of calves
at night from Bega.
Shivering by the side of the road
my breath scatters over dry grass.
Trading
in the soft bones of new lives,
I come with a carload of hope
and inquisitively sniffing noses,

drink steaming coffee at a service station
under fluorescent light,
and drive on.

In colder regions (I reflect,
passing through a patch of mist)
the animals become scarcer and larger.
My tall frame is on loan
from some disgruntled ghost who lived by a peat bog.

The farmers who will buy my calves are asleep.
Past midnight most of the lights
in the district are out.
In my back seat I carry
next year's herds
(how they'll run to meet me at the fence
and butt me in the waist) –
the latest batch from long blood lines.

I travel through a tunnel of trees
over pale gravel,
with my lights on high beam,
the only moving object for miles.

The Amateur Astronomer

People no longer believe what poets
or ministers of religion tell them
unless their senses say it's right.

All those cancelled Utopias,
and syllogisms that just didn't work –
relieved of the incubus of trying to believe,
I walk down my father's mountainside
one night in July, unprotected –
nothing between me and the wind
blowing from Antarctica,

nothing between me and the stars
glimmering at the bottom of space
(the Antarctica of the sky).

The wattles and native pines seem to enjoy
this cold wash of air,
this lack of illusion.
(I do not say disillusion.)

In every large city
there are a hundred or so amateur astronomers
picking their way through the sky.
I'm not that sort of fanatic.
For years if I looked through my antique brass telescope
all I could see was a broken lens
and cobwebs.

Now it's restored
I can train it by day on my father's hill
and see someone hanging out washing
up there, five miles away.
Among tussocks and small blue daisies
invisible in the dark,
I can see the moon as large as a plate
and the rings of Saturn.

Dabbling among solar systems,
I'm as happy as a cow in fresh grass
with no knowledge of botany.

It's time to eat, Olive tells me.
Yes, Olive, I'm coming in
with the moon as my dinner plate.

The Things

My daughter's Bunnikins plate
has had its garden of rabbits
rubbed and washed off.
When she grew up
we lent it to a shingle back lizard.
Now it's my granddaughter's plate.

The things are hallowed by use,
old purple glass in the dust of my yard,
a breadboard of myall wood
with the clear smell of violets,
and a flower pot from my aunt's dead garden.

Things in the mind
become emblems and logical pathways,
a father with a shotgun and Mr Long hiding,
the green eyes he never saw again
and shoes he left on the roof.

The Thrift of Tulips

It's the warmth coaxes tulips out
and makes them flower,
yet they languish in our warm climate.
I'm convinced they love cold
only because the great sterilising sleep
of a northern winter
kills tulip parasites.
The poisonous bulbs, the jonquils,
thrive in our district
(round and fat like spiders' stomachs)
but the harmless tulip bulb
(succulent, shaped like a tear) survives
only when the ground has been civilised (for tulips!)
by ice.

We tried tulip raising only once,
a row of green buds
and one day a bright red flower,
but the calyx in which it came
had vanished.
More flowered – again this conjuring trick.
Nothing clung to the stem
or was scattered on the ground.
Then one day we watched
a green calyx blush
and deepen in a day to red.
The calyx was the petals.
What a masterstroke
in the geometry of growth!
But I've planted no more.
I only grow what's happy in our ground.

Questions for a Winter Night

Why does a cockroach
look like a pressed date?
How does a snake
locomote across water?
You'd expect it to sink like a strip of lead.
You ask the skeleton of a snake,
the fine light rings of bone
among dry grass, they provide some answer.
Why do people shake their heads to say no?
I can answer that one.
Children shake their head from side to side
to avoid food they don't want.
The nod is the acceptance of food.
Why did Sally place her foot wrong
so Cucumgilliga Primary School
had to start each folk dance again,
her embarrassment multiplying her errors?

Why didn't the twenty-four feet
of Cucumgilliga Primary School dance in unison
like the segments of a snake
oscillating across water?

Why is the moon
(high above my radiata pine)
a cross section of frozen apple,
and how did it arrive there?
It's a winter night
and ice is forming at the bottom of miles of still air.
My breath hangs in a cloud.
Why am I on this open veranda in an old iron bed
at this moment of time?

The Old Bath

Two hollows in an old bath
worn by people's bottoms
fascinated Sally as a child.
The old pisé house is stacked full of hay now,
crammed yellow, staring out through glassless windows,
and there's a ghostly army
of thistle sticks, six feet high in the grounds.
It took a lot of lamps flickering
and mothers and fathers and children
sitting in warm water
to wear those hollows.

Impromptu

Every year the weather's unusual.
Stepping from my bed in the dark
I crack the stem of my pipe.

Directing milk jets into a plastic bucket
I'm distracted for a second
and a hoof of polished ebony shifts stance
and tips the white foam on the earth.
That stand of timber all had pipes
(only good
for a collection of giant didgeridoos).
Nothing runs to plan.
Last year who guessed
wool would ride so high?
Could a horseman on the plains of Asia
foresee the numbers of man gone wild?
My father still can't see (he won't listen)
by fencing his large paddock in three
his sheep strip each section in turn
and the feed won't grow back.

We must plan for flaws
(holes to see the sky through
or look at a white horse).
Each generation looks into a new rift,
and history doesn't repeat,
as I amputate the odd tit of a cow with five tits.

The Evening Star

Flickering like a yellow lantern it rises
among an outline of trees on a hill
"the sheep stealer" – Venus, the Evening Star.
("Sheep stealer" to old-timers like Uncle Pat –
"Who's that with the lantern on top of the hill?
Who's that?" – a star.)

At dusk my daughter and her husband
packing clothes and a cot into their van.
As they drive away, all that remains
is a dust haze.

This country cannot hold them –
except with silence.
City,
the son and daughter stealer.
A horse lies on its side in a paddock,
poured out.
Across populations of grass,
with black and green wings
a grasshopper flitters.
This country is haunted,
its children stolen by that Evening Star.

Witnesses

Jehovah's Witnesses, you say with a look of pity.
Well, I'm not one,
but they may well look with pity
at you.

While you and I
despair for the human race
(numbed as reported horrors bombard us)
they can say:
"It is written, this world is mad,
we are not surprised
as we see these ghosts
chasing each other with cutlasses across the quicksands,
the nations sinking."

They refuse to take oaths –
no man can tell the truth.
Bellboys, plumbers, bus conductors,
they live simply in a time of madness,
accumulate few assets
and wait for the day of judgment.

So many of us die trying to right the world,
the widow in her apartment
shrill with anger at students,
the old socialist cooking toadstool soup for "The Bosses".
These Witnesses for all their crazy door-knocking
and Old Testament readings
proclaim one truth –
we are witnesses of the conflagration,
the fires are happening already, all around us.
Our possessions and protests are useless,
our despair is useless.

I am walking down from my father's hill
in another direction
among clean tussocks and granite,
free in the Antarctic night.

Matt Manion

Matt Manion –
matt, dull, unreflecting,
with his small dull fire
cooking chops in the bush –
one day in the kitchen said to my Aunt Margaret
before her spine had begun to curve over
(though her hand since childhood was minus two fingers
laid as a dare on a chopping block,
as her sister Bridge swung an axe),
"You know, Miss McInerney,
I had a funny dream last night."
"Did you, Mr Manion?"
"I dreamed that you and me was married."
"Indeed, Mr Manion, I'm very glad it was only a dream."
"Well, so h'am I. So h'am I."

The significance of Matt's dream (if any)
hovered unexplained, cut off.
My father called this Margaret's only proposal.

Matt had dinner once with my mother and father
terrified to find himself eating inside a house,
holding his cutlery like the reins of a dangerous horse
When she found no peach stones in his plate
Mother, surprised and concerned, asked,
"Didn't I give you any peaches, Mr Manion?"
Matt would have cut a dash
when mosses and ferns ruled the earth,
cooking his chops beside a mild Devonian sea
which was only beginning to taste of salt.

He is one of our guests.

Heat

114 in the shade.

Heat that eats at the very soul –
the early Fathers were right
locating Hell in a hot place.

Plants suffer,
fray in the hot wind and cease to exist,
or else retreat into themselves
in the long siege of the heat.

It becomes a struggle against death
watering the animals twice daily,
dust rising from my boots
as I empty water into the drinking troughs.
The animals suck it straight up,
and I watch for scrub fires.

A neighbour with a pretty complexion
now has a face as florid as butchered meat.
The women are too exhausted to cook or clean,
sweating in armchairs in darkened houses.

I feel sorry for babies and small children.
Some die.
They have no mental resources to fight the heat.
The heat to them must seem a permanent condition,
the world a place of continuous fire.

I remember Sally with beetroot face as a baby
calling out in the hot dark,
staggering around her cot
dazed, like a trapped animal,
wanting to get up and play at two in the morning
folding up in odd corners and panting.

It's night – heat without light,
insects droning and shrilling deliriously.
At two I get up,
boil some tea, answer heat with heat.
Drinking scalding darkness from a cup
concentrates my mood,
gives form to the void.
Lying back again on the veranda
I wait for daybreak,
my mind holding a small reserve of water,
shrinking drop by drop.

A Letter from the Place of Pines

I was born at a place of pines
not far from a place of stones.
There's a town built at the place of stones.

That's where I meet people and go to weddings
and buy and sell,
but the place of pines is my permanent address.

At the place of stones there's a red brick church,
a bridge and willows by the river.
At the place of pines there are rusting cans
and fowls sitting in the dust
and a wagtail that sang all last night in my poplars.

At the place of stones there's a feed mill
and a broadcasting station.
They worry about neighbouring towns developing.
At the place of pines some of us go mad.
Ted Hutt who grew the fabulous tomato plant
shot his brains out in a tree.
My slow neighbour Nat, stickybeaking,
was told by the policeman to scoop them all up.
But there's not much development.

In the place of stones the houses stand in fenced allotments,
there's a high school and a golf course,
and a mad woman tidying up scraps in the street,
screaming obscenities.
People in both places are much the same,
live under the same moon.

In the place of pines
my neighbours' properties are blowing away in the sky,
and there's a lot of dust flying past
I can't identify
from places hundreds of miles further west
(also overstocked).
This dust blows into the place of stones.

In the place of pines
there are damp patches on linoleum
where my dog Tom has licked up food-scraps,
and there are dead branches lying around
they'd collect for firewood in the place of stones.

The place of stones and place of pines
are both part of my mind.
Travelling between them
I stay sane.

Water from My Face

Each year spring occurs
with such vehemence
it's clear the plants don't remember
last summer's dried sticks.

The young discover their bodies
as no one before ever did.
The old say "We remember"
and forget.

Nature has no memory or imagination.
The water falling from my face
into a rusted enamel dish
(washing under a kurrajong tree)
doesn't recall its shape for long.

Iron and Calcium

At night a dozen white cat's eyes
the size of plates,
stare at me down the slope
as I drive up to our house,

the cars and trucks of a lifetime
becoming tons of rust.
(The duco bubbles in lichen patterns
and wild oats grow from cylinder heads.)
When sheep are nibbling grass over our hearthstone
and Spring Forest
is a fine layer of carbon in clay,
there'll be no iron deficiency
in the soil around here.

My neighbour in the pub
said to some bearded scientists,
"So you're up here investigating kangaroos.
Don't waste your time.
How's the joey born?
It's born on the tit!
I've seen it
when it was just two eyes on the end of the tit."

My neighbour's biology
was set, like his drinking habits.

There'll be no calcium deficiency
in the graveyards of our Central West.

Alpine Herbfields

I don't care for alpine landscapes in winter –
I'm more interested in the dead grey leaves
from last summer
pressed flat under the snow.

In summer the herbfield is a coral garden
of constant minute activity
with channels and runnels of snow water
reticulating among daisy and buttercup mats.

It's finely adjusted
between the action of sunlight –
every living thing drinks it –
and the cold down-draught
from snow in high ravines.
After sunset temperature drop quickly.

Portulaca stems, a mesh of red worms,
are just starting to gemmate.
The crushed quartz soil glistens
with moisture,
and the leaf clumps of snow daisies
are a patchwork of silver
up the brown and green slopes.
Criss-crossed by water
the herbfield is a tilted run-off
for dwindling snow banks,
basins of tan rock
spilling into pebbly creeks
through fenlands of cord rushes
where yabbies scavenge in the mud and gravel
of raised ponds.

The richness of the herbfields spoils when grazed.
Cattle would eat them to extinction.
Let them stay unused and simple –
exist only for themselves.
(So this is a botanist's shopping list,
irrigated by snow water,
bare of symbol.)

There's nectar in the shallow tubes
of scented star flowers
and the small brittle flowers of heaths
for bogong moths when they swarm
and leave their skeletons in the grass.

There are no stalks that sudden weather
may snap.
The stems of herbaceous plants
are massed and squash like wire.
Snow gum trunks (on subalpine slopes)
splay from a root
poured like white and brown lava over rock.

If I could, I'd paint snowgrass
on the feldmark pebbled with rocks
like hundreds of sheep asleep.
I'd place a damselfly
among orange flower tufts,
and eyebrights against speckled granite,
and avoid high tors and their drama.

Midsummer snow may bury
a white buttercup overnight.
It's a poor-rich landscape
polished and scrubbed by hardship,
and the terraces of herbfield flower
with such gratitude
(that only desert flowers can match)
clinging to their cold mountain gravels.

The Meat Safe

The day after Jack was killed
a stranger drove
five hundred miles, distraught, to see us,
someone my brother had promised to marry.
We were family she had lost.
She left a suitcase of his starched shirts.

My daughter stayed later at her house,
a large old place,
as the leaves were starting to colour for autumn,

but couldn't sleep for thinking of the birds,
the diamond sparrows, fire-tailed finches
swarming through the old orchard,
three nests to a tree,
and apples stacked loosely in a shed,
and a carcase in a meat safe hanging
beneath an oak
to cool and stiffen.

A child couldn't sleep
for birds and the smell of apples.

Baking at Night

You don't get bread these days
with blue and green beetle wings baked into it
and pink stains from some crimson bug.
On hot nights
the lights of the bakehouse drew
all the insects of Waugoola Shire,
and strolling past you could smell the dough.
But they've given up baking at night.

You don't see the fires of the bagmen
under the bridge by the river.
They're extinct too.
Mr Long sometimes humped his swag
for far-off places,
drinking methylated spirits, shadow boxing
and trying to kiss people.
I've tasted his johnny cakes,
flour mixed with salt and water on a fence post
and cooked on a sheet of galvanised iron,
zinc curling off around the dough.
Burned specks turned out to be mouse dung.

After his long tramp across One-Tree-Plain
with a "cigarette swag"
Jim Long (Old Quizzer) dossed for some weeks
with a dozen other bagmen sprawled drunk
under the bridge at Darlington Point.
He got some meat scraps
and cooked soup for them all in a kerosene tin.
A bagman's three-day-old corpse
when it was noticed
was christened "Hot and Juicy".
The bagmen dug a hole by the side of the river,
a bucket of beer
was sent down from the Punt Hotel,
and Constable Brindle read the burial service.

You don't see many drunkards, wanderers
or blind people
(like Mrs Stinson – as children we loved
to see her holding her missal upside down
in church, poor woman).
There's no Cancer Joe for children to taunt.

If I wanted to join the bagmen by the river
under the weeping willows
I'd find no one there,
only the rumble of semi-trailers crossing the bridge,
the big headlights hurtling over.

We live in very moral times.

With the Stars as My Bed Lamp

Olive, I'd like to wake up under a blackberry bush.
I'd like to go on the road.

Pork chops cooked on a shovel –
Mr Long's favourite method –
it ruins the temper of the steel
but I've never tasted anything as good.

There's something about the moon
just rising above a paddock of stubble,
the light on the dried stalks
and among my silver poplars
that bodes ill for the tax papers on my rickety desk.

I'll be one of those men
of whom Mr Long said,
"He's seen more dinner times than dinners."

Olive, I can see a blackberry bush and a road.
Olive, are you listening?

The Palace Hotel

There are some lusty voices singing
and hands clapping
of fine Aboriginal ladies
(in tune with the jukebox)
as I go past their saloon.

The walls are dirty turquoise,
the floorboards sodden with beer and cigarette butts.
The girls entertain black and white friends,
fall pregnant,
and die of poverty and alcohol.

It's degrading, you say (so do I),
but there's something I like
about the vehemence of their despair,
the way they throw their bodies at life
and don't care.
Black people on a winter night
will sit on boxes and kerosene tins
around a big fire
beneath overcast skies that don't move.

You can tell from the way they sing together
they've more compassion
than most Christian congregations.
Walking past I'm stirred by the voices
of girls in the turquoise saloon,
singing and clapping above the jukebox
with such despair and joy –
something we have lost.

In Praise of Fruit

Fruit is the only food (except milk)
that designs itself to be eaten.
A leaf or cow has no wish
to finish up in your stomach.

But it's my will,
not the will of a slab of beef
putting on weight in a paddock
that counts. Some things
we assimilate by force. (It's not nice,
say cows.)
Nice I am not – and yet
I know fruit has a saving grace,
we need this food without guilt,
these nourishing tons hanging
on twigs.

Get your fruit in bulk,
hastily bottling what you can't eat.
(Overnight the smell of sweetness
ferments,
and your boxes of peaches are snowed
with mould.)

At the markets they've wooden crates as high as your waist
full of pears and stone fruit,
big enough to lie in,
but a rocky bed for your spine –
I'd rather sleep one day
in a pumpkin field in midsummer.

Their Day in Town

Past the third or fourth gate
on marked public roads (dwindling
to an obscure dirt track)
there's a country of broken-down sheds and stunted children
where political ideas
and bailiffs rarely penetrate.
Only the pension cheque
each fortnight on winged sandals
gets past the dogs with pyorrhea
snarling from rusty kennels.
Sons of unpainted shacks
loll on verandas and drink beer,
it's always smoke-oh time, and weeds
and spiders are the hardest workers.

From this land of the two-headed calf
come Madge and her husband each half-year,
both well over six foot,
each with identical haircut done by the other,
clipped short up the neck to the occiput.

Marching along the footpath
when they come to the store of her choice,
Madge swings her arm out to the right,
hard across Tom, who brakes dead.
Hand-signalling pedestrians
are a sign of an advanced civilisation.
They are arbiters of our democracy –
Madge and Tom.

The Spring Forest

Each year we get further away
from the Spring Forest,
the original text.

"Drinking straws" we say,
sipping a milkshake of imitation vanilla
through a thin plastic tube.
My children in summer
used stubble from paddocks
for sipping crushed strawberry water.
These days you don't find tadpoles
boiled up in the washing.

Each year
there are more gaps in the text,
privet in creekbeds
chokes out she-oak,
weeds blot the lettering.

Each place spoke through its plants
and fauna, until we came.

Planting Trees in Old Age

Auntie Bridge and Uncle Pat –
the doors of certain bedrooms
will always be closed.
We speak by not speaking,
like my daughter's diary
hidden in the hollow of a tree
meant only for the wind to read,
and that's how I leave it.

There are certain mad people
whose madness consists of saying
whatever comes into their mind.

Some things I don't wish to know –
how a fine woman wasted herself
on a simpleton
and grew a garden of plants whose names
he mispronounced or didn't know.

Her roses and Dutchman's Pipe have vanished,
and a lifetime of frustration made tolerable
by not being acknowledged.

"What are you planting trees for at your age?"
I asked my aunt aged eighty.
"*Someone* has to plant them," she said.

JMJ

Standing on his veranda
my father holds the teapot high
above his head
(like the elevation of the host)
and tips the tea-leaves on a geranium patch.

My father looking out
over a hundred square miles of dusk,
the landscape a missal
of darkened grasslands and flushed hills.

Priests came on horseback,
each with a blue enamel water-bottle
in its calico case,
over the hard and fast plains.

Our nuns coached their boys well in football
(habits flapping among the forwards)
but they trained no scholars.

The Happy Hour

It's cold, but the cold
won't wake the dead in the ground,
not even whiskey will rouse them,
or the friendly glow of the lights
of the Koorawatha Hotel.
I avoid such friendship, passing
farms where they drink more grain
than they grow.

Driving my tractor home late at night,
standing up to keep warm
in my military greatcoat,
I see a figure
on a horse that has stopped,
swaying in the saddle dead-drunk.
I catch him just as he falls.

I roll up my friend in the coat
and bed him down in the roadside grass,
propping his head on the saddle,

and set out for his household of women
with its blaze of angry lights.

As I walk quickly across the paddocks
already the dogs are barking.

Jack Thompson

The smoke travels with a dead match I fling
in an arc from my veranda.
Under the athel tree in dry moonlight
Jack Thompson's Wolseley is parked,
in good running order except its motor's finished
like Jack who is now underground.

Ethel has given Jack's box of worms away,
the worms for his illegal ghost-haunted fishing trips —
illegal
because he had no fishing licence
in a running war with Fisheries inspectors,
lying low among rushes
blowing out his hurricane lantern,
running out the back door as they knocked on the front,
("Inspector Farrell from the Fisheries Department",
I said to Ethel,
and heard a door bang in the dusk) —
ghost-haunted
because Jack would tell companions on his trips
at a certain point in the river
of this farmer drowned there in a flood,
"a small fellow with a white beard".
Jack was a small fellow
and at three in the morning a small white-bearded ghost
appeared on the embankment.
But where was Jack?

Jack wore the same white beard,
a pith helmet, white silk suit, horn-rimmed glasses
to call on his friends at the Golden Key café
as a "Professor from the Health Department".
After a critical run-down of the kitchen
they still didn't twig it was Jack.

How can I talk about Jack
fading in and out of his illusions
which he half believed in himself?
(like any true artist) —
to define the line of truth
dividing
the innermost skin of the pod of the honesty plant
splitting satin from satin.

Mrs Thompson would speak
an elegy of tears
crumpling her handkerchief in the graveyard.
"Now Jack wouldn't like to see you like this,"
I said, patting her shoulder.

Jack had said
"You know, wouldn't it be nice if Ross called in."
And was dead hours later.

But Jack evades grief
like a goanna running quickly over hot rock
so his temperature stays constant
mixing shade and sunlight
adjusting perfectly to his audience,
but watch that he doesn't run up you like a tree.

Jack's Wolseley is parked outside.
As I take out the engine
and install the engine from the Morris,
Jack is with me opening a cigar box,

showing Aub Adams
his preserved Japanese finger
collected during the war, his own finger
stuck through a hole in the box,
mottled, discoloured and horribly dead.
Aub, a sensitive bachelor, didn't see the joke.

And his cocksparrow ghost haunts Les the gravedigger
who spent three days with Jack digging up
some army issue iron piping
that Jack knew about, forgotten from the war,
which Jack was going to "dump in the river
and sell off piece by piece."

"What do you reckon, Les?" Jack said,
"Shall we have the pipes face into the current
or across it?"
Pointing to a distant figure in a paddock:
"You know Alf Hines?
He drives his car to the trots at six
every Wednesday night
and he's back home at half past ten.
I'll take his truck while he's gone,
load the pipes and dump them in the river.
He won't know a thing.
Twelve quid will be your share,
or if you like, we split the proceeds."

On Thursday Jack reported to Les:
"I almost backed Alf's truck into a washaway
and lost it in the river.
But it's all fixed.
I put the pipes facing into the current,
and I got back with not a minute to spare.
Alf had his headlights right on me
just as I was nicking out."

Les chose to split the proceeds,
but Jack's sales reports worsened from week to week
until he said,
"Les, I've sold just one length this week for eightpence.
As far as I'm concerned
those bloody pipes can *stay* in the river."
Jack paid Les the rest of his twelve pounds.

"If I know Jack," I told Les after his story,
"he never went near the river with those pipes.
He was selling them to Alf
and they didn't want you to know."

On my veranda, in dry moonlight
Jack's ghost is with me,
asthmatic, "a bad nerve case",
Jack calling on Doctor McLaren
(he had been sleeping in a deserted house
away from his wife and daughter
to track down the cause of his asthma)
shook out a red eiderdown from a chaffbag
and, sitting on Bill McLaren's floor
wrapped it around himself and wheezed:
"There you are Doc! A perfect asthma attack!"

As I drive across the Lachlan bridge
I hear Jack's river-haunting ghost
propound his "pre-training school" for horses.
"Ross, some time could you cut us
stringybark rails for the fence?"
For months he talked of his school,
even showed me the block of land
to be balloted by the council.
"A nice job for my retirement.
That chicken shed'll have to go.
And I've got this lady sculpting two concrete lions
for either side of the gate …"

One day Jack arrived with Bill Evans
and I cut them some stringybark rails with my chainsaw.
Weeks later it struck me.
The pre-training school, the concrete lions
had been just an elegant fiction
so Jack could get Bill some stringybark rails.

With me, Jack never tried his Japanese finger
nor his ghost by the river:
I kept him up too late talking.
I thought he was always straight with me.
But even while he was flashing me a wink,
he was leading me into the bulrushes.

A hurricane lantern blows out by the Lachlan.
Jack Thompson ceases to exist.

Night Thoughts Without a Nightingale

I've never heard a nightingale,
but I've been kept awake half the night
by a wagtail's intermittent
"sweet pretty creature"
like a solitary thread of water
in a parched landscape.

We stepped from wooden hulls
and the stale air of Europe
into a land of biblical want and plenty.
Old Testament words,
from some country of the soul
"drought" and "dust", "flood" and "plain",
became acrid and palpable.
To the British mind
dust was the decay of the body
and deserts a place for God to exile his prophets.

We woke in real deserts where men died
and dust could choke the sky for days on end.
A first settler
battling through scrub
halted at dusk
beneath the escarpment of a vast tableland
etched with the quicksilver
of living creeks.

We balanced a Meissen teacup
near a trestle loaded with cream cakes,
at a garden party
where a brown snake was a guest.
Its polished body
followed a circuitous route among high-heeled
and waxed riding boots,
observed only by a boy
who froze his cry of panic
until the snake was well clear.

We gave up red hunting coats to go
eeling in wet tiger snake country with George.
With the flood came the eels.
Out after dark with a lantern and pitchfork
we'd fling the thrashing spines
over our backs into a hessian bag.
But one night coming home
George emptied his catch on the ground
and a half-stunned tiger snake wriggled away.
George's eeling days ended there and then.

We laid out baroque exhibitions of produce
at country shows,
geometric patterns of red and green apples,
capitals of trussed golden sheaves,
fanfared by orange tubas and yellow trombones
of giant gourds.

Blazing darkly like jewels
jars of honey and preserves in pyramids
were our night at the opera.

The parochial claimed precedence
for our home entertainments and wild foods.
We enjoyed the rich peculiarity of transplanted lives
as exotic became native.

But we left no tradition.

Roughriding an unregistered Japanese motorbike
to the edge of my land
I switch off the ignition
It's dusk.
An immense and informative hush of insect noises
proclaims my irrelevance.

The nightingale my ancestors abandoned
mocks the flat square miles they chose.
She mocks their brief, provincial history.
The southern Anglo-Celts
shared some ballads and a way of speaking,
but could not hold this land.

My father
glimpsed a pristine botany
and is scattered minerals.
He cannot recognise
the alien features of his grandson,
or the highway down his escarpment.

The New House

Kev Livio, Chris Parris,
names in strip lettering
on bedroom doors of the new house

(that arrived dwarfing roads
in a cloud of dust) –
The wall of the communal room
is water stained from a fall of snow.
What snow fell on the dreams
of the Carcoar dam builders,
migrant workers, young men
saving a nest egg,
older men on the run from their wives?
Judging from the sticky tape
on their bedroom walls
I guess they dreamed of girls in posters
full-breasted, with no clothes.
A fly door creaks open in the moonlight
as Betty (who's on the Pill)
slips down the hallway in her stockings.

On hot nights in my new house
I'm kept awake
by the dreams of young men building a dam
and the ghost of Betty.

Electricity

It's not hard to choose between
low infant mortality and an art nouveau tile.
There's no nostalgia
about women nursing dying children
on finely carved cedar beds
with embroidered linen.

Through the dusk my wife with quick steps carries
from our old house to the new
my favourite pressure lamp.

Moving across the buff paddocks
its light is softly yellow and archaic,
as today
they've put up powerlines through the trees.

I prefer a world
that's modern, vulgar and well lit.

Man and Animal

Man and animal have needs that are the same.
The animal chooses for his camp
the tops of hills.
The rising sun warms the rocks
and he looks out over the plain.

The man, too, needs light and warmth.
Returning to a darkened camp
is his despondent moment.
His world is unmade and bleak.
Then he coaxes
dead sticks and branches into life.
As the first spark eats into dry leaves
his spirits lift,
and soon the kettle is singing.
He talks to his pots and pans
as though they are alive.
He must, or forget how to speak.

The man and animal are enemies
who do not meet.
They plot and elude each other.
Farmers
punching holes in the night with rifles
are baffled,
and the trapper is called in.

He is paid to have no anger.
He knows and admires his enemy.

Hands sensitive as grass to a footfall
place a twig beneath the plate of the trap.
The twig does not break for smaller creatures,
but it does for the dog.
And steel teeth snap shut.

The trapper is given food and wages by farmers,
but his heart is with a family of dogs
among distant boulders at sunset
who were gone when he raised his rifle.

He arrives in a district,
and dingoes stop howling in the hills at night.
He does not share his expertise.
A few simple secrets
provide him with a living.

The O'Brien Brothers

The shaky O'Briens
(one shook his head, the other always nodded)
long ago shook themselves into the ground.
They didn't die
of too many birthdays.

Death came quickly
and doctors slowly on horseback
when "the diphtheria house"
earned its name.
No one has lived there since.

Now the white Banks rose has been torn away
from the pisé walls,
you can see sky through the hallway,
and sky shines through the eyes
of some of our local half- and quarter-wits,
their hair cropped so short, cold air
permafrosts their minds.

Out in the paddocks
marked on maps
there are phantom roads and a township
no one built.

Harry Adams

"Who made the world?" "Goad."
"Who is God?"
"Buggered if I know, Michael."
Harry Adams was the only unploughed land
our Inland Mission could find,
but he was bare hills with poor catchment,
like our hills where, riddled with cancer,
he came back to die.
Who could smell a cup of tea from a mile away?
Harry, who'd slope through the door to the nearest seat,
and glue himself to fly paper laid by my brothers,
or absorb a puddle in the hollow of an Austrian chair,
but he made no sign and was not caught again.
Where did I last talk to Harry?
In the main street: he was waiting
to be taken to the old people's home.
Who was with Harry when he died?
Not our Inland Mission
as he knotted his tie around a low-hanging branch.

Bush Kitchens

Here's something about our Lachlan valley
kitchen utensils:
some of the Costello camp ovens
travelled from Hill End
across the continent and back.
They'd cook a four or five gallon stew,
and the lids chipped with use.
Now they're iron pots for tourists
in folk museums.

"Don't use that,"
Harry Adams said as someone
shoved a deal stick in the fire
for a pipe lighter.
"That's my custard stirrer!"

When I could run around
on tin roofs without denting them,
our river
was the mother of improvisation.
We drank the Lachlan boiled
with tea leaves.
She washed our enamel plates,
while our cardigans dried our hands
and blew our noses. (Harry Adams!)

Our only dish-washing machine
was George Grogan's:
at meal end he'd call
the dogs to lick his camp oven out.

And kitchens were a moveable
circle of light by the river.

George Grogan

George Grogan's universe
had no numbers.
Droving, he would arrive
minus one or two beasts,
uncorrupted by knowledge of his loss.
Apologetic for a life spent under the stars
George had never seen
the inside of a schoolhouse,
his only forte
the habits of sheep and cattle at night.
Some of his peers had no letters,
but they all knew the numbers of their mob.
The simplest of the simple
was a man who could not count.

Drying Out

One of those times Mr Long
blew his cheque,
then dried out by the Lachlan,
he chose a site for his camp fire
at some distance from his fellow bagmen.

Spreading slices of stale bread
with no jam from an empty tin,
he poured phantom tea
from a boiling billy
and gave colour with his pantomime
to the iron rations.

He'd spar with us children.
"I can fight like a hare and run like a guinea pig.
Put up your claws."

Jim Long and John Manion

Shortage of cash starved
Mr Long into celibacy,
long moon-baked nights
warped by the note of a bird.
Each morning John Manion
removed the kettle from the fire
so Jim Long when he rose
had no hot water,
yet each night Jim cooked their dinner.
When Jim broke his leg
John made some crutches
and sharpened the points one wet summer ...
Bad luck they lived in a time
before sex and money
were a basic right.

The Lachlan

His kirk hidden by a wall of pines
our Scottish parson
gets rid of his religion in the garden.

Harangued by a Jehovah's Witness
across the fence
Mac in singlet and shorts
leans his mattock on a tree,
and welcomes more discussion – in the house.

The Witness settles in an armchair,
when Mac reappears in his collar,
robed for theological debate.

The Lachlan is my church.
River oaks and gums form ecclesiastical glades
of sunlight

for the dragonfly
scooping a mosquito.
Currawongs are Redemptorists
delivering black and white sermons
from high pulpits.
In late winter they hector
blossoms from dull scrublands,
tiny aromatic paper stars
and yellow pollen balls.
Our smaller plants are opportunists.
They temper faith with caution,
flowering in spring before the heat sets in.
But the faith of our river gums is unlimited.
They postpone their blossom for off seasons –
noblesse oblige –
and are the organ pipes of an instrument
with no beginning or end.

Our river is a church with an open door,
but the parishioners are wary and fussy.
Teal nest in thick ground cover,
and musk duck on limbs leaning over the current.
Small finches patrol
the dense understorey
where an eagle's large wings are clumsy,
and blackfish are invited
by moving light and shade,
irregular rocks and snags,
the idiosyncrasies of a known place.

Our river is fed by the spill-off of unstable parishes
by moveable creeks
unloved by surveyors
who would channelise every watercourse.
Public servants
jogging through city parks in shorts at lunchtime
agree and plan policy papers:
"Channelisation and Farm Economics";

"Channelisation and the Controlled Landscape".
Meanwhile fish vote with their fins in denuded creeks.

You don't find our local farmers
jogging around their paddocks,
giving themselves arthritic knees.
Only some streams that feed our Lachlan
run tirelessly,
but with more enjoyment than bureaucrats,
to express certain laws of gravity and motion,
the pleasure of molecules boiling coldly around a boulder
cutting through clay slopes
to granite bedrock.
We observe
their freeplay and turbulence,
individually random but a massed force
scouring basins around roots, engineering shortcuts,
disappearing under sand beds.

The spiny anteater is afraid of my love
and buries himself in bush sand,
as my boots halt and watch.
Birds on the bank exchange passwords
as Jack, my dead brother, is rowing
and my adolescent hand
trails in khaki water, a translucent ghost.
Baptisms, marriages, masses for the dead
float past, with sticks and a drowned page
of the *Cowra Guardian*.
Lights burn on the waters at night
from votive candles of stars
and the isolated homestead on a hill,
where an ageing brother and sister
inherited celibacy and a farm.

Our river was mother to a tribe
of "Murrumbidgee whalers" – swagmen
whose well-stocked rowing boats

drifted through a life of ease.
They saw more reflected sunsets than fence posts,
and odd jobs —
the artfully constructed pile of firewood
that was hollow inside —
passed the time between books.

Our river was a great conveyor of people,
strikebreakers disembarking at midnight
from a paddlewheel steamer,
commercial travellers, itinerants, bales of wool,
but now only the odd party of poets
en route to a festival
travels leisurely waterways by outboard motor,
with their notebooks and binoculars.
We forget our river
was the highway for our invading ancestors,
and we seized these flats by force
from a government of naked old men.

I share a cup of tea with the poets on the bank.

We discuss our river's love of decoration,
garnishing herself with sea tassels and water mats,
painting herself with tree reflections
and glimpses of sky,
and the visiting card she leaves after floods:
the smell of dead frogs and crickets.
Our river is bohemian,
the haunt of lawbreakers and loafers,
watching their reflections in waterholes
and a yabby attach itself to meat on a string,
cautious as a stick insect,
and the middle-aged man who furtively greets you,
puffing up the bank, as you descend,
then find the altar he's built —
male genitals sculpted in sand.

Our river is respectable.
She provides cleared spaces for church picnics
and Mrs Mac teetotal and girlishly light-headed
from "non-alcoholic" cider vouched for and served by Mac.
I yarn with the poets by their camp fire.
My stubble at the end of the day is grey
and they're pink-shaven, black-bearded and hatless.
But they can share a joke with a man who wears a hat.

The river is our confessor,
absolves and dissolves our chemical mistakes,
and our soils are renewed.
But her health is our health.
The flow off of phosphates
feeds a killing blue-green scum of algae.
We can feed our mother too much poison –
our river is mortal.

Yet this evening drinking tea with poets
the river is immortal.
Their boat is pulled up for an overnight pause
in its exchange with the river –
the chatter of water against waxed planks.
A pressure lamp lights a circle of grass
and the souls of the dead join our congregation.
Insects and frogs are a massed choir.
Cooking sausages provide clouds of bush incense,
and we think of the lovers who are married on these banks
in vestries of grass,
experimenting through gaps in clothing.
Her hair is tangled with seeds.
The girl and boy
are vague as they rise,
hardly aware as they pass
of a red glow in the dark,
an old man of the river,
smoking and watching for golden perch and cod
to fill his traps.

Petty crime is an art
which flourishes along these banks.
Lights nod, nets hang from black corks
and ducks are suspicious.
Our river is a church with no gods.
This orchestra of voices from the ribbon weeds
is rich in its mistrust.

Ancient Theft

"You've heard of John Gilbert and Ben Hall,
the bushrangers?
He was on good terms with them.
That big rock on his property,
Gilbert's Lookout, it's called.
Gilbert could peer out for miles.
Now how did a young fellow
from nothing – with nothing –
walk into a property
so well set up, with plenty of stock?"
My father asks about his father,
peering from the rock of old age
into the land before his birth.

If I'm the heir of ancient theft
I sup with silver
my grandfather stole from my grandfather.

Old Testament Country

The camping place of wild horses was a sign.
Horses found the "Wash Pen",
the only permanent water
in this Old Testament country.

Where farms now jostle on the map
my father's father selected
horizon to horizon.
There were granite outcrops
and no fences.
The dark-skinned Canaanites
were soon hunted off,
leaving the wilderness
of leaves to make his own.

In Ireland he called himself farmer,
here he was "on the land".

Bush wildflowers
were a Joseph's coat of colours,
and wild horses, muzzles to the ground
were a sign

in a time before Jesus
and the products of the city.

Gladstone Watts and the Crystal Set

The weirdest night of Gladstone Watts
began near sunset on the plains –
arriving at a tent
while droving a mob
with a "half-Pomeranian" –
that's shorthand for a dog
that couldn't work a chook.
A boundary rider came out,
pumping Gladdie's hand,
talking thirteen to the dozen
(Gladdie wasn't so keen –
he'd spoken to someone a day ago),
and started chopping posts and rails
from mulga; in half an hour

had built a yard for Gladdie's sheep.
After their camp fire meal
the man produced "this wireless thing.
It could darn well near talk."

Given the only bed in the tent
beside some books –
where were those voices?
Gladdie kept eyeing the axe by the fire,
and when the man was snoring
slipped out to bunk with his sheep.

There are questions the western plains can't answer,
voices talking from a man's hand,
lights where no lights should be.

"I've figured since," Gladdie reflects,
"he was a very clever man."

The Two Wethers

"The two wethers"
of Violet Hill
grew old and never read
Professor Fowler's "Science of Life,
Including Love,
Its Law and Power".

The basalt tablelands produced
no pair of sisters
eligible for their sheep run.
Farm economics required
a double match, or nothing.

On Sunday nights they joined
in hymns from "Scottish Paraphrases",
sung only to a tuning fork;

and rode home
through mist and frost.

Nothing of two old brothers
survives, no anecdote:
only a name.

Poverty Bush

We pledged our vows by the poverty bush.
I prepared for your hair
a garland of wiry stems, blue leaves and thorns
that are the first to appear
on scalded land.
At the technical college in town
they're learning the poverty bush dance,
one step forward and two steps back.
When sixty-year-old men ran short
my friend Heather was the first to revolt.
She walked across the floor to Wendy
without self-consciousness,
and watching the movements of the males
guided her among the couples.
Some girls won't get up without a man,
so they sit not budging all night.
But most enjoy dancing with their sex
when gents are scarce –
both step forward, no one steps back.

Law

Law is History, not Science.
We think analogue, not digital.
The same thought travels many dendrites at once.
The brain is a consensus,
not a hierarchy.

Because my son-in-law
wrote a letter
citing a case
about furniture bailed during London air raids
and unclaimed for years,
my antique steamroller
left by me for a decade in someone's yard
came back from its innocent purchaser.

The racket of its arrival
woke the landscape
like a twenty-one gun salute,
and grandchildren ran out to greet
the vast prime mover,
two storeys of red and chrome metal
pulling along our dirt road
through a frame of willow trees,
a bridal train,
with the sun-dappled bride, my steamroller,
chained and suspended
on the long low loader.

The women and children withdrew
when the business of unloading began,
of easing the steamroller's treacherous gravity
from the low platform onto the earth.

Burly and red like their prime mover
the men asked quietly,
"Any women about?"
Then unzipped
to expose hidden parts
that drizzled and hissed steam in dust and dead grass.

Modesty is unwritten law
as precise as legislation.
It constipates women in Bihar by day
who fertilise their fields

only after dark.
It decrees seclusion
for the baboon giving birth.
Only the father can approach.

The law has brought back my chattel,
but she is wearing
an unfamiliar brass horse "Invicta" –
and one morning it's gone.

Nature, like law,
builds with precedent.
The foetus
discarding its gills and tail
has to relive evolution
to become human.
My steamroller and I
are deposited here
by rules that are not simple.

The Golden Wall

Don't ask Uncle Pat why the night sky is dark –
in hot weather
taking his mattress out on the grass
inside his dog-proof fence to sleep.
When Pat lifts his face up to the night –
propped on a pillow
of kapok stuffed in mattress ticking –
he'd fix you with sheep drench if you told him
that his line of sight
should intersect at every point
with a near or distant star
glimmering in the transparency of space
so the whole sky
should be ablaze from end to end
like "a golden wall".

Pat's golden wall was his orange tree.
Like Uncle Pat it had never borne fruit
until I dumped five tons of chicken manure
on its roots.
His line of sight
from the cane lounge where he sprawled
intersected at every point with oranges
twenty feet up in the sky,
a Utopia of fruit
which the district came to visit and eat,
oranges with no ending
like the return veranda
around the four sides of his house
where nephews and nieces ran forever
and their children after them.

Pat forgot his promise to pay for the manure
and the oranges didn't come back.
But he didn't miss them,
so don't ask Pat why the night sky is dark.

Olbers' riddle has hung around
for centuries.
You can't explain it by absorption.
Gas and dust heat up and glow.
Nor by absences or voids.
Every square inch has its galaxies.

Ask the cells inside your head
the same riddle,
why don't they all blaze at once
a golden wall of noise,
each neuron singing its own note
deafening your mind with light.
Political and religious visionaries
promise us this,
every cell singing in unison,
a mass of indistinguishable stars.

But something in the universe denies
the golden wall,
some structure which became Uncle Pat
calling to his nephews from his cane lounge,
"Now don't trample them tomahawk plants!"
(meaning hollyhock plants).

Pat prefers his own company on hot nights
leaving Auntie Bridge inside
with pictures of saints on the bedroom wall.
He takes his bedding
and lies in a darkness
where each star can broadcast as a soloist.

The universe
is a composition of unique bodies
on display,
and the night sky of the mind
allows a single file of thoughts
to light up as a sentence.

Gilbert and Hall

On the road between Boorowa and Binalong
they are inventing morality.
Holding up a black-bordered envelope,
John Gilbert tells his captives, "We must respect death,"
and leaves it unopened.
He fancies a slice of wedding cake
in a letter.
"Don't," says Hall. "It might be poisoned."

After they've stripped all the banknotes
from the mailbags
Hall is for burning the letters and cheques.
"No," says Gilbert. "They might be useful
to the owners."

So they leave them scattered in the grass
for the mailman and a passenger to collect.

O'Meally, the mate of Gilbert and Hall,
has his morality too,
from his saddle pumping shot
into Barnes, the shopkeeper,
who is galloping away unarmed.
"I'm sorry he's dead," O'Meally says later.
"But it's his own fault. He should have stood."

Gilbert and Hall are actors in a self-scripted play.
Drinking port in the firelight with victims
after he's robbed their house
Ben Hall bounces their child on his knee.
"I'd love to take this young 'un on the track –
and make him a man."
"No, no, you can't, you wicked fellow,"
the mother says.
Happy Jack Gilbert commands
the grown-up daughter
to sit at the pianoforte,
and predators and prey sing together.

They are specialists who love their work,
on stolen racehorses
outdistancing police
whom they outgun
with five or six repeaters
slung in holsters around the midriff.
They laugh and discuss the habits of victims,
the miners who challenge them to "a fair fight –
show us your fists",
the squatter who indignantly rejects
the silver change they give back,
the merchant who sneaks a sovereign into his boot.

They have rehearsed the last scene.
One of their "harbourers" for a reward
will lead a group of shadows
to a lonely hiding place
chosen for its dense scrub
where a fugitive can vanish like water.
At dawn a posse of troopers will open fire
on a man scrambling into his boots.

They relish bartering at gunpoint,
a hat, a cloak or saddle.
Death is three days away from Gilbert.
"That's my horse you're riding,"
Happy Jack jokes with his victim.
"You're a common horse thief!
I've a mind to lay a charge.
But I'll swap you this,
if you give me back mine."

They delight in arbitrariness,
stripping an old wayfarer of his life's savings,
robbing a child's piggybank,
staging a party at gunpoint
in Robinson's Hotel.
There are carts and carriages lined up outside –
with valuables untouched.
The captives drink hard liquor
shouted by Gilbert and Hall
who abstemiously sip at bottled ale.
Happy Jack signs
three written passes of leave for an hour.
On the hour Hall goes after them.
"It's not right," he says
as he finds the men strolling back.
"We gave you one hour's leave
and you're ten minutes late."

Driving the Boorowa road a century later
the morality of Gilbert and Hall
is the false apple scent
of roadside briars,
inspiring middle class historians
to romanticise common theft
and paying off a network of spies
as robbing the rich to give to the poor.

I pause to drink tea
from a stainless steel thermos
and the hard good looks of Hall
glitter from translucent thorns.
Happy Jack is cheeky as the pink and white
of rosa canina.
"You've stolen my life," he says.
"They're not your wife and children. They're mine.
Coming home tonight
you'll find me by the fire
sitting in your sheepskin-covered car seat.
I'll be tapping your rosewood pipe on the hearth
and your dog will be sleeping at my feet."

Jack Again

Growing older
the prime numbers come less often.
About to tell you something
at night my thoughts insist
on travelling branch lines
they closed down years ago.
Summer weeds sprout from the bluemetal track.
The rusting rails are two scorch marks
that converge in shimmering heat.

It's fifty years since you dragged yourself,
leg gouged by an axe, felling trees to this spot.
A medical student, not trusting country doctors,
you didn't come home
and flagged down a train for Sydney.

Not Yet Found

I chose the name Spring Forest
and I've yet to find the spring.

Some unfinished equations
are the closest I've come
to the puzzle of why I'm here.

There is a book before our eyes –
the night sky of the universe.
Galileo saw its language was mathematics.
A cricket's encrypted love song,
light from an ancient star
are mathematical messages
arriving in sultry air.

Imaginary and complex numbers
allow life to reproduce itself
endlessly and intricately
without repetition –
the elusive algorithms of a summer night.

Invicta

She is Invicta – head of the horse,
long eyelashes and brown melting eyes,
currency from the copper age.
We are lined up, straggling youths on ponies,
a parody of cavalry at the start of a campaign.

We are lifted through the air,
she has taken our hearts.
Six thousand years ago we mounted her,
plains-dwelling pedestrians,
and she taught us theft and war.

The Two Tents

Late and pragmatic
we arrive with Mr Long in his story
past dusk at two tents on the plain
(a mother and daughter
up from Dubbo on miners' pay day).
Talking to the mother in the first tent;
he finds she's had no customers
and the "titter" six or seven.
He tells the mother, "You'll do me."

Two tents are camped on the plains,
Hygiene and Romance,
and the flap of Hygiene closes,
welcoming Mr Long.

Botany Lessons from Mr Long

Gifts of the mind, not facts, survive.
We would stand under the trees-of-heaven
on the dry creek bed of cool grey pebbles
(large as rocks with not much water to wear them down).
"I think I need a new pipe,"
Mr Long would say.
"I'll go on an expedition to that pipe tree.
A few months back
it had some pretty good pipes ripening on it.
They'd be just about ready by now."

"Mr Long," we'd all chorus.
"Will you pick us a dinky
from the dinky tree!"
A tree hanging with tricycles grew
in a place known only to Mr Long –
and one day they'd be ours.

"Well, I won't be going near there,"
he'd say. "And last time I did,
the dinkies were all very green.
It takes a long time for dinkies to ripen."

On a grey morning the bush
would swallow Mr Long in his moleskins,
as he set out for his pipe tree.

The End of the Pacific War

We were back from a war.
POWs, tall and emaciated
walked unsteadily from ships.
It was spring.
Women were scrubbing brown air raid paper
from window panes,
the neon signs of shops were switched on.

The end of my Pacific War
was rowing out with Jack on Sydney Harbour,
bobbing in a purloined dinghy
among ships and fireworks,
the acrid smoke of detonations
harmless now.
The black and glittering jelly of the harbour
blazed with exploding chrysanthemums
and blue and green starbursts –
an innocent parody.

That spring night in the dinghy
we watched the theatre of the mind,
a spark firing
a consensus of neurons,
the oscillating bursts
of co-operative energy
igniting and fading in the sky.

Later among partying crowds
we wandered "the Cross",
excited by the turbulence
of animal and flower scents
and chasing
some tremendous discovery.

Bell tolling, a fire engine drove past.
Jack hailed a taxi.
"Driver, to the fire."

A Party of Star Gazers

I doubt I'll be the first to report
a stranger lighting the sky,
a moth's eye flaming,
the birth of a supernova.

As the shockwave of neutrinos registers
in water tanks miles underground,
my brass telescope sits on top of a cupboard.

I'm not a disciplined amateur,
watching Jupiter night after night
for subtle colour changes,
interpreting small differences.
My brass telescope
is a family occasion
for husbands and wives and children.

With a heavy duty electric torch
trained on the ground
and deliberately thumping feet
to warn my friends, the venomous snakes,
we walk out into the shockwave of cold air,
under an inflating sky.
We erect the telescope with its tripod
on a gravel crest
looking across the new garden's dense tea-trees
regular as topiary, housing by day
a parliament of honey-eaters and parrots.
Children jostle to look through the eyepiece.
Adults stand back, interested.
I point out obvious features –
the rings of Saturn
that will granulate
after months of patient watching –
and craters of the moon.
Fine details,
a lava flow across the rim
of an impact crater
resolve themselves
for the dedicated observer.

But not for this audience
of talkative appreciators,
sceptical but not technical.
Our breaths are suspended
like the icy detritus of comets.
On the first night of autumn we stand
some in cotton, some wearing wool,
enjoying the riddle of the sky,
not comprehending theory
that says everything came from nothing.
We know our fate is enacted
in light refracted through these lenses.

Blinking, our eyelashes brush
our beginning and our end –
or endless continuity.

The Daisy Picker

Send my corpse home on "the Daisy Picker"
and bury me in my pyjamas –
per "the Daisy Picker"
because it's so hated and loved
for its procrastinations.
Passengers alight
and pick wildflowers by the railway line.
Then with a shuffling of buffers
and whingeing of couplings
with no logic it startles away.

The shadow of our "Daisy Picker",
crossing a bridge
intersects the sun,
as I float on my back,
ears tingling with pressure in the Lachlan.
Cow's toenails and bones would sink.
It's a matter of displacement.
We're judged by quantities.

But don't give my measurements yet
to our local undertaker –
carpenter's rule in his pocket,
as he sells me canaries.

I'm going more trips
on "the Daisy Picker",
journeys with an end
but no destination,
as a red dragonfly
paces the train.

You'll see my face lean from a window,
shaded by a hat brim from the sun,
observing rocks and summer weeds
advance as they recede.

Prickly Moses

These plains and arid ridges
are our promised land.
Driving late at night
past abandoned homesteads
(a rusting sign "Byzantium"
hanging from a gate)
there's not much for the banks to sell,
a ninety year old diary in a derelict shed
recording the erratic rainfall,
some thousands of desiccated acres
and thorny wattles with yellow pollen balls –
the gift of thin, strangely named twigs.
I smell their faint perfume
as I stop and get out
in the empty stillness
of the last continent
where men grew plants.

The Old Buck Rabbit

When the lights are out I step
into my other lives.
The old buck rabbit which bit
a slice from my thirteen year old thumb
(Mr Long egging me on,
"Put your hand in!"
as it cowered in a hollow log)
was nothing to write up
in the CWA cookbook

despite his herb and bread crumb stuffing
and his art in trussing the carcass with twine.
Nor did Mr Long's bird names –
"barker bird" for the eastern shrike tit
and "cherry picker" for the male mistletoe bird
and his "rice eater" –
make it into popular ornithology
unless a man and six boys
are a dialect.
Nor was Ned Flannery's guaranteed method
(before TV)
for keeping children entertained
(he had fourteen)
reported in Hoyle's *Book of Games*
as Jack and I hammered clout-nails
into his wooden leg.

Aunt Margaret's Tea Party

Jack and I spent a summer afternoon
in the cause of science
measuring the correct gap
from the rim of the cup
to the surface of the tea.
Using an ivory and brass pocket rule
and a variety of cups
we found you might vary the gap
by an eighth of an inch
and not be too low or too full.
Later in the year our Aunt Margaret,
who never married, had guests.
Her scones and cupcakes
were lined up like a military parade,
and as she poured the tea
into each cup,
some over-full, others short,
Jack's eyes met mine.

The Rifle Bird's Song

I'm woken by the rifle bird's song –
some notes I know well.
My mother, a policeman's daughter,
always smelt fruit before she bought.
As I was smelling a papaw
an elderly woman touched my arm,
"So that's what you do?" she asked.

Now Olive is gone
and will not come back,
on hot nights I sit up late
turning a few pages
next to an old and noisy air cooler.
I smoke a pipe, using
George Grogan's trick,
a small metal button
or lump of charcoal
lodged in the tobacco –
half an ounce can be eked out for hours.
The unhappy
have no rituals to meet the daylight
each moment
the shock
of meaningless smells
unconnected sound.

The Old German Sailor

Some of my father's fictions were real,
his peacocks
blue and turquoise
picking among fallen eucalypt leaves,
and his pet monkey
who yammered horribly as he died.

My father halted at a mound,
the faint remains of a vanished hut:
"An old German sailor lived here.
'Mr Mac' the sailor would say,
'My mother telled me as a boy,
Jacob my son, you never must steal,
not even a crust to save your life.
And I haf not. Not once.' "
I pause, re-telling my father's story,
and sixty years late
wake to find Jacob and his mother,
the conversation within the conversation,
were a fiction,
puppets in a morality play,
invented for a nine year old boy –
as my youngest brother (the dentist)
woke from his childhood fourteen years old,
late on a cold afternoon
back home from the Goulburn Christian Brothers
at the start of the holidays.

Walking from the gate
no animals were in the paddocks,
birds called from the orchard,
fruit rotted on the ground.
The doors of the house were unlocked
all the furniture gone.
No one answered when he called,
forgotten by his family when the bank sold them up.

At Iambi

My father's sister Bridge had a dream (I was told)
about aircraft crashes.
Poor woman, we thought,
childless, in a big empty house with Uncle Pat.

She imagines herself in nurse's uniform
hurrying across empty paddocks
to the burning wreckage
with painkillers, bandages and antiseptics
to care for the wounded
and say prayers with the dying.
Or she has a tray with cakes and cups of tea
and makes conversation with the survivors.
"See that interesting old tree over there –
with all those mistletoe plants growing from it.
That must be a shire record!
You're just in time for the Morongla show."

One dusk I arrived at Iambi
with a load of manure for their orange tree.
Bridge was enjoying the air.
A large aeroplane flew over, lights flashing in the night sky.
My aunt touched my arm and spoke:
"Wouldn't it be wonderful, Ross,
if it crashed. Think of the loot."

Jack Once Again

In summer an unassuming young man
is travelling in a train
that slowly climbs above the snowline.
Reaching the top of the col
he leaves behind the zone of shade trees
and songbirds,
and becomes detached from his cares and prospects
with glimpses of a grey and distant lake –

The Magic Mountain was among Jack's possessions.
A young man who is dead
cannot explain
why he read about a young man in a train.

I can open the book, read aloud the words
he may have read, or maybe didn't –
and that is all.

A young man with two passengers
is in the pilot's seat
of a plane that slowly climbs above the cloudline.
He becomes detached from the world below:
the sea is a distant corroded mirror.
They sit in a blaze of stationary light
hardly moving at all – or so it seems –
and a moment from now will be plunging
through half a mile of air.
Two will survive. He will not.

Driving at Dusk

I'm driving with just my parking lights.
I switch off the motor
in the dimness under a large ironbark
and can hear a distant sound
of dogs barking,
like the monotheisms of the Middle East.
A water cannon sends a pulse of spray
to drinking fields.
There's a pale yellow sky
fading into blue
and the first stars of a universe
free of meaning
lucid and uncreated
signed by itself.

The Animals

A "domesticated bearded dragon $400"
is not my idea of an animal companion.
A calf asleep on a double bed, perhaps,
or a hare with long ears
crouched under a mahogany sideboard,
thumping the floor.
Or a koala that climbed up a four-poster bed
surprising a seventeen-year-old in her nightie.

They were here before us – the animals –
and we were once them.
Without understanding we watched the sunrise
and the coming of night,
registered the changing of seasons
and dew on leaves that brushed our flanks.
We, the animals,
knew feelings, had a memory,
exchanged sounds and visual cues,
but did not know
what came before
or ask what was to come.

A neighbour sleeps with a wombat in her bed,
and her husband sleeps on the veranda.
Kangaroos watch TV through her sitting room window.

Bottle-fed joeys get osteoporosis
if the composition of the milk isn't right.
The females make better companions.
With shy brown eyes
they hop along beside you
as you collect mail from the gate at dusk.

We were once them,
and now are their custodians.
They know we are different
and their eyes tell us to keep our promise.

Bill came home after a fortnight away.
Pot plants had been kicked off the veranda,
there was an awful smell,
and the front door was ajar.
Inside the house
chairs were overturned,
papers and cushions trampled on floors,
and in the bathroom,
wedged against the washbasin,
her putrid flesh held together by hide,
Twinkle, a pony.
A tractor winched the body out.

Breakfast with a Black Snake

All we have
is circumstantial evidence.
A two year old with white hair like straw,
one of three brothers,
vanishes each morning,
and one day spying parents
follow at a distance.
He crawls across a paddock,
dragging a saucer of milk,
and sits in the grass and waits –
but not for long.
A scolding mother snatches him up.
Too young to explain
or remember –
all we have
is circumstantial evidence
of a child's

conjectured breakfasts with a black snake.
If fate is entropy
and time has no beginning,
why are we still here?
All we have
is circumstantial evidence.
The universe repeats itself.

Mouse Cricket

The four inch gash in the calf
of my sister's granddaughter Lily
is being stitched, subject to interrogation.

"Well, I cut it on the dog kennel's roof.
Because I fell from a mulberry tree.
That's right. The mulberry season *is* over.
You see, we were playing mouse cricket.
A dead mouse is the ball,
a tomato stake, the bat,
and I hit the mouse for six."

Betty and the Cockatoo

In simpler times
the animals also went to school.

"Mu-um! Mu-um!"
Betty would yell,
running along the veranda.
Alice, the family parrot,
was darting at her naked feet,
nipping her toes.

When Betty walked to school
Alice flapped after her
from tree to tree
with raucous cries of "Mu-um! Mu-um!"

Alice was Betty's guilty secret.
"Mu-um! Mu-um!"
mocked her in the school playground –
perched in tall eucalypts
with sulphur crest
a white ghost staring down –
and after school
"Mu-um! Mu-um!" pursued Betty
on the hot and dusty walk home.

Alice was ancient and bitter
and saved her malice (or love) for the young.

Mr Long's Pet Fox

My pet wolves, leaping up on me at dusk
as I feed them,
are a noisy lot.
Mr Long had a pet fox.
When he was out shooting rabbits
it ran with his dogs.
(Years later his hunting companion was an eccentric cat.)
On a trip to Sydney he took his fox
hidden under his calico shirt, in the train
to his sister's house in Woolloomooloo,
and the fox escaped.
People gathered on the footpath
staring and pointing
at a frightened animal.

After sundown
there's a shadow world
where Mr Long is landed gentry,
the fox is man's best friend
and the assassination at Sarajevo
did not take place.

Unlicensed

Unlicensed I drive along roads I know well,
in the same year
a widower and great grandfather.
At dusk my mind takes a short walk
and visits
the burial place on a hill.

With the cattle gone
the land is coming back,
the ruined acres are restored.
Birds I've not seen for years
and perennial native grasses
are plentiful again,
and some interloper crimson roses
among blue wattle foliage and red clay
and dogs – my pet wolves – barking through chicken wire
are wet with the evening dew
of doing nothing.

We stood as a gramophone cranked out
"God Save the King"
then sat on a blanket and watched giant shapes
flicker on a sheet that billowed in the night.

My kin wore wide-brimmed felt hats.
We believed ourselves royalists
but acted like republicans.

We were pink Anglo-Celts who drove
a scattering of dark-skinned tribes from their titles.
We killed as they killed,
and the dead can't apologise.

I drink stolen water
and taste no contamination.
I conserve seeds and flowers and names.
But the world is not a museum – we are not curators.
The ballad's afterglow
is consumed by the future.

LATER POEMS

1976–2013

The Wandering Tattler

I
Faint as a watermark
on the pale wash of landscape
until he separates from granite

grey encyclopaedist
of climates, piping
through the thin reed of his beak

of indecision –
the wandering tattler –
ditherer amongst geographies.

II
Eye the colour of whiskey
piping thinly
as autumn coldly laps
the stones, the wandering tattler
spreads its wings.

III
Black clouds that scarcely move,
a sandbar
midwinter
but where's the wandering tattler?

IV
A lighthouse keeper
played Mozart on a piano,
the wandering tattler
hatched eggs in dry grass.

V
The lighthouse keeper's children
write long letters;
running through the grass,
the wandering tattler
rose up before them.

VI
With his beak
jabbing a hemline in the sand –
if he's frightened,
can freeze into rock
or dead leaves.

VII
The correct temperature is always
a migration away.
Summer in a bay
of grey rocks and marram grass
isn't exact enough,
tasting with his beak
the equations of worms
snatched from sand-slush.

VIII
Why doesn't he fly
into his mind?

IX
He pipes fluently the patois
of log cabins and trappers –
but who's this interloper stitching
by the Gulf of Mexico?

X
Cryptic plumage,
weathered wood or exposed rock,
but his meaning is easy
as red berries clambering
in stubble,
belongs to no colour, mottled,
undecided to the end.

XI
Short of breath
an old man fumbles
with the latch of a gate.
Sand dunes are covering
his fences.
At the end of a season
about to die a bird
faces cold
such as it's never known –
or heat,
it's a matter of accident.

Herbal Teas

I
I don't like herbal teas.
I can't
gulp mothballs and old fur coats.

II
Ninety feet above the rainforest floor
the lost pilot
watches his parachute settle
amongst butterflies and orchids,
but doesn't want help
from herbal teas.

III
The enjoyment
of church-going, abstract art
or herbal teas
requires effort.

IV
Camomile and dandelion tea
have the taste
of burned grasshoppers
and uplift you.

V
In his study watching the dawn
through bare tree-tops,
the subject for his thesis arrived:
herbal teas.

VI
He drank
a funeral of leaves.

VII
His love for infusions
of dried vegetation
proclaimed a new aesthetic,
became an industry.

VIII
Uncorrupted by herbal teas
the red face
of the blonde
teenage learner-driver
caught in a traffic-jam
says, "I'm fed up!"

IX
At the herbal tea-party
our glances are furtive.

X
Our minds savour
their variety
like flowers in a catalogue.
Psyche flutters
amongst the quartz gardens
of ox-eyes and gentians
and grey woolly leaves
you could sew into tea-cosies.

XI
Mind and eye
are radical,
stomach's a conservative.

XII
Hair blowing in the firelight
he leaned in my tent-door:
"Herbal teas will cure
brittle fingernails, heart attacks,
cancer and you."

XIII
Scorched by candle-flame
undecipherable letters arrive
from friends in Herbaltealand:
"What a night ... happy as plants ...
dropped my glasses
in the alfresco john ...
don't need them ...
see a greenfly on a thistle leaf
at two hundred yards ...
marigold tea
cured my attack of the nematodes."

XIV
For my holiday I've packed
a toothbush and silk shirt,
and *South Wind* in paperback.
My herbal teas
are at home in the pantry.

The Antarctic Botanist

I
In summer the ink melts.
He boils Kerguelen cabbage
(with its pale yellow juice).
Good for scurvy,
good with grilled fish.
Antarctic flora
paint the rocks.

II
He has grown a beard.
No insects fly and pollinate.
Flowers open to the wind.
In his tent after sundown
by the hissing light of his pressure lamp
he writes to a girl.

III
At night
the crashing of waves,
the creaking of whales.

IV
As the roaring forties
buffet his tent,
he thinks of subtropical suburbs,
cars parked under poincianas,
windscreens splattered with petals.

V
Wearing a yellow shirt
he collects specimens
in a summer too chancy for annuals.
His suede desert boots
brush the rhizomes of Kerguelen cabbage
meandering for a yard or so
as he scrambles up ledges
of green perennials.

VI
He stares
at splashes and blisters of lichen
on granite.

VII
One night he gets drunk
on his island.
Standing at the open flap of his tent
his shadow tilts down the herbfield
seawards to the pack ice
at the bottom of the world.

VIII
To be a prince of botany
and pin his name on a species,
Jacksonia glauca,
but an ice age overnight
from a thousand miles away
will mill the names fine
as dried camomile.

IX
No room for more princes,
as the sea booms on the reefs.
He lurches over living specimens
to shout at the waves.
New orders break

and glisten on the rocks.
Jacksonales ... Jacksonia imperialis.

X
His island flora fill
three issues of a learned journal,
as lying face down he sees
the moon rise over the tree-tops
of a moss tuft.

XI
The light from his tent has gone out.
In wet moleskins he slithers
down gravel banks,
and spreads his trousers on a rock.
His magnum opus will begin:
"The rocks of this island
sometimes sprout trousers.

XII
"Yellow shirts may be found
floating in the sea,
and on summer nights
a long pink lily
flowers from a suede tuber.
The prostrate form is most frequent.

XIII
"The lights of the aurora
entertain the scientist
sitting naked on a rock.
Green veils 'form and dissolve',
flicker and chase each other.
He came to observe plants
and studies his soul instead."

Tourists and Visitors

I
Graded like cultured pearls, from small to tiny,
from young to old,
the Japanese family, humble peasant folk,
and not well off,
stands at a railway station in remote
Australia. Why
their careful family councils led them here
air-freighted south
from their volcanic rice fields is not apparent.
They silently huddle.
The great-grandmother high as the eight-year-old,
but broad in the beam,
is holding currency, Australian notes.
Her palm is flat.
Her face hunched over these strange pieces of paper
is lost for words.
Her open hand is like an open mouth.

II
The absence of observers and the light
in the damp gardens
make a perfect setting for the Hong Kong mother
to photograph
her laughing late teens daughter posed before
a naked boxer
threatening the setting sun with marble fists.
The girl is pointing
to manly parts screened by a marble vine-leaf.
The long deep shadows,
the daughter's laughing eyes and pointing finger
blink through a lens,
as my appearance on the curving path,
shoes crunching gravel,
intrudes on this domestic triad of mother,
daughter and statue.

I smile. They smile. My steps maintain their rhythm.
A quick look back.
This pantomime of skittish daughter mocking
a marble prude
is snapped again – before the light has gone.

III
A boy and two men call out by the highway.
They'll never catch
a taxi here, but there's a rank, I explain,
behind the railway.
"You're right," they say, "the cars go by so fast,
too fast to stop" –
and gesture with their hands. We walk together.
"You're from New Guinea?"
I ask. "Yes, we're from Bougainville," they say,
"You know our country?"
"No," I reply, "not yet. But I've two friends.
One married a Chimbu,
the other married a Tolai." We all laugh.
The spokesman says,
"I'm Joe, and he's Joe too. He's living here.
His son's my subject."
The boy who is an education thesis
holds Joe Two's hand.
"We're black because we come from Bougainville,"
Joe One explains.
"Other New Guineans are mostly brown –
they're like Fijians.
We're *very black*," he says, as if surprised.

IV
The airport lounge is packed with Japanese tourists.
I start to sew
a button on a cuff. A Japanese bride
sits by my side
and indicates in mime that I should stop.
She swiftly sews

with expert hands, then deftly bites the thread.
The Australians cheer.
An old man says, "Hey, my buttons need sewing too."

Not a Winter's Tale

For Rob Darroch and Sandra Jobson

If on a winter's night a tale proposes,
and you look up, hand frozen to your hair,
your disarray displayed in the cheval glass,
so that you fidget, leave the room and pace

the empty grass, exhaling wraiths of breath
to scatter skywards through bare whips of plum,
you'll hear at last that hound intone through woods
too dry for frost. You now retrace your steps,

reclaim the polished brass knob in your hand,
and treading on the milled green tufted carpet,
collapse relieved, back at your desk,
the page open where you began, the winter's tale

leading you to this table and six glasses,
these spoons reflecting six conspirators,
and under every serving mat, this message:
"Calvin once rode to Rome and wore a hat."

Noah's Woods

As the plate of the landscape sank
peat-bog swallowed oak and birch grove,
then open sea swallowed peat-bog and fenland.
Noah's Woods sailors called them,
tearing their trawls on fir-trunks
and elk bones twenty fathoms down.

At Dogger's Bank
a country the size of Denmark sank
as the channel cut through mild limestone.

A man would not suspect
waves breaking on a nearby beach,
sucking up crushed white shells
and throwing them back.
But year by year
family graves and fields, his childhood
go under the sea.
He trawls nets above his parent's house,
then one day after a week of storms
can find no trace,
only acres of grey sea and kelp.

The dispossessed remember.
Centuries later an old man summons his clan:
"This shrunken pasture grudged to us by strangers
is not our land.
Our land and history are beneath the sea.
Tell your children:
we are Noah's people from Noah's Woods."

Neighbours

The Roaches and Jameses are neighbours.
Mr Roach owns shoe shops, the old style of shoe shop.
He appraises you as a ten or eleven if you're male,
and eight, or an eight and a half if you're a female.
His eyes undress your feet and detect
fallen arches and pigeon toes without even thinking.

Mr Roach used to fold his newspaper neatly
and listen every night to the seven o'clock news.
Then television came and he gave up radio.
A flickering grey screen held him in his armchair,

the same programs, week in, week out,
with a cup of hot meat extract at ten o'clock, brought
by Mrs Roach before retiring.

Mr James lived as an artist for a year,
then decided to try his hand at glue.
He spent nights researching in the public library
and purchased a failing business
for the trade name Parson's Glue.

At all hours of the day and night
Mr James came home from his glue factory.
To unwind, he played Chopin mazurkas and ballades.
His magenta, plastic containers with gold label
announcing "Parson's Glue" in a copperplate script
were loved by children and by artists.
The formula, label and container
were all his own invention – as he hid with a smile
behind the name of the shadowy Parsons.

With the coming of television Mr James
added lithographic plates to his product line.
And when the Roaches bought a colour TV
he set up a factory to make plastic small arms –
not toys or limbs for dolls, but actual weapons.
This business failed, but two out of three
isn't bad for a lifetime.

Mr James sometimes slept in a tin garden shed,
to get peace and quiet from his five children.
Mr Roach's two children went into the shoe business,
and Mr Roach retired.

At about five to ten each night Mr Roach shut his kitchen window.
He would listen in summer
for the sound of Mr James's air conditioner in the tin shed.
If it was on, this meant Mr James was spending the night there.
Perhaps he had quarrelled with Mrs James,

perhaps he was reading *War and Peace*
into the early hours of the morning.
Such questions did not concern Mr Roach.
All he knew was Mr James was in his shed
and this was something to tell Mrs Roach.

The oddness of Mr James took its toll on his wife.
She would go with the children to their beach house
and leave her husband to his piano
and late night feasting on cheese toast.
The bachelor summers of Mr James
were a worry for Mr Roach.
He and Mrs Roach were lovingly inseparable,
a left and right shoe.
But his next door neighbours
had come from different manufacturers.
Mr James was a fancy suede model with a gold buckle,
stitching that fell apart,
and a warranty that was not worth two bob.
Mrs James was a reputable make, a natty lace-up
with sensible heels, dependable when it rained.

The predictable routines of the Roaches
meant their house was always being robbed.
Thursday visits to his sister Lilly were a favourite time for thieves,
as were Wednesday morning shopping expeditions.
The Roaches lived next door to a Catholic church and school.
Vehicles came and went like a gannet rookery.
Non-catholics waited
in cars outside the Roaches' house while their wives were at mass.
But some of these men were not waiting for wives,
they were observing the metronomic ways of the Roaches.
Bars appeared on every window,
an advertisement for burglars to call.
Burglars knew by heart what brands of appliances
the Roaches always bought,
and the three places where Mrs Roach
kept the house-keeping money.

The Jameses' house was immune from robbers,
except a bicycle stolen once from the garage.
A house whose seven people
were in constant crisis
had no appeal for professional thieves.

Life is bitterly unfair.
Each household had an equal stock
of theftworthy items.
Matters became worse in the neighbourhood
when young Eric James bought his father's house.
The Catholic priest confided in Mr Roach
that the church would be an anxious purchaser
when – of course – the Roaches were ready.
So the Roaches made a clause in their wills
that the house was to be auctioned on their death.
Let the priest buy at auction – no one could say
that a Roach had sold to the church by private treaty.

The new James neighbours
made the parents seem conservative.
The tin shed was demolished
for a swimming pool,
and after dark they swam naked.
Mr Roach made a mental note on young Mrs James:
"No make-up and no clothes."
Garments and toys were trampled in every room
and Roberta befriended flying foxes,
walking around with an injured bat
clinging under her t-shirt.

Eric, her husband, was some sort of stockbroker
who loved spiders.
He had a pet name for each pair of small black eyes
spinning in the corners of his study.
He built brown wooden verandas and an aviary
where finches multiplied in shaded light,
then a brick barbecue of Aztec proportions.

When he started a two storey cubby house for his girls,
the brown wooden posts, twenty feet high,
looked like a gallows to the Roaches.
Weekends and late afternoons
working on his cubby house
were the happiest time of Eric's life.

The moment for nailing down the ridge capping came.
Eric manoeuvred himself out onto the roof
more than twenty feet up in the air,
flat on his stomach,
several times seeming to fall.
It became unbearable for Roberta and her mother.
They went inside.
But Mr Roach, deaf in old age, busied himself nearby
on his side of the fence, weeding and raking up leaves,
watching and anxious that his neighbour might fall,
and ready to be of service as neighbours should.

Mr Roach went flying one night,
not one of his flying demonstrations at the bowling club,
when he glided shoeless above the green,
showing his friends how to follow the curvature of the air
like the bias of a bowl.
This time he was over the sea, very high.

There was a rookery of gannets on a cliff,
thousands of birds,
but he couldn't find Mrs Roach.
The households of birds replicated themselves like human suburbs.
In the cacophony of calls there was no voice print he knew,
no place was his own.
Then a gannet with no make-up and clothes
caught his eye.
Her nest was littered with fish scraps.
Where there was a James, a Roach must live next door.
Ignoring young Mrs James, he landed beside Mrs Roach.

Children's Games

I
The screen lights up as he switches it on.
The letters of the poem
are lights on a dark page,
and plastic toys, orange as summer
roar past the window on the flagstones.

A book of games
appears on the page.
Windblown stems
blow white, blow green.

Mother where are you?
Father where are you?
says the girl in a pinafore
standing at the crumbling
edge of the path.

Mother has her lover
over the sea,
father from the bedroom
telephones a lady.

The girl sits down
and chalks on the path
a book of games.
Who will wash my dirty face?

II
As he writes at night
a black and white cat jumps
on the sill and stares in.
Slides off
and re-absorbs in the dark.

We'll play Prohibitions.
We'll dress a lady
but we can't use green,
yellow, pink or blue.

How will you dress my lady?
I'll zip the back
of her white silk dress.

How will you dress my lady?
I'll place a tortoiseshell comb
in mahogany hair.

And you?
I'll get her blue silk shoes …

Forfeit.
The phone is slammed down.
A door crashes shut.
Feet hurry down the path
and will never come back.

Children are crying.
A telephone rings
and rings.

We'll play Prohibitions again.
In the dark of the bed
who'll undress my lady?
Forfeit.
Weeping.
And a mouth stretches in agony.

III
In the picture
the girls each touch a tree.
The trees are full of apples.

Only puss in the middle
has no tree.

Puss, puss, is the call,
give me a drop of water!
The girls change trees,
run with grim jaws,
then touch wood
and compose
themselves again as a picture.

Puss in the middle.
Too slow.

IV
The girls are mocking under the tree,
his head is knocking against a wall,
she hears him as she lies in bed.
He'll kill himself in the rose garden.
His head is knocking against a wall.
She hears him and she lies in bed.
Already he's dead. The smoke of the gunshot
hovers among October roses.
From her bed she hears him knocking his head.

V
A rabbit is jumping and jumping
on the back steps.
Tears are in her eyes, screaming.
"Who'll sew my pantomime dress
for school, where
is my lunch and satchel?"

A rabbit is screaming
and her eyes
are red.

VI

The looking glass is shattered.
The white rabbits
have lost their silk waistcoats
and they huddle in a cage.
They squeeze up tight,
eyes closed in the wind.

Feeding them tufts of grass
the small boy bursts into tears.
"I want my green plate back.
The rabbits can't have my green plate."

VII

When plates and doors are angry,
the cup-of-tea bird sings,
"Cup-of-tea mumma."

The wind bells are arguing with the air,
there are raised voices in a bedroom
and the cup-of-tea bird sings,
"Cup-of-tea mumma."

There are violet abysses in the sky,
her parents play a deadly monopoly,
smoke fumes from the kitchen oven
and the cup-of-tea bird,
fluttering to keep
the red checked curtains she knows,
is ignored as she sings,
"Cup-of-tea mumma."

VIII

Puss has left the picture book
and become a character.
Ambling out of the frame
of two dimensional apple trees
where the girls run with set

jaws in their set piece,
he arches his tail and jumps
with soft paws onto a window sill.
He sneezes at the smell of chicken soup.

At sunrise to catch the warmth
he balances
on the rim of a cactus tub.

The woman hides in the shrubs past midnight
with wild dry eyes.
The man shakes a baby under a tree
as the moon sets, towards dawn.
Puss is the witness
of these non-events in his life.

IX
The King and Queen are fighting.
Lightning and thunder
shake the board.
In the house of cheese
the small pieces cower.

"Get-another-mother," the two-year-old calls out.
The three- and five-year-olds
giggle hysterically.
Day after day the battle goes on
and the small pieces laugh
as the two-year-old shouts
"Get-another-mother."
The King becomes a father,
"What do you mean, Annie?
Do you want another mother?"
"No! You get another mother!"

X
The children play, two girls, one boy.
An apple falls in the walled garden.
The children follow the rolling apple,
run down a path and through a gate.
A clap of thunder, a sudden mist.
"Where have we been?" the smallest asks,
"All I remember is a path and a basket."
"Our old home is gone," the eldest says,
"Hold hands, the mist is slippery and cold."

XI
The children are asleep.
The mother has gone to live in her own house.
The father comes home with the Queen of Diamonds.
Lying against him on a couch
she touches the buckle of his belt.

XII
The cup-of-tea bird is shut outside crying in her tantrum.
She watches the reflections of gardens and clouds in glass French doors.
She flies away from the house of cheese, her mother and the Jack,
Her father and his pageant of ladies. She hangs above the map,
All the clockwork lives, the children's games, the wilderness of roses.
There are black clouds boiling in a blue sky. Her mother is burning cakes.
The cup-of-tea bird sees herself after school, lying in the grass,
When her father comes to pick her up. Now in his car her grief
Empties onto her cheeks with overheard talk about her mother.
"One day, Daddy," she says as rain begins, "you'll find your princess."
House-hunting with her mother, the two year old complains,
"Mumma, I'm too tired to walk." "This is a nice area,"
The cup-of-tea bird consoles. In the house of cheese the telephone
Is ringing, the wolf consults his watch, Red Riding Hood's cheerful clogs
Will clatter down the path in a minute, but the cup-of-tea bird
Warns the visitor, flying down on the path to drive her away.
The cup-of-tea bird discards the book of games, she calls out when cakes
Are burning, she flies where skies are breaking apart, she carries the grief
Of parents, she is the protector of the house. She is five years old.

Death of a Seagull

I
Pigface were flowering in the sandhills.
Struggling in the sea-wind
bees gathered nectar.

II
From sandy ditches
invisible siblings yelled
at each other.

III
Moist from the ocean
Isabel fitted her body
into warm dry sand like a plaster cast.

IV
In her neighbourhood magazine
of stories and drawings
she'd announce under "Coming Events":
"Jack Tennant
and Helen, his wife, will divorce …"

V
On the night her parents told them
a black moth flew through the beach house window.
Anne screamed.
Isabel shouted,
"You only knew each other one month
when you married.
You should've waited."

VI
A family seven days ago,
and now their father
was a postcard signed, "love, Dad".

VII
In her sand-oven Isabel
heard William's muffled shout
"Look! A dead seagull!"

VIII
For the rest of the day they dug,
and nailed together a driftwood cross.
They sheathed in plastic
a cardboard plaque inscribed:
"Here lies
Sam the Seagull buried by Isabel Tennant
William Tennant
Anne Tennant
2. 10. 1980."
Bees visited cerise pigface
picked for Sam's grave.

IX
At dusk they poured a cup
of sea-water on his mound,
and clouds were a cast of thousands.
Lights from the beach house
and cooking smells
meant dinner with Mother.

Child in the Dark

I
The sunset faded from the windows
and lights switched on
inside *her* house.
Curtains on tracks slammed shut.
The bikes of one of her kids
lay flat on a pebbled deck.

II
Waiting behind a gardenia bush
as dusk phased into night
he felt the silence grow
between each passing car.
The throb of the pool filter
became the voice of his fear.

III
"That's *her* house!"
Mum said that morning
as they drove past.

IV
He ran, while rocks
were still smashing the windows.
A block away Mum's car was waiting.
The engine started and headlights switched on
as he ran up and was pulled
with bleeding knee through the door.

V
Mum patted his bandaged leg in bed
and the conspirators kissed good-night.
But his blood remained
on the limestone rockery
where his father's flashlight
was probing the night.

The Flight of the Children

On Friday afternoons and back on Sunday
routinely strapping themselves in, they fly
each week or fortnight, unaccompanied
except for teddy, digital watch or headset.

Snow splashed on mountain ranges, cumulus
at sunset puffed in sumo wrestling poses
are as familiar as the stippled lines
of rain that race across the perspex porthole,

repetitive as the safety demonstrations,
the juice and biscuit balanced on a tray.
Always there is a room, which is their own,
with battered animals, where they can't be,

a parent they must leave, to see the other.
They dream of moving cities by some act
of childish will. Maps, coastlines are transformed
and two rooms are a skateboard ride apart.

Senryu for Age 40

A beer glass in one hand
and vacuum cleaner in the other:
the single father.

He plans his social life
like a campaign, so every night
has some event.

The curry from the party,
six kilos dumped around a rose bush
still scents his garden.

It's now his turn, and children
are a returning tide of voices
through empty rooms.

At first they call
him "Mumma". Do they ever call her
by his name?

Twenty per cent come back:
and for a year of nights he made
love to a number.

Carrying the last child up
the icy steps: and now he puts
himself to bed.

Home drunk, he has to stop
Puss galloping on the piano
demanding food.

The primal claim of mothers
each day to cut the children's lunch
gives him a viewpoint.

He must learn leadership:
it's two days since they cleaned their teeth,
three since they bathed.

His desperate expertise
in bed could win him a pentathlon –
yet he's still single.

His overgrown tennis court;
he is armed with tin snips, secateurs
and spider repellent.

Shirt ripped and hacking weeds
and honeysuckle, he is sweating
through leaf-dust.

The summer night which becomes
his second marriage – long black hair,
her naked approach.

She was changing flats next day.
His children ran up and down her stairs
like porpoises.

Watching her private rites,
her hair-wash in the shower, he asks
himself, "Why me?"

With Father Before Christmas

THE FIRST YEAR

No bigger than her pencil's point, at night
baby grasshoppers, green with bright red eyes
land on Isabel's homework, jump at random,
ricochet from her desk lamp's brilliant circle,
then reappear upon a page of music.
Her eyes close and her mind fills up with trees.

Spiders descend from overhanging trees
on babysitters (yuk!) who come each night
(or so it seems), as Father's bachelor eyes
lust after girls at bars. Desperate, random,
he finds few eligibles in his circle.
His brass bed rarely tinkles its wry music.

Anne dances, Isabel practises her music,
William builds cubby houses in the trees,
Puss jumps up, scratching on glass doors at night,
and, while they eat, stares with refracting eyes.
The route of fall for William's spud is random.
He hunts beneath a dark and kicking circle,

potato mashed on knee, confronts the circle
of sisters uttering their derisive music,
and wants to strip and hang them from the trees.

Father will read from a "good book" tonight,
but custard pools on cedar nag his eyes,
toys on the floor and clothing dropped at random.

His garden's pageant is intense but random,
loving yet starved by his small family circle,
he craves intelligence, a woman's music.
Deafened by the cicadas in the trees
they stand on the stone patio at night,
following bats and meteors with their eyes.

Anne stinks with scent, paints blue around her eyes,
as milk teeth go, her smile is gapped and random.
She carries Puss draped in a semi-circle
upon her chest, swaying with him to music.
"Hey Puss, don't try hiding up those trees.
Don't claw like that. Now you be good, tonight."

Home late that night, Father checks sleeping eyes,
then falls with random limbs through a bright circle
of toys and music, laundered sheets and trees.

THE SECOND YEAR

(A seaside holiday begins with hundreds of cicadas in a tree at a bedroom window)

Isabel wakes to greengrocers and white ghosts,
metallic toys with small wire legs and feet,
heraldic clockwork flying in to land.
She loves each one, yet more arrive in waves.
She strains her comprehension to its edge.
They squawk no answer in vibrating air.

Alone she sends her love into the air,
and watches, framed by curtains like pale ghosts,
a black prince walking backwards on prim feet.

Wearing the garments of some foreign land,
Father drives off to get the milk. She waves.
Beach sounds and cries break in at a blurred edge.

The children jostle at the ocean's edge,
as breakers heave and splinter in the air
and hermit crabs in shells like tumbling ghosts
roll in the surf which races round their feet.
Laughing at foam, toes gripping at the land,
they stage concerted screams at bubbling waves.

Eating with friends at night they hear the waves,
and someone, absent, at the table's edge
sets a branch knocking on the window, air
rattling through papers. Father's angry ghosts
blow in, lifting the curtains, nightmare feet
escaping from some mangrove hinterland.

Fishing, a toady's all the children land,
but Father eyes off women in the waves.
One day Anne's glance has an accusing edge.
"You're dumb. Sticking your bottom in the air!"
William, obsessed, reads about spies and ghosts
and stands in pools which magnify his feet.

Back at the house, they hose sand from their feet,
fine sugar grains, dissolving back to land.
Bathing for bed, they set up monster waves
so great lakes trickle from the tiled floor's edge.
Father harangues them with a flustered air.
Anne makes him sit and watch their game of ghosts.

Abandoned by his ghosts, he lets his feet
pace on the interim land between two waves,
a mirror edge, bleeding in violet air.

THE THIRD YEAR

(Hot days in the suburbs are followed by a country holiday)

The jug wakes with its pounding water.
They find his bed is tenanted, a woman
has sorted laundered clothes into heaped order.
Vanilla neatness permeates the house,
flowers dwell in vases, tables glint with light.
Anne gazes in a mirror, watching clouds.

Cicadas fly over William in dark clouds.
He shakes a tree. Squawking and peeing water,
one flies off, lurching like a pregnant woman.
The deafening chorus has a sort of order,
droning, croaking in gusts around the house,
massive as saturating heat and light.

Their station wagon sets off at first light …
They halt and dust subsides in thinning clouds.
Glasses, a jug of lemon barley water
appear, and at the porch a dark-haired woman.
Their sharp cries, dirty feet and lack of order
invade the high rooms of an old white house.

There's a raised lily pond beside her house.
They lunch beneath a crabapple's mottled light.
Grasshoppers land upon reflected clouds
and gold fish sip the surface of the water.
A foot beneath the table seeks a woman,
toes rest on toes, lips drink to the new order.

Teeth tearing grass, deaf to her tiniest order,
Anne's horse won't even trot around the house,
and Anne's so jodhpured, saddlewise and light.
But after she climbs down, he races clouds,
canters on river sand and rolls in water,
as Anne sits bellowing that she's not yet woman.

Father and Jane in bed are man and woman,
the curious presence of an adult order.
Children are voices in a summer house
discovering ancient farm tools in dim light.
Isabel, chasing, starts grasshopper clouds,
legs afraid of love and running water.

Hair dripping water, a towel-swathed young woman
slips through the fragrant order of her house
switching from dark to light with moonlit clouds.

PING-PONG AT NIGHT ON THE TERRACE

The metal fretwork of a camellia bush
suspends a ping-pong ball. Anne gets it back
and serves to "Dad", who carries the limp form
of Puss. Pupils dilated in the dark,
Puss follows the ball with eyes of yellow water,
jostled on Father's hip, a bag of leaves;

at last offended, scrambles down and leaves.
Anne calls as a tail steers behind a bush,
"Dad, where's your handicap! Now get Puss back!"
A desk lamp lights the match. Giant shadows form
on lawns and balls fly stinging through the dark.
Tongue rasping on a hose, Puss swallows water.

Funny, Puss never decorates trees with water,
Anne thinks, yet he loves scratching up dead leaves
for poos, and squats, fur like a cactus bush.
Her heel treads on the ball, while stumbling back.
Squashed celluloid swells and regains its form
beneath a hot tap, brought in from the dark,

but William's teasing laughter from the dark
ridicules Anne about a speck of water,
her tears on the green table. Torn iris leaves

rub Puss's chin, and a grey lavender bush
combs hairs from his decrepit, knobbly back.
At meals Jane requires etiquette and form.

Wedged on a cactus tub a tabby form
bobs up, deprived, gazing in from the dark,
scratching the glass. A tumblerful of water
from Father soon bespangles Puss, who leaves.
A soggy mat befriends a privet bush.
But nights of clambering on their father's back

watched by Puss from a sill, will not come back.
Isabel's left breast has begun to form,
the children talk pedantically in the dark,
cake recipes are swapped in bed, mouths water.
And one night Puss is gone, dissolved in leaves.
They knock up neighbours, call out through the bush.

But he's gone bush, cannot be whistled back,
his stiff form decomposing in the dark,
as sprinklers pulsing water splatter leaves.

Lenin's Question

"As Lenin said, 'What is to be done?'" Your words
were naked like our bodies as we lay,
mid-morning on a working day, the sheets
rolled back, your long black mane of hair undone.
The bed was like the Russian steppes. The horse
on which we rode veered unpredictably,
its spirited hooves took us beyond all landmarks,
and looking back, all we could see was wheat.
That day we planned children, the bourgeois response
to Lenin's question. But we could not plan
the vehemence of the young bones you would carry,
voices demanding, small fists grabbing breasts
years after they were weaned. The farm we planted

was older than collectives or kibbutzim,
it could survive these fires and summer storms,
monogamy, our oldest cultural unit,
where women own the gate and men are guests.

Parenthood

I have held what I hoped would become the best minds of a generation
Over the gutter outside an Italian coffee shop watching the small
Warm urine splatter on the asphalt – impatient to rejoin
An almond torta and a cappuccino at a formica table.
I have been a single parent with three children at a Chinese restaurant
The eldest five years old and each in turn demanding
My company as they fussed in toilets and my pork sate went cold.
They rarely went all at once; each child required an individual
Moment of inspiration – and when their toilet pilgrimage was ended
I have tried to eat the remnants of my meal with twisting children
Beneath the table, screaming and grabbing in a scrimmage.
I have been wiping clean the fold between young buttocks as a pizza
I hoped to finish was cleared from a red and white checked table cloth.
I have been pouring wine for women I was hoping to impress
When a daughter ran for help through guests urgently holding out
Her gift, a potty, which I took with the same courtesy
As she gave it, grateful to dispose of its contents so simply
In a flurry of water released by the pushing of a button.
I have been butted by heads which have told me to go away and I have done so,
My mouth has been wrenched by small hands wanting to reach down to my tonsils
As I lay in bed on Sunday mornings and the sun shone through the slats
Of dusty blinds. I have helpfully carried dilly-dalliers up steps
Who indignantly ran straight down and walked up by themselves.
My arms have become exhausted, bouncing young animals until they fell asleep
In my lap listening to Buxtehude. "Too cold," I have been told,
As I handed a piece of fruit from the refrigerator, and for weeks had to warm
Refrigerated apples in the microwave so milk teeth cutting green
Carbohydrate did not chill. I have pleasurably smacked small bottoms
Which have climbed up and arched themselves on my lap wanting the report
And tingle of my palm. I have known large round heads that bumped

And rubbed themselves against my forehead, and affectionate noses
That loved to displace inconvenient snot from themselves onto me.
The demands of their bodies have taken me to unfamiliar geographies.
I have explored the white tiles and stainless steel benches of restaurant kitchens
And guided short legs across rinsed floors smelling of detergent
Past men in white with heads lowered and cleavers dissecting and assembling
Mounds of sparkling pink flesh – and located the remote dark shrine
Of a toilet behind boxes of coarse green vegetables and long white radishes.
I have badgered half-asleep children along backstreets at night, carrying
Whom I could to my van. I have stumbled with them sleeping in my arms
Up concrete steps on winter nights after eating in Greek restaurants,
Counting each body, then slamming the door of my van and taking
My own body, the last of my tasks, to a cold bed free of arguments.
I have lived in the extreme latitudes of child rearing, the blizzard
Of the temper tantrum and my own not always wise or honourable response,
The midnight sun of the child calling for attention late at night,
And have longed for the white courtyards and mediterranean calm of middle age.
Now these small bodies are becoming civilised people claiming they are not
Ashamed of a parent's overgrown garden and unpainted ceilings
Which a new arrival, with an infant's forthrightness, complains are "old".
And the father of this tribe sleeps in a bed which is warm with arguments.
Their bones elongate and put on weight and they draw away into space.
Their faces lengthen with responsibility and their own concerns.
I could clutch as they recede and fret for the push of miniature persons.
And claim them as children of my flesh – but my own body is where I must live.

Harold's Walk

He turned and waved.
He was one year and a month.
With cobweb-light hair,
the colour of leatherwood honey,
brown poet's eyes
and refined cheekbones
burnished red like the blush
on a white Shanghai peach,

he turned and waved.
There was a graze in his left nostril,
a thin scab in the fold where it met the cheek.
He was wearing a white singlet
and plastic pilchers.
Having farewelled us
he headed off down the road
like a tottering upright tortoise.
Propelled by an unstoppable busyness,
his pink feet imprinted the hot soft dust
of the road that led
into that Old Testament afternoon,
the biblical vastness of southwest Queensland.

He escaped as we were placing
a small native pine in the back of the utility.
A single blow of the axe, a sharp smell of resin
and we had a Christmas tree.
But Christmas and tomorrow had no meaning for him.
His sole interest
was the random stagger of his short fat legs
and this curious ability
to distance himself from objects.

No birds or insects
announced their presence in the heavy stillness
as water and life withdrew.
The rapid and twittering dialects
of finches and wagtails, the warbling of magpies
that had made the morning into a watermeadow
of sounds and activity
were a hypothesis cancelled in the oven air
by the axeblade of sunlight.
There were no geckoes, whose ghostlike transparent bodies
attracted by insect harvests
frolicked on flywire screens at night.
They too were hiding.

But the child, an escaping particle, whose energy had no objective,
who woke and could not be contained,
small fists hoisting the face up to look
over cot-bars
and grab for the horizon,
ran tottering and uncompromised through hot dust.
If we had tried to stop him
he would have squealed, "No, no,"
one of his three words –
the others "oh" for surprise
and "mamy" for need and distress.
He ran with no sense of history
through brigalow country unreformed like himself,
that was cleared long ago with crowbar, axe and shovel,
cleared again by bulldozer and chains,
and cleared once more
by a blade cutting beneath the surface.
But the seeds and roots are unrepentant
as the tortoise-child
who runs with no fear of marks in the road
that may lead to a death-adder
in a camouflaged coil of dust.

His momentum was unadulterated by knowledge.
His hypothesis rejected our evidence.
He ran falling on his plastic pilchers
and picking himself up,
unwilling to learn
except what he could teach himself
from placing stones in his mouth
and tearing leaves apart with his fingers.

The night sky above brigalow country
is a Joseph's coat of stars,
but if your finger tracked the Southern Cross
or saucepan for him,
he grabbed at the finger and not the stars.

Because there was hot available air
into which he could run, he ran.
Balancing himself with arms apart
his stops and starts were unpredictable,
the play of free will –
liberated by chaos from classical physics.
The wild purple verbena scrambling by the road,
milk thistles,
and grasses bending with the weight of seeds
were the instantly touchable aromatic kingdom
through which he tottered,
startled only by the grasshopper's sudden parachute
of lemon splashed with a blood drop.
Some hundreds of yards further on
he turned and waved again
a last farewell
from eyes set in an oval whimsical head,
before entering his chosen land
of wilga and blue native pine.

Second Chance

I
I telephone late.
"How nice for you,"
you say above the howling,
"to be at work.
The boys won't eat
those pork puffs you bought."

The house is silent and dark.
A voice calls from a bunk bed,
"Tuck me up.
I'm so hungry. I've had nothing to eat."

II
There is a technical problem
with the threatened puppet show.
The bossy puppeteer
has fallen asleep.

III
Years later, aged nine,
he has a recurrent dream.
He's goalkeeper for a hockey game in a maze.
There's a sound of hooves
and he has to field
a lead ball, as tall as his mother.

IV
I'm cutting my lunch in the early morning dark;
half asleep, my three-year-old appears:
"Are we going to have our shower?
My eyes are open."

As I soap my hair, I warn him,
"Shampoo coming down."
We wake the house each morning
 chanting our male chorus,
"Shampoo coming down."

V
Summer rain vibrates
orange nasturtiums trailing
from a cracked concrete pot.
It soaks cacti amputated
by the shears of a helpful child,
and thunder is a broom
banging in a distant wardrobe.

VI
Our older son telephones me at work:
there's a crisis, Mum's rushed to the chemist –
walking backwards to watch
his kitten trapped on the roof
he sat on a cactus tub,
the one with the red thorns.

VII
You leave wet footprints
on the polished boards of the white hall
coming naked from the shower.

VIII
Mowing ground
from where I've hacked out black bamboo
dust blows from the spinning blades
onto your washing.

IX
Our youngest goes to bed.
Chanting voices issue from his room
and fill the house,
as his finger follows
the letters on a page.
Next day:
"Was my expression good?"

X
I'm about to drop a lolly on a stick
into a garbage bin.
"Hey! Mum and you drink wine,"
he protests. "You can't do that.
Lollies are the child's wine."

XI
Smaller he would protest
as I trimmed foam with my razor.
"I can shave too," he'd say,
"My whiskers are in me."

XII
Our older boy reprimands me:
"Those are Mum's good dress-making scissors."
As I'm cutting my toe-nails.

XIII
It's a wintery night. In his bed
I read *The Hound of the Baskervilles*.
We pause to turn a page
and hear a creepy sound
from under his floor,
the Mouse of the Baskervilles –
a small wheel turning in a darkened laundry.

XIV
In summer at dusk the storm bird calls.
The "bossy puppeteer" now eleven years tall
holds out wet rye bread in his palm
so rainbow lorikeets
perch eating with crumbed beaks.
His younger brother on a swing
jumps to do a "360" – and so
a small soldier bears his arm in a sling.
The night-flowering cactus that he hacked
flowers for the first time –
a flower the size of a cantaloupe –
choosing for its debut
the hottest day in a hundred years.
By noon it's dead.
On sultry mornings, lying in bed we hear
the storm bird calling, a contralto voice,
here and far away.

Your hair cascades upon the pillow, black
except for five or six white hairs.
I ask: open your eyes and look into mine,
your eyes and skin like theirs,
my privileged summer, a second chance.

The Messenger

Late, he was fifteen minutes late.
She'd drive herself to hospital.
Fed up, she switched on the ignition.

"Mum's left, she left – just now, this minute",
high voices chorused, agitated.
Astonished, too enraged to speak
he thought, "I've had enough of this."

Two short and desperate legs ran out –
the car was gone – ran up the hill
and caught her at the traffic lights.
"Mum," he called out, "Dad's here, Dad's here!"

He had diverted the tornado,
a house and marriage safe again.

A Short History of Europe

He badgers, jostling on black cobblestones.
I let him climb inside the cupola,
and wait in the piazza, writing postcards.
A lady in a fur coat cycles past.
"Dad, now the bell-tower." "No – the dome's enough."

I'm startled by the long, lopsided curve
of arm fondling her golden cataract,
a secular Virgin balanced on a shell;

Uccello's soldiers jostling in the dark;
Bronzino's "Bia", the child who died. He sees
white feathers falling in a long dim courtyard –
snow silencing the sparrows of the Uffizi.

I drink espresso and his busy spoon
stirs circles in his ciocalata calda.
We eat gelati, dodging motor scooters,
and pace the Arno with its many bridges,
one of us twelve, the other fifty-eight,
under a sky of smoky creams and blues –
a frieze of domes and spires, smudged palaces.
Sticks float past in the yellow flood, and mats
of rubbish, a mass movement of detritus
towards the roar of the Vespucci weir.
Looking back from the parapet we spot
a soccer ball that bobs behind some willows.
It pauses and meanders, undecided.
We make a silent pact. That ball's our ball.
We walk and track its progress down the river,
its drift towards the weir … and now it's racing
and sucked into an avalanche of spray.

We peer across the wild and churning acres,
the Sturm und Drang whose clamour fills our ears,
but there's no ball with is red hexagons.
We've lost our reference point. It's dark and cold.
Time to trudge back through frost to our hotel.

Florence 1998

Father and Sons

I
He's been away for a week,
so I telephone.
"Dad, your voice is too loud."

II
Two weeks with my sister-in-law
and her ordered parenting:
my boys are like polished silver.

III
As I wash his dirty feet in the bath
his toes curl coquettishly.

IV
The cap still on the lens
he points his new red telescope.
"I can see the craters on the moon!"

V
Between courses my two boys
leave the Peking Inn
for a yoyo break.

VI
Hiding in a distant room
crying under a bed
sobbing to himself in gasps
I can't see him in the twilight.
"I was cleaning the car as he said,
but he kept on at me, finding fault.
It's always like this.
He doesn't want to pay me the money."

VII
Your flight aims toward Delhi at midnight.
Brown eyes gaze up, his arms reach up
and draw me down, planting a chaste kiss on my lips.
Then he says: "And good night Mum, wherever you are."

Next morning
taking his school bags from my car
face blank as a wall, he doesn't say goodbye.

VIII
"There are eighty seven different vegetables in this shop
and you'll eat only three.
How boring to be your father."

IX
Looking for a poem to read
at school assembly,
my ten year old packs in his school bag
Frank O'Hara's "Lunch Poems".

X
"Good night, Mr Bubby," I say.
"Bubby," he says
testing the word doubtfully – a pet name or an insult.
Years later, aged 14, he still wants to be tucked up
and a good night kiss.
He smiles: "Good night, Mr Lovely One."
"That's what I was just about to say," I say.

XI
The teenager's unblinking gaze: "Dad,
you're too kind to be any good as a lawyer."

XII
I pick up a beetle struggling in illuminated water
and launch it at some bushes.
Both taller than me now, we swim at night
in the blue glass mosaic pool
(affordable only at the end of their childhood –
inhabited by childish shouts and screams
for just two or three summers).
The heater's on and steam rises from the surface.
As we swim lengths
the underwater pool light refracts through wobbling liquid
and a ghost light bobs in distant eucalypts.

I stand at the shallow end
watching a large aircraft fly over, red lights blinking,
as young baritone voices
call out my given name.

The Ring

I
He loved an amethyst and two green garnets.
He paid. A box snapped shut upon the ring.

II
As he produced the ring, her eyes lit up,
intrigued by green and purple stones, compelled
to touch its antique gold – love at first sight.
"If you come back," he said, "it's yours to keep."
His wife did not come back
and six months later she returned the ring.

III
The meanings of the ring: a beautiful object
that he could love and own (or so he thought);
a husband's gesture of goodwill and love;
a small morality play that he had planned
with simple plot and unambiguous roles.

IV
He packed the ring away with all its meanings
among some socks and slowly shut the drawer.
Years passed. He met the woman of his life.
She wore a bridal sari, red and gold.
Their wedding party "cheap", some guests decided.
They had no money. Hope and happiness
come free – and they were young, or almost young.
More children came, two boys, intense brown eyes.
Weeds were cut back, the roses flowered again,
rubbish was emptied out of dusty rooms.

She civilised the beast that kept a ring
and gave him love, community and family
(her sisters on the phone, three girls conspiring).
He kissed her as she stepped out from the shower
and joked about the "poison ring" (his phrase) –
"It's got no meaning now." "Oh yes it has."
And so it stayed unwanted in a drawer.

V
There was another who would love the ring.
His shadow crossed the grass, a spider web
blew faintly as he passed. A glass pane shattered,
an expert hand reached in, a door clicked open,
a phantom of the sunlight slipped inside.
His image registered in mirrors, shoes
flitted across the polished wooden floors.
He moved from room to room, making no sound,
fastidious, leaving no mess behind.
Gloved fingers opened drawers, selecting quickly,
and rummaging in darkness found the ring
and loved it for the heroin it would buy.

Conversations in a Family Van

I
There was a pale green van.
I called it "Bulk"
after the BLK in its number plate.
If cheap vinyl bench seats
purchased second hand through the classifieds
could reassemble themselves and speak
(twenty years after their trip to the wrecking yard)
this is what they might repeat.

II
Between marriages I'm driving
with my children aged two, three and five.
"We're having lunch with a lady.
She has two little daughters
called Nova and Buffy."
"That's not their names.
No! You're tricking,"
small lungs angrily chorus.

III
So each detail of my story is complete
for years I've been trying
to recall a name –
something to do with stars
but not Astrid.
A small grubby sedan
overtakes on my right,
the grimy chrome letters
on its boot spell the model name –
NOVA bursting on my mind
like a supernova.

IV
My children aged eight, nine and eleven
are on the benches in the back,
their step mother with me in the front.
We've picked them up
after a childbirth class.
"When that baby's born,"
the eight year old says,
darkening her voice like the witches in Macbeth,
"IT's not going to last long.
I'm making sure it's just Baby Bones."

V
Baby Bones is two years old,
strapped in a toddler's seat,
singing a meaningless song
to his sisters and brother as we drive.
At the end of his meaningless song
he loudly claps his own applause,
and his sisters and brother
laugh and clap too.

VI
"Those glasses you're wearing are women's glasses,"
the young adults critique my spectacles
purchased from a hardware store.
They are oversize
and large gold medallions
decorate the frames.
"When I bought them I had no glasses on.
I couldn't see what they looked like."

VII
When the pale green van is young
I place my only child at the back
a baby girl
in a basket of white plastic wicker,
a tiny human being.
Driving down a busy highway
the rear door, not properly latched,
swings up of its own volition.
In the mirror I see a mass
of following traffic,
and the white basket,
poised at the back, as though about to fall out,
held only by its own small gravity.
I stop the van
and there's no conversation at all.

VIII
The vinyl benches launch into direct speech,
the left and right sides of my brain speaking together:
"When he bought us second-hand
through the classified pages of the newspaper –"

The near bench:
"Another of his bargains – "

Both benches together again:
"his pale green van
was like an empty house,
just a driver's seat and passenger seat up front
like two little tomb stones.
We furnished his van, we made it a home.
But what was the point of his van and us,
eight places for just two people?
There were no children then."

The near bench:
"Another of his whims."

The far bench:
"Perhaps they had children
to fill up the van and sit on us."

IX
The near bench:
"On the days he had the children,
picking them up from school
he was chronically late.
Always excuses.
A traffic pile up. Or he'd run out of petrol.
They'd be standing on the footpath
almost in tears as he drove up.
He was a poseur, not a parent."

The far bench:
"Remember that hot morning
his cheap reconditioned motor cracked in half.
The engine oil ebbed down the road like blood,
and we watched
the father and three little children
with their short fat legs
set out on the three miles to school."

X
The near bench:
"He'd drive for hours along mountain roads
to buy a blue or red rhododendron
with his last ten dollars,
and they'd start crying to go home."

XI
The far bench:
"Remember that time he filled the van
with banana palms
to plant along his front fence.
He threatened to call his house
'Banana Castle'."

The near bench:
"All because they were a bargain –
more than a fast-growing screen,
in eighteen months, a banana palm jungle,
with fruit like shrivelled fingers
so he had to hack them all out –
a year of week-ends with a mattock."

The far bench:
"But spiders and fruit bats loved the big leaves
glinting in the streetlights at night."

XII
The near bench:
"He was young and stupid.
That marriage was a joke.
I'd see his hand reach out for hers
and she'd snatch her hand away.
Those banana palms were a big mistake."

The far bench: "Nothing is a joke.
I was the bench at the rear,
further away from children bringing up their milk,
the changing of nappies, the little quarrels.
I could watch the dawn
through the back window
grey clouds in the blue
that changed to burning pink.
What happened is what happened."

Thirteen Long Playing Haiku

For Warwick Arnold

I
A cigarette stuck to his lips,
at night the amateur broadcaster
washes his precious vinyl LPs
in warm soapy water,
and coughs himself to sleep.

Next day the needle sticks in the grooves
and his voice is a croak on air.

II
Small silver discs whose binary code
is read by a ruby laser
obsess my days and nights,
colourful illustrations in their jewel cases,

and sleeve note stories
of Ravel walking along the beach
at Monte Carlo,
Brahms's hopeless love for Clara.

III
Our demographic:
aged over 50, male.
Some buy numerous versions of a single piece,
others – "completists" – want
a composer's every work.
Some study ratings in guides for hours,
want no repeats in their collection
and insist on original instruments.
Others go crazy at sales
and emerge from an orgasm of spending
loaded with CDs,
blinking in the sunlight.

IV
I replace Allegri *after* Alkan.
I'd forgotten
there was a double "l" in Allegri.

V
Members of a Masonic order
standing apart from wives and partners
we furtively exchange information
about bargains and rarities.
As our collections grow
we abandon the mainstream,
and develop bizarre tastes.

VI
Some of us file composers
in alphabetical order,
and have systems
for filing within a composer.

Alphabetists avoid compilations.
Do you file
the string quartets of Debussy and Ravel
under D or R?

VII
"Where's *Einstein on the Beach*?"
the free-filers ask their overflowing
and continually circulating collections,
stacked under beds, in broom cupboards,
discs piled in drawers
and detached from their jewel cases.
For a week Philip Glass hides
between Louis Armstrong in Paris
and Monteverdi's *Orfeo*,
then moves on and finds new companions.

VIII
The older dealers understand their clients.
A woman is buying *Figaro* for her daughter:
"Isn't Mozart a bit light?"
"Madam,
is the ceiling of the Sistine Chapel 'a bit light'?"
Wrapping my purchase,
he diagnoses me
through Henry Kissinger glasses:
"If you can't make up your mind what to play,
play your collection
in alphabetical order."

IX
Arriving home at night
with my newspaper neatly
folded under my arm,
I'm bailed up by my son
at the top of the stairs:
"Mum, he's hiding more CDs
in his *Financial Review*."

X
Driving a carload of young women
to a tax class I'm giving,
I turn the ignition key.
Will I switch off John Cage's
Sonatas and Interludes for Prepared Piano?
I let the CD play unannounced
and roll back the sun roof.
The car fills with sunlight and young women's conversation
punctuated by strange and luminous percussions.
Gulls and the grey arch of Sydney's Harbour Bridge pass over us.
They thank me as we park:
"That was very pleasant."

XI
A second hand music shop
leaves a message on my voicemail.
Within minutes I'm sorting through
thousands of baroque and early music CDs.
"A deceased estate,
he was a baroque man – "
they quote an amateur broadcaster's name.
"I'm a baroque man too," I say.
But not like this,
every little byway explored,
volumes of duets for recorders,
lute music that would play for weeks,
lovingly assembled
by a narrow and exact mind.
Shaken, I buy just some Ockeghem and Handel.

At home I open a jewel case and smell ash –
the dead man's cigarettes.
"Dad," the voices say,
"it'll happen to you – to your collection."

XII
The collector writes his own valedictory:
"We approve
how you studiously play
almost every CD you buy.
We forgive the occasional omission,
one or two missed in a boxed set of Schubert lieder,
and those you never play, but love
as a memento
of the same performance on much played vinyl.
We admire your urge to know and experience blues,
minimalism, a capella masses,
Alkan to Zelenka – even Broadway musicals.
The collector's life is solitary and odd,
his assembly of objects
meaningful only to himself."

XIII
I'm tipping CDs into the 10 stack
in the boot of my red car,
constructing my new identity:
Handel's *Saul*, Schnittke's *concerto grosso*,
some John Lee Hooker,
Lou Reed's *Transformer* –
some of the dead broadcaster's treasures,
his Buxtehude *La Capricciosa* variations.
I'm also removing my old self,
replacing the discs in their cases.
I have the jewel cases laid out
like a neurosurgeon's instruments,
as I withdraw and insert,
fingertips gingerly holding each disc by its edge,
checking each label is up.

Tonight I'm driving to a beach house
three hours of tunnels and freeways, past dairy country,
through eucalypt forests
and along a moonlit peninsula,
the music and the road
a single line of thought.

Thirteen Ways of Looking at Twelve Cinnamon Buns

For John Weerden

Hartford Accident and Indemnity, of which Wallace Stevens was later a vice president, had guaranteed a contractor who went broke and Stevens decided this required a meeting in Philadelphia. The year was 1928. Robert De Vore recollects: "I stood at the gate in the station, and when he came through I didn't have any trouble spotting him... tall, austere, very dignified, an unusual-looking man. He said 'Let's get on our way. We want to go to the attorney's office and get into this thing right away. We don't want to waste any time.' I said, 'No sir!'

"Then he said, 'The attorney's office is down in Chestnut Street, so on the way down what do you say we get some cinnamon buns... I always, whenever I come to Philadelphia, buy these cinnamon buns at Lahr's.' I thought, This is strange to do... He ordered a dozen to send to Hartford. I thought, Oh, that is it. Then he wanted a dozen more... And I thought, My gosh, I wonder when he's going to eat these things. Well, we got to the attorney's office... and into the conference room. There were about seven of us. He opened up his bag, put it in the middle of the table, and said, 'Let's have a cinnamon bun.' Everyone, trying to be polite, agreed with him, and we all reached in and got a handful of goo. And we started our conference." From Peter Brazeau, ed. *Parts of a World: Wallace Stevens Remembered* (San Francisco: North Point Press, 1985) 12–13.

I
"Let's have a cinnamon bun,"
he says, opening the paper bag,
placing it on the mahogany table.
Twelve cinnamon buns are twelve facts.

II
Twelve cinnamon buns are not
red and green saris,
cans of jaggery,
milk punch
or tea-chests
on a beach in Ceylon.

III
They are coated with pink sugar.
They are from Lahr's.
The seven in the conference room
including Mr Stevens
gaze out at Chestnut Street.
They see a sycamore tree and people
strolling freely on the sidewalk.

IV
When he visits Philadelphia
he goes first to Lahr's,
buys twelve cinnamon buns.
There is a correct sequence of events
that admits no escape.

V
Let's get cracking
get on with it
straight on with our business
no time to waste
waste no time at all
and get twelve cinnamon buns.

VI
As he opens the bag
the room is perfumed with spices and pastry.
The perfume questions
his motive for calling the meeting.

VII
The churned milk of a cow,
the milled seeds of a wheat field,
the crystallised juice of sugar plantations,
a droplet of cochineal,
the fragrant bark of a tree
converge at Lahr's.
Fastidiously transformed
oven-fresh
they give seven communicants
a brief epiphany.

VIII
Twelve buns
divided by seven mouths.
History does not record
the unlucky two
who had no second bun.

IX
He has the build of a retired footballer,
imposing and austere,
and speaks slowly.
He falls silent
munching a cinnamon bun.

X
This is high art:
One man sharing
a supreme bliss
with six astonished conscripts.

XI
The seven will not recall
the pieces of paper they signed.
One image will survive:
the impressive sweetness
and gravity

of a tall man tearing open
a paper bag.

XII
The last crumb has gone.
The last pink sugar has been licked
from the last sticky finger.
There is relief.
The seven can talk again,
revert to the routine of their lives.

XIII
They do not notice
through the pattern of sycamore leaves
framed in the window
a delivery van
setting out for Hartford
with a cargo of twelve cinnamon buns.

WALLACE STEVENS REPLIES

My salutations for your thirteen ways.
But there's one way of looking at the buns,
And only one, and that's the Hartford way.
The buns were never an aesthetic statement.
Stevens the poet was somewhere else that day.
I had people at loggerheads – not speaking.
I get my wrangling parties in one place
And play my opening gambit – cinnamon buns!
The glances say that I'm a trifle daft.
The hands reach out and rummage for the buns,
And meet and almost touch across the table,
The goo, the sticky scent, the morning freshness …
And in an hour I have my settlement.
Forgive me, but I kept my poetry
And life in separate boxes. You don't make it.

Self Portrait at 62

Aged 62, I like what I do.
Minus a prostate, I have erectile dysfunction,
but we make love in our way, and still with fervour
within my altered body map.

I lunch outdoors at a Buddhist restaurant
with three of my children
between the white pendulous flowers of a datura
and a giant ginger plant.
Lucy, to show she's in recovery,
closes her eyes and touches the tip of her nose
with her index finger.
Her elder brother does the same.
They laugh and explain –
if you have MS, you're OK
if your finger can locate your nose.

It changes your consciousness,
he says at another lunch,
eating gado gado with chopsticks,
and sometimes you remember a time before MS.

Aged 62, I like what I do
and remember an earlier body map.

A young person has left a message on my voice mail.
"I have an insoluble problem," she says,
"with untaxed profits in a unit trust,
and if you could call me, I'd be oh so grateful."

A young person has donated the body I inhabit.
Its shins tend to flake,
so I rub in a white medicinal cream.
It makes the skin supple and smooth
and pleasantly fragrant.

My body sits in an office tower (one of a pair).
The twin towers overlook a geometrical garden
with a family of three bronze wombats
through which I walk
to lunch at the Buddhist restaurant.

The eyes of my body peer at a screen,
a diagram of forty or so companies,
connected by coloured arrows and dotted lines.
My fountain pen leaves red ticks on a sheet
where the companies are sorted by class
then stops at a name
I can't classify.

I am married to beautiful, argumentative you.
You say, "When I'm talking about me,
how do you always change the subject to you?"

I'm completing a survey for prostate cancer survivors.
"Do you have feelings of worthlessness?" I circle "Never".
"Do you feel positive?" I circle "Always".

My son Harry, six foot one,
has a gentle manner.
We drive in each morning,
have coffee in the travertine foyer of the twin towers
and he walks to school.
He dismisses the applied sciences
at some traffic lights.
I brace myself, unsure where this leads.
"Electron clouds interest me. Air pollution doesn't."

Now we come to the day of this self portrait,
an ordinary day when no one dies or falls in love,
aged 62, a few days south of 63.
I forget to say good-bye to the dog.

(Your job is to make his breakfast,
my job is to play –
sometimes I lie on the grass
my hands shielding my face from his tongue.)
After squeezing orange juices for three
my sixteen year old and I
are strapping ourselves in.
The garage door rolls up.

We drive through refrigerated stillness,
early, to beat the traffic,
not for the poetry of empty streets,
blue mornings and a white winter sun.
He abstains from catching the train with friends.
Perhaps because he's my youngest
"estremo unico fior" – but for my child
I hope the cold earth is a distant prospect.

I order two cappuccinos in the travertine foyer.
"He's your son?" they ask.
"My fifth and last child."
"He must be spoilt."
Not so, I say inwardly.
He's the last of siblings
who've grown up and left,
ignoring his hey wait for me.

I unlock the glass door of my office
and am hemmed in by pale wood and papers.
My window doesn't look out on the geometrical garden.
Switching on my computer
I look down at three freeways, some hotels,
a construction site for a cross-city tunnel
as mechanical shovels empty earth
into waiting trucks.

The cars are army ants that do not stop
until one detaches from the flow
and hesitates
where a freeway splits in two.
Indicator flashing,
it creeps across a white hatched dividing strip,
locates the missed route and speeds up.

I answer phone calls and emails.
Eight levels above the construction site I hear
a jackhammer faintly tapping,
almost inaudible through plate glass.

Mid-morning there's a panic. By tonight
I am to write a fifteen page opinion
on a fictional gain
that would stop a large transaction.

I assemble my thoughts.
I look across at a slowly moving cloudscape,
university towers on the rim of our planet,
aircraft tilted upwards, gaining height.
I search my hard drive for text that I can paste.
After two hours
I've little to show, a few unimpressive sentences.

So I lunch by myself in a deli –
antipasto and salad leaves.

Mid-afternoon my edifice of words
is taking shape on screen.
My opinion balances hope and risk,
and with a flip of logic
eliminates doubt.

Below my window
a screw drill suspended from a crane
withdraws from the hole it has bored,
swings free with a reverse twist,
cascading dirt.

I hardly notice, as the day declines,
the flashing orange lights of mechanical shovels
moving about in compacted mud,
the cold earth, an approaching prospect.
I'm absorbed in formatting
the analysis of facts,
the cadences of reassurance.
The pages compose themselves on my screen,
the cursor lifts and re-arranges text.

At twilight, land and sky
are a pool of luminous indigo-violet,
my office and image, brightly lit,
suspended on the glass.
The red tail lights of the army ants head west.
I speak to you on the phone.
After 23 years your voice still thrills me –
Aphrodite or Pallas Athene or both?

Outside it's gone black, there's no construction site,
just a void,
as my two fingers tap into the night.
The people who were waiting for my opinion
have gone home.
Finally I type
yours sincerely, my name, Tax Counsel.
It's marked draft, more refinements are needed,
and I push the send button.

There's a distant alarm.
I consider the fire stair while I wait.
The lift arrives.

Crossing the deserted travertine foyer,
I pass abandoned coffee machines.
The alarm is ringing loudly, intensely.
Someone must have breached a security door.
In the car park my ignition key starts the motor
and sound system – Pandolfi Mealli's "La Stella".

There's a fire engine outside the building,
its lights blinking lazily red, white and blue.
I swing across oncoming headlights,
head up a lane, turn left for home.
Poetry is incidental.
I am my poem.

Ada – Dies Natalis

I
"As rare as rocking horse shit" –
one in 15,000 the internet says.
Standing in the corridor
of a children's cardiac unit
I'm surrounded by coloured diagrams,
the blue veins and red arteries
of wrong connections.
Each map is wild and unique
as a snowflake,
but they're all actuarial possibilities,
and each is a life.
Ada's is the supracardiac version.
The veins from her lungs join
in a single vein that seeks
and almost touches her left ventricle,
and loses its way and veers
in an improbable backwards loop
to her right ventricle.
Ada is simple to fix
if five hours under surgical lights are simple.

II
"Isn't she beautiful! Isn't she beautiful!"
the young aunt, ardent, repeats.
Feeding from aureoles like brown dinner plates,
Ada (pronounced "Ardour"
after Nabokov's heroine)
breathes heavily, gulps air,
turns blue as she starts to cry.

III
Tomorrow the veins from her lungs
will be cut
and joined to her left ventricle.
The grandmothers wash and scrub the house,
a grandfather (that's me) standing on a stool,
instructed by the grandmothers,
ties a clothesline to an iron spike
set in nineteenth century brickwork.
Eight days from now Ada
will be carried through a narrow dim house.
Her eyes will open like dark butterflies
and lungs inhale
this nectarine tree, ripening muscatels
and staked tomatoes in the summer heat.

IV
On any day 300,000 are born
of dust from exploded supernovae.
There was no witness when a point
became the universe
and the first stars started to burn,
billions of galaxies lighting up.
The 300,000 all have witnesses,
the nurse who spotted Ada's laboured breathing –
"There's something wrong with that baby."

V
"Hibiscus" – one of her first words.
It's night and the passerby
can look over a gate past pink and red roses through a clear glass door
and see a shadowy figure in a hallway
gyrating and shaking a maraca and tambourine
to inaudible music,
who's wondering if neighbours think he's mad,
but he has a daughter to entertain –
she's hidden in a cot –
Ada, two years and a bit.

VI
In the dark of early morning
I hear a muffled voice talking to a child,
and a solitary cry.
The child's translation:
"Daddy's wings have gone and he's lost his fairy dust."

VII
Her father has been dead for three weeks.
She's restless in the restaurant.
Hoisting her on my hip
we go out in the street –
as my veal parmigiana arrives.
I identify flowers in gardens lit by street lamps.
"That's a strelitzia," I say,
"a relative of the banana."
We head towards an illuminated shop front,
with cut flowers in buckets on the footpath
and shadows standing in doorways.
"I saw Daddy," she says.
At the house where she's staying, she chooses
Sonia and the Flying Babies.
"Read it again."
I do, but Sonia has a father.
In a private voice, as I'm leaving, she says:
"I want you to stay."

VIII
A month later, at two years and nine months
she's still finding questions and answers:
"How did your Daddy die?"
"He was quite old and had a heart attack," I reply.
"He was in a room by himself
and ran out into the street and died."

IX
Ada has become herself,
the miniature parts,
all in working order, are complete.
Aged three she mounts a platform
to wash her hands,
looks down and sighs –
the cares of adulthood.
The rectangular box-basin
of sparkling white porcelain
(an aesthetic manifesto of her architect-mother)
has a reddish-brown smear of water,
tannin-stained rivulets.
She flicks on a tap
and her small plump hand
decisively sluices out the discoloured water,
face averted, absorbed in her task.

Self Portrait at 65

i.m. Quinton Duffy 13.11.1971 – 10.9.2005

I
I sit alone watching a Japanese anime film
on a large screen.
A moth flickers across projected light.

II
I've been trying to write about a death,
my granddaughter's father, aged thirty-three,
a perfect human being
who loved Japanese anime films.
Past midnight in a hospital ward
my daughter kisses his inert head
while her mother and I look on.

III
There was a "famous" incident in his childhood.
His mother hears him, aged five,
chattering to his one week old sister,
asking questions.
He appears crestfallen in the kitchen doorway:
"That baby doesn't seem to like me.
She won't talk."

IV
My daughter's regret – and she laughs –
he missed the fifth season
of *The Sopranos*.
The Brothers Karamazov
is buried with him, unfinished,
his shirt sleeves as he liked them
partly rolled up.

V
The females of the household
(my wife and daughter) resolve
Ada, not yet three, and I
will shower together –
"a male presence."

VI
Three weeks after Q's death I fly down to Julia.
She wakes me after midnight.
We drive the old brown Volvo to the hospital,

the same car as three weeks earlier.
It feels like the same journey
as a small child struggles for breath.
By three a.m., after antihistamines,
Ada's pedalling a plastic car
across vinyl tiles
in the fluorescent calm of Emergency.
There are lurid flowers painted on the wall.

VII

I read about an improbable event:
one of the archaea
that light up marshes at night
fused with an oxygen eating bacterium
and became us,
all complex life,
and the improbable fungus
too small for hospital microscopes
that killed Q as he lay in an isolation ward.

VIII

It's six months since Q's death.
I sit in a glass room typing letters
for a research foundation.
The garden wilts in the sun,
overgrown with climbing roses.
Tomorrow I stay with my daughter
who carries his unborn child.

As the sun declines I switch off my screen –
I've an hour to mow the lawns.
I change into a torn t-shirt
and faded trousers
ripped with splashes of white paint and yellow chlorine.
My mower starts with one pull –
a surprise – but now it can't stop
until the petrol runs out
or I jerk the lead from the spark-plug.

Its staccato roar consumes the grass on my driveway.
In the street a young man
is packing his young family into a car.
They hurry to close the doors,
alarmed by this obsessive old man,
red-faced and sweating in his clouds of dust,
as I reach the grass on the verge
and mow beside their car.
The blades are spitting out topsoil fines and dead leaves.
A pebble ricochets.
On the opposite footpath an Asian girl
holds a handkerchief to her nose.

The young man parks down the road and is back,
mild-mannered, fair hair and egg-shaped head.
I depress the throttle to hear his reproach:
"You could at least have waited!"
"I was embarrassed," I say,
"I do the lawns in a particular order
 and I've a tennis court to mow before it's dark."
He nods and walks away.

IX
My postscript, aged 68.
Julia telephones
and reads a poem of nineteen syllables.
She asks how many syllables for a haiku.
"Seventeen," I reply.

She'll send the corrected haiku
as a text message:
"and you can put it in a poem –
So it will be preserved."

This is Julia Lehmann's haiku,
(now a syllable short):

"Widowed 4 years, I find
the wig you made from your hair,
(still scented)."

X
A postscript to the postscript:
I have to set up the camera again
with my self portrait
for a final tracking shot.
I'm 69
and having radiotherapy.
Lying on the slab
surrounded by lights
in an empty room with pop music playing
I shut my eyes
so I don't panic.
That night my daughter
texts me another haiku for Q
(the number of syllables correct):
"Always fluorescent
in the room where you died,
my howl is a ghost there."

Travels in Peru

I
City of cathedrals and altitude sickness – Cusco –
the melée just before dawn
as we board at the railway station.
The narrow gauge blue train
climbs up the pink adobe slopes,
slums inhabiting the sky,
hollyhock and yellow helianthus
flourishing in a spew of garbage and plastic,
skinny dogs at dawn
asleep on cold doorsteps.

A moment of fright as the blue Vistadome
starts rolling back –
then shudders and resumes its ascent.
The climbing and rolling back are repeated,
slicing through backyards,
broken glass on top of mud-brick walls,
makeshift corner stores with American cola signs –
roller shutters down at sunrise.

II
Climbing out of the Cusco valley,
the friable slopes held in suspension
by proclamations to Christ and Peru
etched on the hills,
we have a teetering view
of a dilapidated basketball court,
a pink Queen Elizabeth flowering
in a dusty courtyard.
Trotting by the track
a schoolgirl jams her fingers in her ears
as we speed up through the early morning.

III
Ten thousand feet above sea level
staring up through the curved glass roof
at slender 80 foot eucalypts
populating austere slopes with leaves,
a universal tree,
we ask if these Australians
were the first trees
to colonise these rarefied altitudes.

IV
The train stops and she is there,
looking up at the carriages,
with large felt hat
and face of red brown leather,
old bony hands

clutching a bunch of arum lilies
fringed awkwardly with pink dahlias,
no longer fresh.
Railwaymen chat by the line.
Materialised from fields of dead maize
at our unscheduled stop
the old Quezchua woman walks up and down
clutching her hopeful flowers.

V
At Ollantaytambo
Manco Inca routed the Spanish,
and there's an influx of Japanese tourists.
As the blue Vistadome loses altitude,
the eucalypts vanish.
Orchids cascade from the forks of trees.
Gesturing like an orchestra conductor
a stentorian Japanese guide
instructs his elderly listeners:
"Junguru asoko desu."
Here we are in the jungle.

VI
My memento of a hatless Machu Picchu –
a sunburnt scalp.
At the high point of the ruins,
the Intihuatana,
big Marco, our guide (twenty years' experience)
scans his tour group:
"Any more question marks?"

VII
There's a kindergarten of local plants,
cloud forest inhabitants.
Marco identifies
a tall terrestrial orchid
with purple and red flowers.
He points: "That's a passion fruit vine."

Red-haired Marianne from Canada
with gold cross flashing from her cleavage asks:
"Does it make you passionate?"
Marco, pointing to a baby shrub:
"You've had coca leaf tea?"
We chorus yes.
"That's a coca plant.
To get high
an addict would have to eat
eight kilograms of leaves."
(Or did he say four?)
"Of course we know how to make cocaine.
It's pleasant now in Machu Picchu,
75 degrees Fahrenheit.
But *it gets hotter in winter*,
a month from now, very sticky,
85 degrees at midday in June."

VIII
Amanda of Bill and Amanda,
an older Australian couple,
gives the Intihuatana a miss
and goes to sleep
in grass beneath a tree,
behind a low Inca wall.
Back from the House of the High Priest,
the Temple of the Sun
and the Head of the Condor,
Bill – imagining what it's like
to be here at the full moon –
walks straight past Amanda.
"Bill, you've forgotten Amanda."

IX
We buy a rug of pastel-coloured ducks
and a small cotton doll –
in Melbourne its two and a half year old owner
will call it Jolene.

To set up their stalls
at the Agua Calientes handicrafts market
some vendors walk for ten hours.

X
"South Americans love a party" –
(a Washington military attaché's verdict).
Our blue Vistadome heads back to Cusco
with non-stop piped music,
and between snatches of sleep we glimpse
the cold boiling river,
a deserted highway.
Mountain peaks, pink canine teeth
in the fading light
appear and are gone.
Shrilling panpipes announce
a prancing blue and gold devil
(a Peru Rail official).
The music switches to catwalk.
The young man and woman
who checked our tickets
have become fashion models,
pace up and down
and pose in alpaca wool garments,
hands on hips,
with radiant shy good looks.

XI
Flying into Lima next evening
is a different sort of party.
Massed hungry faces in the dark
stare through the glass wall of the terminal
as we circulate like tropical fish.
We sight a placard with our name.
The locks on the car doors click shut.
We drive through a city of walled compounds,
cars parked behind high, iron gates.

XII
Glancing from our hotel window
on level 10, in Miraflores
there's a fog –
the morning fog that nourished
a carpet of wild flowers
on this rainless, coastal plain.
In simpler times
when the city stayed within its walls
they'd visit this place,
families with their horse and cart:
"Mira flores –
come and admire the flowers."
In less simple times
it's come and admire the cars,
the shops and the bars.

XIII
Laura from Brazil
is an accompanying spouse – like me –
from the 10th International Consumer Law Conference
on this tour of archaeological sites and museums.
She and I converse in sign language.
As our car proceeds along Avendida Jose Larco
Antonio turns around to explain.
His commentary for Laura
in a mixture of Spanish and Portuguese
he'll repeat for me in English.
I've a nagging concern as the morning progresses:
the paltriness of Antonio's stipend
from this privileged tour for two.

XIV
After the stone gods with fangs and claws,
painstakingly chiselled to scare and subjugate
we're cheered by the polychrome funerary cloths
of the Paracas necropolis
(I'm heading there tomorrow)

red and blue birds and flowers,
as though new, from a handicrafts stall —
and the elongated skulls,
of the people who wove these cloths
eighteen hundred years ago.

XV
I've arrived at the heart of my travels —
unplanned, unexpected
at 700 AD
in a Lima museum,
the pots of the Moche —
Antonio calls it his "favourite culture".
Each pot, with stirrup handle and spout,
is a sculpture —
a pale blue pumpkin, yellow maize,
a penis and balls displayed like colourful fruit,
copulating llamas (the doe
looks wistfully over her shoulder),
a laughing face, eyes almost shut,
a thick-featured man
slaps a drum,
midwives pull and support at a birth,
a dance of humanity, a party.
And after the party,
a blind man stares into space,
there's a Downs syndrome child,
a dance of corpses holding hands.
"When they took this country from us,"
Antonio says,
"they said we were primitive."

XVI
I dress in the dark,
mouth an inaudible goodbye.
At two fifty a.m.

I'm in a car headed for a bus terminal
"in a poor neighbourhood … notorious for theft."
We pass boarded-up shop fronts, rubbish in laneways.
I've a hundred soles in my shirt pocket
(thirty dollars)
some travel agency papers,
and the clothes I'm wearing, nothing else –
no passport, credit cards or wallet.
With no Spanish, I've no identity.
I'm an almost naked sixty four year old man
of little value.

XVII
I'm sitting in the bus terminal,
a cavernous interior
alone at three-ten a.m.
My bus doesn't leave
until three forty-five.
I didn't ask for this long wait.
Helena, my glamorous Lima travel agent
is taking no chances I'll be late.
A woman sometimes guards the toilets,
sitting at a table, taking coins.
More often she's in a lounge,
with back turned, watching TV,
idly switching channels.
I worry I've no small change
for a visit to her toilets.

At three forty-two I decide it's time to board the bus,
and present Helena's accreditation papers,
where she designates me "Americano"
(a comical source of confusion
if my corpse is found by the side of the road).
The driver shakes his head: "Boleto."
That isn't me.
I retreat inside the terminal.
Who is this Señor Boleto?

I notice other passengers
are presenting some white paper with orange print.
I have one of those.
One minute to go.
I walk out again,
present my paper with the orange print.
Impassive as Charon
the driver motions me to board.

XVIII
I'm heading down the Panamericana
at four a.m. in a window seat.
We stop at tollgates.
Workmen join and leave the bus.
The desert flows past – a phantom landscape.
Boleto – billet – ticket!
Señor Boleto's ghost dissolves.
The bus lights up a passing universe.
An older woman takes the seat on my left,
thick, solid clothes,
and leaves the bus after an hour or so.

A pale dawn sky
reveals a Martian terrain,
strange isolated buildings,
like discarded shipping containers,
one every few miles,
by the road or on a distant hill
 "built by people from the Andes
refugees from the Shining Path"
Ricardo my Pisco guide will explain.

A first glimpse of sea on the right.
The bus descends from the plateau.
We are driving through a flat land
of ruined sea resorts,
abandoned fast food outlets, faded cola signs,
miles of derelict chicken sheds

open to the wind,
strips of black plastic dangling from roofs
that stretch back hundreds of feet
to the beaches of the cold Pacific.

XIX
There's a road sign:
"Bienvenido a Pisco".
I'm on high alert.
I have to choose the right stop.
With no Spanish, I'm a man who's deaf and dumb.
The bus halts. Some workmen get out.
Not much activity, so I stay in my seat.
We start and stop again.
This time it's a major intersection.
As I step down from the bus
I check with the driver. "Pisco?" He nods.

There's a collection of people,
 and just one placard, and it has my name.
The glamorous Helena becomes St Helena.
Driving into Pisco, my driver asks:
"¿Hablas español?" "No español."
"No ingles."
But I've made my connection.

XX
Peruvian sea-birds love a party.
There's a constant uproar in the sunlight
from hundreds of thousands of cormorants
nesting on rocky amphitheatres and arches
of the Islas Ballestas.
Hundreds of sea lions lounging on ledges,
pelicans and penguins
join in the party,
and Peruvian boobies, tall black and white birds
with giant chicks in fluffy white baby-suits.

Large starfish and crabs glitter on the rock-face
as the swell falls and rises.
Mid-morning the power-boats head back to Paracas.
We leave these spectacular islands with regret.

XXI

We're in the Reserva Nacional de Paracas,
where four hundred funerary bundles were exhumed,
in foetal position, waiting for rebirth,
colourful textiles, perfect in dry soil,
eighteen hundred years old.
Ricardo, our guide,
bends down and chips at the road.
He holds out what seems to be asphalt.
But darkened by decades of passing tyres,
it's salt – the road is solid salt.
There are mounds of bleaching scallop shells
dumped by unlicensed fishermen on the run,
and a small museum,
its prize exhibits stolen.

XXII

Twelve hours or so after I dressed in the dark
(it seems like a week)
I'm sitting in Ricardo's cramped office
"our new office. It's even got a toilet."
I've handed over a ten soles tip
(worrying if it's the right amount).
Emma from Texas has a string plait.
Fifteen or sixteen years old,
she's been here for three months.
"This is *my* country," she affirms,
"Peru is where I'm going to live my life."

"She helps with my English" Ricardo explains.

"It's not b-e-e-n" Emma expounds,
"That's British. You say b-e-n."

Ricardo shrugs. "How do I know what to say?
B-e-n when it's spelled b-e-e-n?"

A tourist vacates the toilet.
I close the door and fumble for a light switch.
It's dark, completely dark. I can't see a thing.
I edge forward, feel the bowl against my knees
and unzip.
My urine splashes on a lid that's shut.

XXIII
Composing my face for Ricardo and Emma
I open the toilet door.
The driver who'll take me to the bus
and get my ticket is here.
We retrace our early morning drive
to the Pisco intersection.
Excited he guides me to a large crimson bus
that's already starting,
and gestures – I can get a ticket on board –
and hands me my ten soles note.

XXIV
It's seventeen hours since I dressed in the dark.
Between sleep and waking
I've watched this morning's landscape
roll past in reverse order,
people who were grouped at the edge of a cotton field
just after dawn,
sitting at the end of the day,
surrounded by cotton they've picked,
irrigated landscapes alternating with desert,
hundreds of abandoned chicken sheds,
ruined sea resorts,
buildings like discarded shipping containers.
It wasn't a dream.

As the slums of Lima
flow past in the dark
I stop worrying about
hassling for a cab at the bus terminal.
faith replaces doubt,
I'm filled with a trance-like certitude.
I step down and there's a placard with my name.
A hundred votive candles for St Helena!

XXV
The Pacific Ocean at sunset
is the finale of these travels.
My cab collects you from the conference
with Jean, your friend from Arizona,
past noon, our last day, a fast forward tour
of selected museums and sights.
I become the guide
to elongated skulls
Paracas funerary cloths and Moche pots,
and a late afternoon courtyard of frangipannis.
The planned denouement of our day.
The cab deposits us in a hotel driveway.
Across the road we find we're at the edge
of the Peruvian coastal plain,
cliffs of grey shingle dropping
three hundred feet
to the expanse of the Pacific
(a puzzle for Australians
who know it as wild and blue,
but Spaniards happened on the naming rights.)
The massive ripples stretch for half a mile.
Placid, forming like molten silver,
they do not know their name.
The waves roll in,
a procession of civilisations,
a huge *pax vobiscum*, a twilight of the gods.

Marriage and Seduction

Reading a memoir "Cuban Missile Crisis 1962"
I revisit a floodlit beer garden at night, a student laughing:
"Are any of us going to be alive tomorrow?" But for me
There is no crisis. All my thoughts are concentrated on X.
I hardly know her. I am charmed by X's faint American accent,
Her reticent beauty, her compact, almost oriental grace.
At closing time we drive off and regroup at X's flat ...
Her party's breaking up. We're heading for the door. Her hand
Touches my sleeve. She stretches up, speaks in my ear. "Please stay."
I'm startled by the aureoles of her nipples, large brown-purple discs.
I can't believe my arms are holding her, so sudden, so exquisite.
I phone X twice that week – brief and evasive conversations.
The Cuban missile crisis passes and we meet by chance.
Her short, strained sentence: "Let's be friends." For forty years
I've driven past the red-brick block of flats where we loved once.
I didn't ask for what X gave and then took back. I ask myself
If there was some mistake I made, and what was in her mind.

What's done to us, we do to others. Stranded between marriages
I start seeing Y and then my phone calls stop. I don't explain.
Months pass. We meet by accident in the street. Y's with some colleagues,
We're chatting and I notice tears and quickly say goodbye.
Years later at a funeral there's an unfamiliar eulogist.
I'm curious, filled with admiration for this passionate young woman,
Then realise with a shock that she is Y whose womanhood I snubbed.

A marriage if it's right is not seduction. It's an equal meeting.
A slow learner, aged thirty nine, I stumbled on this commonplace.
At my first lunch with G (that's you) – fate had us share the same initial –
You argued eloquently for arranged marriages. That gave me hope.
Three decades on I wake and find your face and you're still beautiful.

Sunglasses

I
My twentieth century began
when Jacqueline Kennedy placed
her first pair of polaroids
on the bridge of her nose.

II
And ended
27 December 2007
with a motorcade and detonations
as Benazir Bhutto
(another lover of dark glasses)
stood up to wave through a sunroof.

III
For two years I was in love
with an impossibly beautiful face
hiding behind sunglasses.
She dealt with the unwanted beauty
by giving her boyfriends,
strictly equal treatment,
leaving us all with the taste
of lipstick on our teeth,
propping her head on our shoulder
in the back seat of taxis,
allowing her breast to be touched,
but no buttons undone,
her nights a succession
of holding hands in cinemas
and candlelit dinners in restaurants
with young men she liked, but did not love.
Aged twenty-one, the shades
fell from my eyes.
I lost my virginity, but not with her.
I gave up tormenting and being tormented.
"This happens to all my men," she said.

"I'm surprised you took so long."
We shook hands and said goodbye.
She was waiting for something, not me.

IV
As the cameras flash like intermittent artillery,
flanked by lawyers with files,
the defendants emerge with dark glasses.
They are actors in someone else's play.

V
I was driving with a psychiatrist friend
down a valley.
He gestured (from behind dark glasses)
at a house on a hill.
"That was my house. With the blue roof.
I was married and gave my wife a terrible time."
Years later he was in bed
with an avant-garde composer
(later a defector to tonality)
who woke and mumbled, rubbing his eyes,
"What ship are you from?"
Earl haunted exclusive jewellers,
trying on necklaces, brooches, bracelets.
He enjoyed his absurdity in the mirror,
avuncular, short black hair, slightly plump,
shiny pink skin with pores,
sparkling like a duchess for a minute or so.
He had a miserable end in an old men's home
without sunglasses.

VI
Edwin Land's polymer film between two layers of glass
polarising ultraviolet light
and cutting the incidence of cataracts
was a post-war romance.
His patent gave new colours to the world.
Arid landscapes became a cool blue-green.

For the first time we could watch,
with our eye movements undetected.
We found a new mobility.
Two ellipses of dark glass
allowed us to switch between identities.
We became free
to write the novel of our lives.

VII
My wife and I are on a train to Pompeii
in an almost empty carriage.
An unshaven lurching man
is starting an argument,
waving his hands at fellow passengers.
From the far end of the carriage
a well-dressed woman (a local) gets up
and totters on high heels towards us,
wanting a front stalls seat for the altercation.
She sits as close as decency allows
and politely puts on dark glasses.

Thirteen Reviews of the New Babylon Inn

for Nicholas Lehmann

I
"The world's *eighth* worst hotel?
I vote it Number One!
I've known better in the back-blocks of China.
I was offered heroin at the entrance.
The narrow stairs shake when you tread on them.
I couldn't get my door to lock
and the sheets have holes and strange stains.
Read the reviews before you book."

II
"The manager yelled at me
when I asked where's the free internet."

III
"Don't be deluded by the photos and location.
My room was like a horror film,
dank, the tiniest I've ever seen.
I could hardly wrestle my suitcases through the door.
To sit on the toilet I had to twist my legs around
or have one foot in the shower."

IV
"Their free American breakfast!
A small piece of white bread, a droplet of jam
and microscopic package of cottage cheese."

V
"No cold water. Both taps had hot water!
And a power point in the shower cubicle.
See the photo I've posted."

VI
"Six panels were missing in the ceiling –
something to look at when you're lying in bed."

VII
"My wife woke up thinking I was tickling her feet.
I felt a tickle too,
and switched on the light.
Two beady eyes of a small rodent!
Grabbing bits of our pizza
he vanished through a hole in the wall."

VIII
"I complained about mice eating our chocolate.
'What do you expect?' the man at front desk said,
'Mice like chocolate.'"

IX
"Extra friendly staff
found my lost passport under the bed.
They attend you like a princess *aus Deutschland*. Five stars."

X
"My secretary
will never book for me again.
My secretary isn't going to be my secretary."

XI
"I didn't expect pre-warmed bed linen,
residues of bodily fluids
sandwich wrappings and cigarette ash.
A hooker and her John
pulling their clothes on
hurried out the door
as we checked into our room."

XII
"Just out of college
we were sucked in by the price and location,
and were review-skeptics.
OMG, they were right!"

XIII
Dreams are explained.
8½ Avenue has five lanes
of bumper to bumper, humid traffic.
The beautiful grid
of this flat, granite island,
its horizontals and verticals of space,
are a psychic phenomenon.
I step out from my air-conditioned limousine
with tinted windows,
and recognise the facade from the photos:
a fire escape zigzags down the front,

the New Babylon Inn
is backed by a tangerine sunset.
A young price-conscious family with luggage
is staring from the sidewalk.
I walk up and open the glass door
with precision.
They pick up their things and follow.
Management greets me
and my credit card
like a friend back from the dead.

Elizabethan Evening

In the long twilight on a balcony
A red-haired queen laughs at the ribaldry

Of joiners whose oaks swords and spears beat back
A Viking horde of cobblers' mock attack.

The villagers look up at her amazed –
Her turquoise dress, pale face, enameled, glazed.

Mastiffs leap at a bear chained to a stake,
A mechanical dolphin rises from the lake

And in the rising mist, the sound of flutes
Mingles with torch-lit singers plucking lutes.

As fireworks paint the sky of nearby farms,
A fair-haired child slumped in his father's arms

Is carried through picnickers on the grass
Who quip and call out: "Let the glover pass."

(Shakespeare's father was a glove-maker: Stephen Greenblatt's *Will in the World*.)

The Rush Cutters

Variation on a theme of Thomas Hood

Dust-streaked, sunburned, we had been cutting rushes,
And were surprised and hid among the bushes.

There was a troop of horsemen and the high
Droning of bagpipes under a flushed sky.

Riding sidesaddle in a red silk gown,
She had blonde plaits and a small silver crown.

A soldier planted a banner on the sand.
Helping her down, an equerry held her hand

And bowing to her, offered a gold cup.
Her pageboys raced the waves, breeches rolled up.

We saw her speaking, then she turned and smiled,
Looking at us, sixteen years old, a child,

And stepped into a boat, taking the light
With her, as oarsmen rowed into the night.

Exotic Postcards

I
I am in Paris, London and New York –
so excited I can barely believe it.
No. This can't be real.
I wake up, sixteen years old
in Burgoyne Street, Gordon, NSW.
Australia is yet to get postcodes.

II

ESTONIAN MATURE AGE STUDENT
I can't decide if my name
in English is Les or Leo —
You are pissing in the woods.
You hear Germans behind you.
Soldiers.
You have to be able to —
what is the English word?
Like a knife. *Abschneiden!*

III

YOUNGER STUDENT FROM HUNGARY
I hate this time of day.
(He is gazing from a stone balustrade
over the university grounds at dusk.)
It is so indecisive.
Where I come from I'm a Count.
(We are now in his parents'
small attic.)
That means nothing in my country.
We have hundreds of Counts.
(He has hardly any accent —
an unidentifiable spice in food.)

IV

As the nondescript middle-aged woman
(in white uniform
with gold-framed spectacles)
hands wrapped bacon across the counter
I notice on her forearm
a pale aquamarine tattoo —
six numerals.

V
I'm just twenty-one
and lose my virginity in Woolloomooloo, Sydney.
Waking up, I hear
small children in the lane chatter in Italian.

VI
The postcards arrive.

VII
AUSTRALIAN PAINTER IN PARIS
There is a problem with his trousers.
He is gesticulating
in a Paris department store
pointing at his fly.
The uncomprehending saleswoman
wants to call the police.
He gesticulates more wildly –
bursts into desperate Franglais:
Le zippeur! Le zippeur!

VIII
AUSTRALIAN POET ON BROOKLYN BRIDGE
As he collapses
he calls out to his muggers:
Back pocket!

IX
A DIFFERENT AUSTRALIAN PAINTER IN SPAIN
He is in the city of the man
who painted *Kronos Devouring His Sons*.
He takes a break from art-viewing.
At the end of the day
a steaming cup of hot chocolate.
*?10#@
as he spits out a cockroach.

X
My friends go away and come back.
Instead I marry, have children and divorce,
too cautious and provincial
to become a sender of postcards.

XI
Driving into Delhi from the airport
an old woman
bent insect-like beneath a vast load of sticks
is a black silhouette
against a primrose-yellow dusk.
At noon in a bus
on a decayed rural highway
we pass overturned trucks
and chillies drying on the road edge
in great red carpets.
We are three-quarters of the way
across a 900 metres long bridge
over the almost waterless sacred Falgu river –
we jerk to a stop.
An oncoming truck has just moved onto the bridge
and blocks the way.
An hour of angry unintelligible negotiations.
2,500 years ago on a nearby hill
Gautama preached his fire sermon.
Hundreds of vehicles pile up in both directions.
Officials arrive.
We cheer as the truck slowly reverses.
Five minutes later
we start moving forward into Gaya
where night has fallen.
Vendors sitting in white dhotis
in shop fronts lit by petrol lamps
are surrounded by sacks of beans
ghur (pads of crystalised sugar)
bolts of silk and white metal water pitchers.

Young men with guilty smiles are stealing
sugar cane from small trucks
stalled in traffic.
I inhale wonderful smells and dust.

I'm in the Calcutta General Post Office
(in 1983 it's not yet Kolkata)
queuing with Indians
who place their stamped letters on a counter
and watch as postal workers post-mark their valuable stamps.
I'm sending my first postcards,
forty-two years young, no diarrhoea yet –

XII
My forty-two year old head is full of pink forts
and white marble palaces on lakes at night
and beggars pleading at car door windows.
As we halt at each railway station my fellow travellers
drink sweet tea from clay cups they smash on the platform
but I'm buying bundles of Amar Chitra Katha comic books,
and read about Indian gods and goddesses
as the train passes across bright arid landscapes –
my colourful collection of "quintessential Indian stories"
32 with only one duplicate – but only a fraction
of hundreds of titles.
(Thirty years later Indian friends say:
You are very fortunate. They are quite a rarity now.)
On the hill-fort of Chittor I stumble through grassy ruins
into an abandoned temple
and find a trio of huge stone heads in a dry moat,
one face expressing grief, one laughing, one serene,
the equal of Michelangelo's *David* I convince myself.
In Jaipur I ask a young bicycle rickshaw driver
to take me to a puppet maker.
I take you to a very good puppet maker, he says,
pedaling through the dusk.

Suddenly over his shoulder he asks
as we pass red stone buildings in the fading light,
Do you like poetry?
Yes, I say. I write poetry. Do you?
He says, Yes,
and explains his poems are in Hindi.
We are silent. He pedals.
What is your religion? he asks.
Atheist, is my reply. I've no religion.
He considers as his legs pedal.
Then asks: What is your caste? (pronounced karsht)
I have no caste, I say.
There are no castes in my country.
What, you have no caste, no religion,
he exclaims.
You are like a –
I don't know the English word –
anatha – a man with no father or mother.
An orphan, I reply.
The puppets his friend makes
are crude and disappointing,
but the man is poor with a wife and small children
in a cramped canvas shanty
lit by sooty oil lamps
and I'm expected to be generous.

XIII

I did not see the rickshaw driver again.
That ride through the night was thirty years ago.
Our interest in poetry was something
we shared in our brief monosyllabic exchanges,
yet I troubled him.
Although affluent, I was to be pitied,
a displaced man with no ties,
an exotic postcard.

Why I Write Poetry

For Pat Eldershaw, 50 years late

In my childhood dead poets have a habit
of making unexpected appearances.

I'm five. We've moved to a skinny house by the Harbour.
As the last crates are carried in at dusk
blue gas rings burn in a darkened kitchen.
"This is the house
where the poet Henry Kendall lived,"
my father says in his sententious voice,
reserved for important announcements.

I'm eight. A radio voice is saying:
"A Melbourne publican, Joshua Mooney
used to light the fire in his saloon
with the IOUs of poets –
Adam Lindsay Gordon, Marcus Clark ..."
My mother blushes with excitement:
"That was my grandfather.
And when he was an alderman
he named the streets of St Kilda after the poets."
So an Irish-born publican left a road-map
of English verse circa 1870.
Milton intersects with Browning and Tennyson Streets,
Chaucer curves into Wordsworth,
and he didn't forget Shakespeare, Spenser, Cowper or Southey.

I'm ten. We move to a house among tall trees.
Magpies steal my hair.
I make friends with a small old lady weeding her stone wall:
"The poet Louise Mack used to live in your house."

It seems
everywhere my child-eyes look
poets are growing like wild lupins.
But that's not why I write poetry.

At thirteen my mind is made up.
I'll be an artist.
But what sort of artist? It's like sitting
a multiple choice exam.
Singing with my mother
I can't hear notes she hears.
I'm not a natural draughtsman.
And fiction's too hard – where are the stories?
Poetry is my default option.
But that's not why I write poetry.

I despise it at first. I don't "hear, O hear"
Shelley's West Wind.
My life-long love affair is prompted
by a five foot eight, sixty year old man,
a first rate cricket coach
with silver hair, purple cheeks, small brown eyes
and sarcastic, nasal twang,
who carries his rotund body
as though he's wheeling a neatly stacked trolley.
In his acid, Australian bush accent
he asks thirty boys:
"Is there anyone here
who isn't *absolutely* certain there's a life after death?"
I'm the only hand raised.

He gives us poems to read:
Blake, Eliot, E. E. Cummings, Crowe Ransome.
He analyses, asks questions, doesn't enthuse,
observing quietly, letting us decide.
Poems are detective stories with hidden meanings.

Our honours group meets after school in his study
surrounded by the bleached jackets
of Lawrence, Gide, Virginia Woolf and Joyce.
A smoky sun goes down and lights of buildings
and boats tremble on cross-hatched harbour waters.
Our voices recently broken, we inhale the printed word,
poetry – the mystery of everything.
A boy puts up his hand: "Sir,
I've just thought of a terrific image –
red sails in the sunset."
"Jackson, you've been beaten to it."
There are brown and blue-black clouds through bay windows,
dim lawns as we pack our bags
and leave our reticent guide to catch our trains home.

I work out this poem –
another multiple choice exam –
baby-sitting a small person.
Her teeth crunch passionfruit seeds.
I tell her: "Your mouth sounds like a concrete mixer."
Poetry is our human love of metaphor.
We see one thing and think of something else.
A green wool dress becomes the woman we love.
Poetry is non-local causality.
We are bathed in a mysterious glow.
That's why I write poetry.

www.ingramcontent.com/pod-product-compliance
Lightning Source LLC
Chambersburg PA
CBHW020634230426
43665CB00008B/174